CREATING COMMUNITY on COLLEGE CAMPUSES

SUNY Series
FRONTIERS IN EDUCATION
Philip G. Altbach, Editor

The Frontiers in Education Series draws upon a range of disciplines and approaches in the analysis of contemporary educational issues and concerns. Books in the series help to reinterpret established fields of scholarship in education by encouraging the latest synthesis and research. A special focus highlights educational policy issues from a multidisciplinary perspective. The series is published in cooperation with the Graduate School of Education, State University of New York at Buffalo.

CREATING COMMUNITY
on COLLEGE CAMPUSES

IRVING J. SPITZBERG, JR.
and VIRGINIA V. THORNDIKE

State University of New York Press

Published by
State University of New York Press, Albany

For information, address State University of New York
Press, State University Plaza, Albany, NY 12246

Production by Christine M. Lynch
Marketing by Fran Keneston

Library of Congress Cataloging-in-Publication Data
Spitzberg, Irving J.
    Creating community on college campuses / Irving J. Spitzberg and
Virginia V. Thorndike.
        p.   cm. — (SUNY series, frontiers in education)
    Includes bibliographical references and index.
    ISBN 0-7914-1005-6 (alk. paper) . — ISBN 0-7914-1006-4 (pbk. :
alk. paper)
    1. College students—United States. 2. College environment-
-United States. 3. Community. 4. Universities and colleges—United
States. I. Thorndike, Virginia V., 1948– . II. Title.
III. Series.
LA229.S58   1992
378.1'98'0973—dc20
                                                            91–17847
                                                            CIP

10 9 8 7 6 5 4 3 2 1

*We dedicate this book
to the memory of two educators
and creators of community, our fathers:*

Irving J. Spitzberg, M.D.

*(December 7, 1899–May 6, 1989),
committed his life to teaching at the
University of Arkansas School of Medicine
and to practice in pediatrics in Little Rock, Arkansas.*

Robert L. Thorndike, Ph.D.

*(September 22, 1910–September 21, 1990),
committed his life to teaching teachers at
Teachers College, Columbia University
and to research in educational psychology.*

Contents

Foreword
by Ernest L. Boyer

In the spring of 1990, The Carnegie Foundation for the Advancement of Teaching, in cooperation with the American Council on Education, published a special report entitled *Campus Life—In Search of Community*. That study, which argued for a "more integrative vision of community in higher education" and set forth six principles around which a *college compact* could be established, inspired widespread interest on campuses from coast to coast. Now, the two key researchers for the Carnegie study—Irving Spitzberg and Virginia Thorndike—have followed up with their own thorough and thoughtful report that is sure to enrich the debate over how to make colleges and universities more intellectually and socially vital communities of learning.

The portrait of campus life the authors paint in *Creating Community on College Campuses* is troubling, but it is not, as they acknowledge, without hopeful signs. For example, while alcohol abuse remains, in their view, a "major" social pathology, they describe important efforts on almost every campus to educate students about the risks of overdrinking. As for campus crime, which Spitzberg and Thorndike say, has "captured the imagination of the media," they make clear that college campuses are "substantially safer than their surrounding communities." And in regard to fraternity and sorority life, the authors find that most institutions are working actively at ways to "empower the positive aspects of Greek life and curb the negative ones."

Even with these hopeful signs, however, Spitzberg and Thorndike find that many conditions on college campuses remain unsettling and in need of far greater attention. They note in particular the breakdown of civility and efforts to regulate speech. In their view, some colleges and universities are putting freedom of speech at risk because of their understandable desire to protect students against incivility and harassment of a sexual or racial nature. In addressing this vital matter, the authors focus on what we also found to be one of the most vexing issues facing administrators. In *Campus Life,* we argued against restrictive speech codes, for both practical and legal reasons,

xi

and urged colleges and universities to define high standards of civility while condemning in the strongest possible terms any violation of such standards.

On this issue, Spitzberg and Thorndike are unequivocal in their support for freedom of speech, while making, I believe, two fresh and wonderfully important larger points. First, they assert that challenging bigotry forcefully and thoughtfully represents "an essential opportunity to teach by example." They call for institutions to acknowledge the existence of bigotry in our society and take "serious steps" to educate members of the campus community to "understand and respect both diversity and the constitutional principles that frame interaction in a pluralistic democracy." They raise, in essence, what ought to be a core value in our colleges; namely *education* in both intellectual and moral terms.

After examining, thoughtfully, a wide range of student life issues, Spitzberg and Thorndike turn their attention to student and faculty relationships. Here, they voice grave concerns. For the majority of students, according to their carefully documented report, student-faculty relationships hardly exist, characterized mainly by an "absence." They provide the following picture: "Large classes that effectively block interaction continue to be the norm. Few students seek assistance outside the class and few faculty offer much of it. Repeatedly, individuals compare their institutions to fast food restaurants—providing efficient mass production that contributes little to the long-range intellectual health of the student or the institution."

In part, the distancing of students from academic participation can, according to the authors, be explained by several changing patterns of campus life. Most students, partly by necessity, partly by choice, Spitzberg and Thorndike say, spend the "bulk of their time on activities other than going to class or studying." Traditional-age students tend to do paid work for at least twenty hours a week, reserving weekends for partying, and spending three to four hours a day in casual involvement with friends. Most adult students who make up an increasing proportion of the undergraduate population, they also note, are doing paid work thirty-six hours or more a week and committing weekends to family and friends. Where is the teaching and learning community that ought to be at the heart of a college?

In *Campus Life,* we suggested that a college and university must, above all, be an educationally *purposeful* community—a place where faculty and students work together to strengthen teaching and learning on campus. Yet this principle, the authors of *Creating Community on College Campuses* make evident, is at odds with a climate in which "both students and faculty appear to be quite satisfied with the status quo of teaching and learning. Since they have never been socialized to value an intellectual community, most students do not expect or desire interaction with faculty and, therefore, do not regret its absence." Moreover, while most faculty, Spitzberg and Thorndike assert, express concerns about what they say is a decline in academic standards, "few take the time and expend the energy to create more interactive and demanding classes."

In the days ahead, reaffirming the intellectual life as a central dimension of community must be more vigorously pressed. A college of quality must, after all, be measured first by the commitment of its members—students *and* faculty—to the *educational* mission of the institution. It is in the classroom where community begins, but learning also reaches out to the various departments, residence halls, and the campus commons. The distancing that Spitzberg and Thorndike describe is not acceptable.

In their final chapters, Spitzberg and Thorndike urge the creation and implementation of what they call a *Compact for a Pluralistic Community.* The core ethical principles that they propose for such a compact are: the centrality of learning; the priority of freedom of thought and expression; the priority of justice; and the importance of differences. They also propose a series of specific implementing recommendations, which they acknowledge would have to vary from campus to campus according to differing needs, goals, and constraints. This carefully constructed framework is, I believe, a good basis for reestablishing a campus community of consequence.

What is particularly helpful in relation to the principles Spitzberg and Thorndike define is that they provide many compelling examples of institutions that are addressing such principles productively, in the process enriching the quality of campus life. This represents a valuable road map to possible change.

In the end, building a vital community is a challenge not just for higher learning, but for society at large. In our hard-edge competitive world, more humane, more integrative purposes must be defined. And perhaps it is not too much to hope that as colleges and universities affirm a new vision of community on campus, they may also promote the common good in the neighborhood, the nation, and the world.

Preface

This book is about community on campus. Occasionally we found it. Usually we did not. Everywhere we looked we found both paradox and promise.

The very concept of community on campus is paradoxical. Even small campuses are complex and diverse societies. To aspire to community, then, is to see the promise of wholeness in the apparent contradiction of competing individual and small-group needs and rights, and to seek to connect individuals and subcommunities with community of the whole.

Our book owes its existence to the Carnegie Foundation for the Advancement of Teaching's commitment to enhancing the quality of student life on American campuses. In 1989, we were privileged to work as Carnegie's principal researchers on a year-long study of the health of community on American campuses. This study began as a response to campus leaders' concern about the perceived deterioration of student life, as illustrated by racial separation and tension, alcohol abuse, violence against women, and retreat from participation in the extracurriculum. It quickly broadened to include inquiry into undergraduates' experience of academic community as well.

In April 1990, The Carnegie Foundation released *Campus Life: In Search of Community,* a special report that drew on our work. Since the Carnegie report was a relatively brief research essay, we now publish our full manuscript with the permission and cooperation of the Carnegie Foundation for the Advancement of Teaching and its president, Ernest Boyer.

In this book, we examine undergraduates' experience of community in both the academic and nonacademic realms. We structure this broad topic around three foci: (1) student diversity, particularly racial and ethnic diversity and the climate on campus for women students; (2) individual and small-group rights and responsibilities in relation to institutional authority; (3) student-faculty relations and the learning community. Since the central mission of higher education on the cusp of the twenty-first century is educating students, we offer recommendations for creating on campuses a revitalized, pluralistic learning community, not looking backward to a Golden Age that never was, but looking forward and taking into account the magnitude of the task.

We gathered evidence for this book from diverse sources. First, we and a team of colleagues visited eighteen campuses representing a cross section of American higher education: community colleges, comprehensive universities, liberal arts colleges, and research universities. Our sample included more public than private and more large than small institutions, because we wanted to draw a portrait of the campus reality experienced by the overwhelming majority of undergraduates today. These visits took place on campuses across the country so as to tap regional diversity as well. Finally there was a distribution among urban, suburban, and rural institutions. Thus, we span the diversity of American higher education, from a small historically black college in the South, where everyone relates to one other as family, offering unconditional love, to the enormous flagship university intent upon becoming one of the top ten research institutions in the country, where the students and faculty interact minimally in bulging classes and where there is little connection to the university. We and our site visitors conducted small-group discussions with scores of students, faculty, and administrators, talking with between seventy-five and one hundred people on each campus.

Although the campus visits served as the core of our book, we also drew on the results of three national surveys conducted in 1989. The Carnegie Foundation updated its 1984 survey of faculty, *The Condition of the Professoriate*. The American Council on Education (ACE), in collaboration with Carnegie, surveyed college and university presidents, asking them about their views on the current condition of student life. Likewise, the National Association of Student Personnel Administrators, in cooperation with ACE, surveyed chief student affairs officers, posing similar questions.

In addition, we reviewed the most recent scholarship on the topics we cover. We also read dozens of campus studies, perused many campus newspapers and general publications, and communicated with dozens of scholars and practitioners across the country.

We completed our primary research in 1989 and finished the original manuscript in January 1990. In early 1991, we modestly revised the manuscript for publication.

We accept full responsibility for the inevitable lacunae and any errors of commission in this study of a complex topic carried out in such a limited period of time.

Acknowledgments

This enterprise of exploring community on campus was enabled by the collaboration and assistance of many individuals.

First, we acknowledge the personal role of Ernest Boyer, President of the Carnegie Foundation for the Advancement of Teaching. His concern about the life of the undergraduate in the United States, publicly documented in *College* and eloquently stated everywhere he goes, led to this project. Our conversations with him and his encouragement have left their mark on every page of this book.

Other Carnegie colleagues were also active members of our community of inquiry. Gene Rice, then Senior Fellow, now Dean of the Faculty at Antioch, played an essential role. Gene Maeroff and Gene Haas, Senior Fellows as well, were discussion partners, readers, and campus visitors. When he joined the Carnegie Foundation as vice president, Charles Glassick became enabler-in-chief. Bob Hochstein often focused the conversation with Hochstein hooks.

We had as partners in our campus visits four outstanding scholars of higher education in the United States: Professor Steven Diner of George Mason University, Dean Barbara Moran of the University of North Carolina at Chapel Hill, Professor Martin Finkelstein of Seton Hall University, and Professor Jack Schuster of the Claremont Graduate School. The quality of their research reports and the insight of their comments on our drafts provided an excellent foundation for this book.

Dr. Elaine El-Khawas, Vice-President for Policy Analysis and Research of the American Council on Education, and Dr. Elizabeth Nuss, Executive Director of the National Association of Student Personnel Administrators, coordinated the surveys of presidents and chief student affairs officers, respectively. Partners throughout 1989, they offered useful comments on earlier drafts of our manuscript. Ms. Jill Bogard of the ACE library generously gave of her time, helping us find myriad books and articles.

On each campus a senior student affairs administrator coordinated the work of the campus visitors and arranged the interviews with the dozens of individuals who took time out from busy schedules to talk with us about community. Since we have promised to maintain the confidentiality of these campuses, we cannot thank each of these hosts by name. But the record must show that their energy and their impartiality form the foundations for this study.

Throughout the year, dozens of scholars and builders of campus community across the country generously shared the results of their research and their experience. To them all, a most heartfelt thanks.

In addition to the support of the Carnegie Foundation, we gratefully acknowledge the Henry Luce Foundation grant to Carnegie to support this work. The Henry Luce Foundation, through the good offices of its president, Henry Luce III, its executive vice-president, Robert Armstrong, and its program officer, Mary Jane Crook, has generously supported Irving Spitzberg's service to leadership education in American universities. The Henry Luce Foundation has a distinguished record of philanthropy to strengthen community and leadership in the United States. This book is a continuation of that philanthropy.

We extend special thanks to Mariann Kurtz, 1988 graduate of the University of Louisville, and currently a student at the Kellogg School of Management at Northwestern. Mariann was our colleague throughout 1989. She collected and interpreted vast amounts of data, participated in campus visits, provided invaluable administrative assistance, and continually contributed a much-needed student perspective. Her wise presence was a special gift.

Alicia Durán, 1990 graduate of Bryn Mawr College, and a staff analyst for the Knowledge Company, has been our associate as we have prepared the final manuscript. She has been a vigilant, energetic, and trusted companion throughout the process.

All of our colleagues in this exploration of community have helped us understand community at its best: we all have shared the common ground of commitment to improving community in higher education.

Part 1

Introduction

CHAPTER 1

Overview

"On my campus, we seem to have more crime than ever before." "On my campus, black and white students live in separate and sometimes conflicting worlds." "On my campus, students are apathetic." "On my campus, community is dead." "Alcohol is such a problem on my campus."

So went a conversation among the presidents of some of America's most important colleges and universities at an American Council on Education board meeting in late 1988. These campus leaders have not been alone. Feelings of fragmentation and disconnection, even alienation and anomie among students, faculty, and staff in most sectors of American higher education are not new. Indeed, there are many who worry that these feelings have been intensifying. And, as the eighties evolved, more attention was focused on a perceived deterioration of campus life: increased intolerance and bigotry, in word and deed; increased crime against property and person; increased alcohol abuse.

Not surprisingly, in the last few years, there has also been an upsurge of interest among many on campus in seeking new forms for connection with each other (both between individuals and among small groups) and with the campus as a whole. There is renewed aspiration for community. If the metaphor of community runs deep in American higher education, it is because the term evokes both the central aspiration of a social and moral order grounded in the reconciliation of the individual and society and the yearning for an academic experience that connects the learner to ideas, to other learners, and, ultimately, to society. As evidence of social disintegration seems to proliferate, we ask ourselves, dismayed, Is community on campus possible?

Many of us continue to say Yes. Examining and revitalizing community on American campuses should be a central component of the national higher education agenda in the 1990s. This means discussing openly the limits to community of the whole that increasing complexity and diversity on campus impose, as well as the enrichment of the whole that pluralism offers. This means thinking creatively of ways to strengthen subcommunities without jeopardizing the whole, and ways to strengthen the whole without jeopardizing the parts.

The Challenge of Change

American higher education has evolved significantly during the past twenty-five years. Students are different. There is greater ethnic diversity—more Hispanics, more Asian-Americans, more foreign students, modestly more African-American students. The range of age is greater and the average student is significantly older. There are more women than men. Almost half of students attend part-time. The American higher educational system, with its more than twelve million students, is the most diverse college and university system in the world. This diversity is its strength and its challenge.

Faculty have changed too. They are older, since there has been only a recent and modest influx of new appointments in higher education. They are less mobile because there are fewer jobs to be had. They are publishing more because the reward system continues to be skewed toward research in much of higher education. (In large part, this is due to comprehensive universities' aspirations to become research institutions). Faculty are "perishing" less, though, because a larger proportion of them have tenure.

The typical American university has become much larger and more complex. Its priorities have become more diverse. It now is even more committed to serving external constituencies—government, business, and industry—while keeping the students minimally happy. On campus, student and faculty diversity has been accompanied by greater diversity of goals as well. Institutions must advance knowledge, provide applied expertise to social problems, offer special programs to poorly prepared students, and raise more money for research, physical plant, and intercollegiate athletics from diverse sources. Educating students has become a lower priority.

More than 77 percent of American students now attend public colleges and universities. So when we talk about American higher education, we are talking increasingly and overwhelmingly about publicly controlled education, accountable to and dependent upon state governments.

This increasing diversity of students, faculty, and goals has led to campuses that are complex confederations of subcommunities. In the face of this diversity and complexity, many people see no common ground at all except physical proximity. Physical proximity itself is more time limited. A greater percentage of those affiliated with our institutions of higher education are commuters and part-timers. Most students spend only part of their day and part of their year on campus. Many regular faculty, though now spending most of their adult lives on one campus, limit more the number of hours and days per week in attendance, although this varies by type of institution. Only administrators spend whole days, weeks, years, and lives on campus. Generally, individuals' connections to their campus have become more time limited and more narrowly instrumental.

Research Findings

We have structured our broad examination of student life and community on campus around three themes: (1) student (in)tolerance of difference; (2) the boundaries of institutional authority; and (3) the nature of student and faculty (dis)connections and their impact on the learning community.

In "Campus Life in Perspective: Historical Snapshots," we trace the major forces that have brought changes to the areas of student life that are our foci: (1) the opening of higher education to a more diverse student body; (2) the changing concepts of authority and responsibility within the institution; and (3) the changing nature of student-faculty interaction. Not surprisingly, the tensions that characterize American campuses are rooted in the history of higher education. There is little new under the historical sun.

We chose to single out two of the most problematic aspects of difference on campus: race and ethnicity, and gender. We found that American student culture is essentially segregated in terms of racial and ethnic-group relations, but that many individuals have significant and friendly interaction. We found little evidence of overt or premeditated racism, but ample evidence of misunderstanding and insensitivity. African-American students experience significantly more alienation than do other minorities, and therefore we have devoted more time to examining this tension. In regards to undergraduate women, we found that the climate on campus has improved substantially over the last decade. Nonetheless, sexual harassment, in its subtler and grosser forms, continues, and students rarely learn about the contributions of women in their courses.

We found campuses more regulated than they were in the 1970s and early 1980s. Although *in loco parentis* is no longer the basis of campus authority, many of the regulations that were supported by the theory are alive and well. We found everywhere more and better programs to educate students about responsible and safe behaviors, that is, about mature participation in the campus community and society more generally. As we inquired into student behavior and student attitudes toward peers and the institution, we discovered:

- that alcohol abuse remains the major social pathology. However, on every campus there are greater efforts being made to educate students about the risks of overdrinking.
- that Greek life remains important at most institutions despite the small percentage of students involved nationally. Attitudes varied from campus to campus and on the same campus, because fraternities and sororities raise complex questions about the role of cohesive subgroups in building or undermining community of the whole. Most institutions are trying to find ways to empower the positive aspects of Greek life and curb the negative ones.

- that the regulation of speech is a major problem on our campuses. Indeed, under pressure from minority and women's groups and aggrieved individuals, and deeply concerned about protecting students against incivility and harassment of a sexual or racial nature, some colleges and universities are putting freedom of speech at risk.
- that crime on campus, an issue that has captured the imagination of the media, is not epidemic. At present, there are inadequate data to determine whether or not it has increased. There is no doubt that most campuses are substantially safer than their surrounding communities. Concerted efforts over the past decade have improved security everywhere we visited. Facilities have improved, student awareness has increased.
- that the initiation and enforcement of most regulations on campus occur within a complex system where students often play responsible roles, with support from student affairs professionals and faculty.

After examining important aspects of student life outside the classroom, we turn to the heart of the matter—the academic experience—and look carefully at the relationship between students and faculty. We found that students on research campuses (almost 29 percent) have little contact with regular faculty; those at comprehensive institutions (almost 28 percent) have somewhat more; and those at community (38 percent) and liberal arts (5 percent) colleges have substantially more. For the majority of our students, though, faculty-student relations can be characterized as an absence of relationship. Large lecture classes that effectively block interaction continue to be the norm. Few students seek assistance outside the class and few faculty offer much of it. Repeatedly, individuals compared their institutions to fast food restaurants— providing efficient mass production of a product that contributes little to the long-range intellectual health of the student or the institution.

We have found that the majority of students are less engaged in all aspects of academic and nonacademic campus life.[1] A number of factors contribute to this minimal contact and minimal connectedness. Most students, partly by necessity, partly by choice, spend the bulk of their time on activities other than going to class and studying. Most traditional-age students tend to do paid work for at least twenty hours a week, reserve long weekends for partying, and spend three to four hours a day in casual interaction with friends. Most adult students work thirty-six hours or more a week for pay, and commit their weekends to their families or friends. Academic work may actually be the lowest priority of both traditional-age and adult students.

Faculty culture varies according to each institution and its commitment to the priority of teaching. At community colleges and liberal arts colleges, we found faculty quite committed to the classroom and providing significant academic support to students. At aspiring comprehensive campuses and research institutions, teaching was the lowest priority for regular faculty. Students saw mainly adjuncts and graduate students.

We found that students rarely experience the campus as an academic community. Since they view it primarily as a place to acquire the credential necessary to get a job, this lack of intellectual community does not distress them. Faculty and academic administrators, for the most part, do little to strengthen learning communities on their campuses. Faculty, indeed, understand that reducing their demands on students can free up time for research and publication.

It is ironic and disturbing that neither faculty nor students find this lack of interaction a cause for serious concern. Surveys show the great majority of students "satisfied" with the quality of their instruction. Many faculty, by choice or by necessity, do not place a high priority on fostering intellectual community in their classrooms.

Perspectives on Community

In seeking to understand the reality and the aspiration on today's campuses, we have chosen the analytical lens of community. The theme of community, or more precisely, eclipse of community, in America is an old one. For more than one hundred years intellectuals, activists, religious leaders, and educators have bemoaned the decline of community in our increasingly urban and modern society. In the history of higher education, too, the growth of the large and complex university, which has accelerated exponentially since World War II, has been accompanied by the concern that we have lost community.

Certainly the term "community" is ubiquitous, in higher education as elsewhere. The cynic might propose as axiomatic that the actual experience of community exists in inverse proportion to the frequency of the use of the term by important group members. Indeed, today, a term that traditionally described a relatively small number of people living in the same area and linked by common values, practices, and goals, is often used to denote sheer proximity (neighborhoods within large suburbs, for example) and narrowly focused interest groups (the environmental community, the business community).

Yet, although usage has been watered down, it is quite clear that the term "community" still elicits a strong response from many of us, even when we are not quite able to explain why. The word carries with it historical resonance and metaphorical power, linking us to a personal saga of family and neighborhood and, perhaps, to a national saga of westward settlement and democratic ideals. In higher education, it conjures up enclaves of scholarship and learning (community of learning) and also college spirit associated with the private clubs, fraternities, and sororities that have figured so prominently in student life. Everywhere we went, people responded strongly to our topic: the campus as community. It excited strong reactions and lively debates.

In exploring community on campus, we have reflected on values, goals, and practices that individuals share and that constitute the basis for coming together and staying together, the basis for a sense of belonging. This search for common ground that connects individuals to groups and to the whole has informed much of our work. We have found affirmative community of the whole on campuses today relatively circumscribed.

To explore community on campus also has meant being attentive to a range of complexities. Since we have emphasized large institutions that are structurally complex and that have substantial socioeconomic and racial and ethnic diversity, we have been inundated with complexity of all kinds. We have examined complex questions to which there are no easy answers: To what extent can a given community include contradictory values? What are the costs and benefits of difference and dissent? What factors are weakening the campus learning community and how can institutions reinforce this foundation of higher education?

The invocation of community always refers to interests and values that transcend a single individual and therefore constrain his or her choices. Thus we have focused on the relations between individuals and the community. For example, does a pledge's individual right to security and privacy limit the ritual of initiation through hazing that contributes to the continuity of the community in a fraternity? Or does the university have the right to require students to take courses in ethnic or women's studies?

The relationship of subcommunities to other subcommunities and to the community of the whole has been likewise central. In some cases, values may be completely consonant, but we found many examples of partial or even complete dissonance. And in these cases, who decides which community should prevail? Dartmouth is a well-known example. The members of the *Dartmouth Review* seem to constitute a community (some of whose members are off campus). The values they espouse conflict strongly with minority ones, and also with the more liberal values of the community of the whole at Dartmouth.

We evoke these complexities, not because we shall be able to resolve them into simple formulae, but rather to underscore the limits of our *tour d'horizon* of life on American campuses as we enter the 1990s. We have found some interesting surprises and have also come to confirm some earlier conclusions. But as you continue through this book, it is essential to remember that our conclusions are informed by the understanding of community as a complex concept, one that incorporates the values of a democratic society encouraging learning and participation by all citizens of the campus.

Since we believe that the health of community on campus is essential to the mission of American higher education, we articulate a post-*in loco paren-*

tis theory of campus community that can guide renewal. This Compact for a Pluralistic Community includes four major principles: (1) the centrality of learning; (2) the importance of freedom of thought and expression; (3) the standard of justice in assessing all individual and community actions; and (4) respect for difference in the diverse campus communities manifested in civility of action. The recommendations that conclude our book are meant to support the creation of pluralistic learning communities on our nation's campuses.

In our vision of pluralistic campus community built on the foundation of a principled compact, implemented with honesty and integrity, individuals and subcommunities representing the pluralistic society of today have substantial autonomy once they enroll in the core values of the campus. They also have the right and responsibility to participate in the governance of the community of the whole. Finally, and most importantly, they enter into a compact for caring that acknowledges the mutual responsibility to respect individual and group differences and to promote high-quality relationships with others.

Lack of engagement, social fragmentation, and packaged and passive learning do not an academic community make. This nation and the world require men and women who are intellectually and civically well prepared, who have been educated to sustain and appreciate community. Our colleges and universities have a privileged role to play in this worthy endeavor.

CHAPTER 2

Campus Life in Perspective: Historical Snapshots

Introduction

Dramatic changes in size and structural complexity have affected every aspect of campus life. Since size and structural complexity are overarching factors influencing any experience of community on campus, we begin this historical overview with a brief reference to these changes before turning our attention to our three central themes of diversity, the boundaries of institutional authority, and faculty-student (dis)connections. We can best appreciate the changes in the size and structure of American higher education by looking at two snapshots: the first taken on the eve of the American Revolution, the second taken in 1980.

On the eve of the American Revolution, there were nine colleges, most of which awarded degrees to four or five candidates a year. Harvard was about to graduate its largest class—sixty-three proud men—in 1771. In 1770, there were only three thousand living graduates of all of the colleges in the country.[1] All students took the same courses, taught by teachers who were relatively young and temporary. The only long-term fixture, unless he was dismissed because of student riots, was the president, who, with his lay board, had absolute power. The state legislature may have provided a modest subvention, but it exercised little real power. Almost all of the operating money came from student tuition. A few wealthy landowners and an emerging cadre of wealthy alumni funded scholarships and capital expenditures.

In 1980, there were more than three thousand universities and colleges, ranging from small, two-year community colleges and four-year liberal arts colleges to gigantic state universities with up to sixty thousand students. These institutions enrolled approximately 11.5 million students in programs of study ranging from an associate's degree in cosmetology to a Ph.D. in cosmology. Approximately 675,000 faculty taught these students, almost 500,000 of whom were full-time, tenured or tenure-track, professors. The total current-fund expenditures exceeded $56 billion.[2] The money came first from the states, next from the federal government, and finally from student tuition. Most of the campuses were large, public systems governed by politically appointed boards of trustees and powerful but temporary presidents.

Indeed, between 1770 and 1980, higher education was transformed. The dramatic changes in size and structure mirrored the changes in the larger society. In the Jacksonian period, when America was moving West and becoming more populist, the higher education system expanded. By the eve of the Civil War, there were 250 colleges and universities, of which 180 still survive today. After the Civil War there was another boom, so that by 1870 there were 500 colleges and universities serving a fast-growing American population. Americans wanted a college for their children, a college nearby. By the time of the Morrill Act, two types of colleges were emerging—the traditional, religiously oriented institution, and the growing state university serving many diverse and utilitarian needs. The Morrill Act, with its grant of lands for universities to serve the public interest, rapidly accelerated the expansion of these public institutions. But even this expansion only generated by 1870 a full-time enrollment of 52,296 students taught by 5,563 faculty. By 1900, when the American population had grown through immigration to about 76 million, there were 237,592 students taught by 23,868 faculty. The number of institutions had almost doubled to 977 in thirty years, while enrollment had quadrupled.[3]

In the first twenty years of the twentieth century, enrollment more than doubled again to 587,880. In the next decade, it doubled yet again to 1,100,737. The Great Depression slowed, but did not stop, enrollment growth, which reached 1,494,203 on 1,708 campuses in 1939–40. The next dramatic surge occurred after the hiatus of World War II, when the GI Bill brought the enrollment numbers to 2,659,021 in 1949–50. The wave of baby boomers hit American higher education in the 1960s, so that by 1969–70 there were 8,004,660 students attending 2,525 institutions. The surge continued, and in 1980 there were 11,569,899 students taught by 675,000 faculty in 3,152 colleges and universities. The scale of American higher education had become gargantuan.

This dramatic increase in scale led to more structurally complex institutions, as did the increasing complexity of the knowledge that was being discovered and transmitted. By the early nineteenth century, colleges started adding new subjects to the trivium and quadrivium of the colonial colleges. The debate at Yale in the 1820s illustrated the tensions nationwide between proponents of the classical curriculum and reformers who advocated more utilitarian courses, such as science, engineering, and modern languages. By the Civil War, modern science and engineering disciplines began to emerge: chemistry, physics, civil and mechanical engineering.

The influence of the German university model at the turn of the century led to even greater disciplinary specialization. The emerging research universities organized themselves into academic departments around narrow specialties, led by research scholars. In regard to academic matters, the locus of power began to shift from the central administration to these departments. Specialization created both political and intellectual fragmentation:

> It is not putting it too strongly to say that in no American college today, with equipment sufficient to entitle it to the name, can a faculty be found in which all the members are bound together by any single important connecting link of past scholarly acquirement or current intellectual interest. It is the merest chance if a professor of biology in the younger ranks can meet the professor of Greek understandingly even within the narrow limits of the root meanings of the Greek terms in his technical vocabulary...[4]

After World War II, structural complexity increased much more. New disciplines, subdisciplines, and programs proliferated in response to scientific progress and student demands. These trends increased the power of the academic department. Administrative components, such as the business office, the development office, the sponsored research office, and campus security, became more complex. New ones appeared, such as affirmative action and computing. The research bureaucracy expanded. New categories of faculty became important: adjunct professors to teach undergraduates, soft-money researchers to work on grants and contracts. The universe of higher education became more complex in response to an ever more complex postindustrial society.

Having briefly acknowledged the sweeping changes in size and structural complexity that have created the campus of the 1990s, we turn to historical snapshots of the three themes central to our exploration of community on campus.

Opening to Diversity: Women and Minorities

The history of American higher education has been one of an ever growing and diversifying group of participants. Until the nineteenth century, students and faculty alike were overwhelmingly white Anglo-Saxon Protestant males from middle- to upper-class families. During the nineteenth century, colleges and universities began to admit men of less affluent means and some women. Black and women's colleges emerged after the Civil War. In the early twentieth century, urban universities began to admit new immigrants, particularly Jews, who, by 1918, were 48 percent of the enrollment at New York University, 21 percent at Columbia, and 10 percent at Harvard.[5] This prompted a transformation of the curriculum: the creation of general education courses to teach these bright young men the traditional preparatory school curriculum quickly. Campus life, though, changed very little.

Between 1920 and 1930, earned bachelor's degrees increased from 48,622 to 122,484, or two and one-half times—the fastest decade of growth in the twentieth century, except for the fifties. Much of this growth came from women. In 1920, 16,642 women earned BAs; in 1930, 48,869, almost three times as many. In 1920, 31,980 men earned BAs; in 1930, it was 73,615, almost two and one-third times as many. In 1930, one and one-half times as many men as women earned the BA. In 1900 the ratio had been 4.23 men to 1 woman. It was not until 1970 that this ratio was reduced to 1.32. By 1980, parity was reached at last.[6]

As we can see, most of the "feminization" of the classroom had occurred by 1930. However, society's view of educated women as wives and mothers responsible for managing the home did not change significantly until the 1970s. The separate and unequal division of gender roles was reflected in higher education through different curricula for men and women, and through different faculty attitudes and expectations.

As was the case during previous wars, World War II briefly expanded options for women. They enrolled in more science courses; they entered medical school. But the return to normalcy meant a return to domesticity. Whereas 12 percent of medical school graduates were women in 1949, 5 percent were women by the mid-1950s.[7] Arguments against professional training for women resurfaced. Helene Deutsch's *Psychology of Women* (1944) and Lundberg and Farnham's *Modern Woman: The Lost Sex* (1947) both cautioned against professional aspirations in mothers.[8] Women's behavior, however, quietly belied tradition. In the 1950s and 1960s, more and more women graduates worked for most or much of their adult lives. Although most male professions remained closed, the expanding economy accommodated larger numbers of women.

The first significant feminist movement since suffrage developed in the 1960s, as social reform became an important national issue. The civil rights movement, in which many women participated, gave impetus to women's demands for greater equality. Vocal African-American and white women activists denouncing the subordinate role of women in civil rights, free speech, and antiwar activism launched the new wave of American feminism. The impact of the women's movement on campuses took various forms: the formulation of new regulations to decrease discrimination against women faculty and staff, the growth of women's athletics, the development of women's centers providing a broad array of services, and a reappraisal of the knowledge base on which scholarship and teaching had been premised, a knowledge base that excluded half the human race. By the end of the 1970s, women's rights and women's difference had a stronger footing in the academy than ever before.

After World War II, the GI Bill provided support to large numbers of mature men, and some women, from diverse backgrounds. However, it was not until the 1960s, thirty years after the feminization of campuses, that the number and percentage of African-Americans, the second wave of ethnic diversity, increased significantly. Responding to the civil rights movement, higher education opened its doors wider. In 1965, there were 274,000 African-Americans enrolled in institutions of higher education in both under-graduate and graduate programs, 4.8 percent of the total enrollment of 5,675,000. In 1970, this rose to 522,000, or 7 percent.[9] By 1976, the increase mounted to 948,000, or 9.8 percent, and it peaked in 1980 at 1,107,000, or 10.2 percent. By 1982, African-American enrollment had begun to ebb, dropping to 1,101,000, or 9.2 percent.[10]

The wave of students of Hispanic origin is more recent still and lower than that for African-Americans. In 1976, the National Center for Education-al Statistics reported 384,000 people of Hispanic origin enrolled in under-graduate and graduate programs, 3.5 percent of the total. By 1980, this had increased to 472,000, 3.9 percent of the total, and by 1986, Hispanics num-bered 623,000 and 5.0 percent of all enrollments.[11] Another report indicates that the percentage of Hispanic high school graduates enrolled in college declined in the second half of the seventies. The aforementioned increase, then, is due to the growth in the number of college-age Hispanics.[12]

The increase in Asian-American enrollment is quite dramatic. In 1976, 198,000 students constituted 1.8 percent of the enrollment. By 1986, 623,000 students constituted 5 percent of all of the students in American higher edu-cation.[13] The Native American student population has remained constant at 0.7 percent even though it has increased absolutely from 76,000 in 1976 to 91,000 in 1986.[14]

On American campuses, the experience of increased racial and ethnic diversity is barely twenty years old. Until most recently, it was limited to the increased presence of African-Americans on white campuses. It was the community colleges that saw the greatest influx of minority students and adapted the most to their needs. By the end of the 1970s, despite increased access, minority students still did not attend college in proportion to their numbers in the population as a whole and had higher attrition rates than white students. However, the issue of minority access and achievement had become a top priority in the higher education world.

Ironically, the arrival of more African-Americans on campus coincided with a change in attitude toward difference that was international in its scope. In America, by the 1970s, the aspiration to assimilate had lost ground against new affirmations of racial and ethnic pride. The ideal of "America [as] God's Crucible, the great Melting-Pot"[15] has never recovered. The 1970s also saw the growth of white resentment of affirmative action. These atti-tudes crystallized in the 1977 *Allen Bakke* case. Denied admission to a Uni-versity of California medical school that had accepted African-American applicants with lower test scores, Bakke sued and won.

Changing Concepts of Authority and Responsibility

The relationship between the student and the campus has both changed and stayed constant over our history. The ethical and legal framework for understanding this relationship and enforcing the boundaries of authority changed quite recently, in the 1960s, from the doctrine of *in loco parentis* to a dual framework, a contractual one, and, particularly in public institutions, a constitutional one.

The challenging of institutional authority by students has always occurred, although the intensity of protest appears to wax and wane. There was greater intensity and frequency during the American Revolution, in the early nineteenth century, in the 1930s, and lastly, in the 1960s. One must qualify the assertion of the constancy of challenge by noting two things: first, that, since the 1960s, parental authority in our society has weakened, changing the nature of adult-adolescent interaction on campus; second, that, for the last twenty-five years, given the influx of adult students, campus conflict over authority has been less and less reducible to intergenerational conflict.[16]

Students in colonial times came to college when they were fourteen or fifteen. Their parents expected college authorities to take responsibility for and discipline these young men during their adolescent exuberance. The concept of *in loco parentis* was both an ethical and legal concept that correctly identified the socializing function of higher education. The colleges responded to this challenge with suitable pontification. In 1792, President Nisbet of Dickinson College, explaining the collegiate role to parents, summarized well the reigning expectations:

> A Parent cannot but be anxious when his Child is at distance from him, and exposed to Dangers of different kinds, but as in Education a certain Risk must be run, in order to gain a certain Advantage, every good Parent, as well as every good Teacher, ought to be satisfied when he is taking the best means for preserving the Morals of his Child, as well as for improving his Understanding.[17]

This extension of parental authority to the campus also guaranteed generational warfare, not only figuratively, but literally. Throughout the eighteenth and nineteenth centuries, rebellion was part of student culture, and students resisted institutional efforts to regulate their social and academic behavior.[18] There were riots over such things as bad food and excessive discipline. In the early nineteenth century, there were riots at Penn, Yale, and Princeton; indeed, the students bombed a building at Princeton.[19] The disturbances were generally successfully quelled, but occasionally the president lost his job because he could not control his charges. Student residences, whether on the campus or in town, became the sites of organized rebellion. The foresighted founders of Yale urged its first president not to create student residences because of all the trouble young men living together got into. Over the years, most student rebellion has been local and nonideological. In an example from the 1950s, a "Pogo for President" rally turned into a riot with the police.[20]

The campus has also been the setting for politically motivated dissent. When revolution came to the new United States, the students at King's College (soon to be called Columbia) forced the Tory president, Myles Cooper, to escape from his residence over a back fence to an English sloop of war in New York harbor. They then took over the college. One Alexander Hamilton, class of 1774, held the mob at bay while the president escaped and then led his fellow classmates in the take-over.[21] During the 1930s, on urban campuses, a number of radical students experimenting with communism held occasional demonstrations. During the 1960s, politically motivated student dissent became commonplace on campuses. Sparked by student involvement in the civil rights movement, the free speech movement at Berkeley, in 1965, was followed by Black Power incidents (San Francisco State, Cornell) and antiwar demonstrations that mixed with protest against various university policies. Sit-ins, strikes, marches, and the systematic disruption of classes were the most prevalent forms of protest. There was also violence, including the bombing and burning of university buildings. The killing of students at Kent State by National Guardsmen marked the end of a tragic and perplexing era. As the war in Vietnam ended, campuses normalized. That is, there continued to be occasional student protests of varying degrees of intensity.[22]

From the beginnings of the colonial colleges through the flapper era of the 1920s and the Joe College 1950s until the present day, student drinking has been the root of much conflict. During the early Harvard days, local merchants were warned against serving alcohol to young scholars. Prohibition in the 1920s offered a special challenge to colleges that was widely debated. Little effort was put into enforcement on those campuses where drinking was a tradition, and little was needed in the small sectarian colleges where alcohol had been prohibited since their founding. Until states raised their drinking age in the 1970s, colleges and universities for the most part maintained a laissez-faire approach to alcohol use. In the 1960s and 1970s, drug use became widespread in student culture, exacerbating regulation issues at a time of acute student rebellion against authority.

Student journalists have, since the early nineteenth century, used campus newspapers and magazines to assert radical and conservative positions and have often conflicted with campus administrations. In the 1930s, President Nicholas Murray Butler expelled the editor of the *Columbia Spectator* for criticizing him and his administration and for writing radical opinions. Over the years, only a small number of students have created controversy through exercising free speech and press on campus. Conflict around the exercise of these freedoms has been a locus of frequent testing of institutional boundaries. In the wake of the free speech movement at Berkeley, court decisions confirmed that campuses could regulate the when and where of expression, but not the what.

Social fraternities have provided an enduring organizational setting for avoiding and rebelling against institutional boundaries of authority. In the early nineteenth century, during the first major expansion of American higher education, students devised this new form of organization to structure their social life outside of the controls of the college. At Union College in New York, a group of wealthy young men formed the first fraternity, Kappa Alpha, and clothed it in vaguely Masonic ritual. By 1840, fraternities had spread to most of New England; they took solid root in the Midwest and the South by the time of the Civil War.[23] They comprised elite groups of students pledged to secrecy and committed to creating a select friendship group. By the late nineteenth century, the dominant model of campus life had become that of the fraternity and later the sorority, even though on most campuses few students ever joined. The Greeks created a setting where students controlled their own social lives and a culture where extracurricular, not academic, achievement was most highly valued.

Enforcement of authority on campus has historically been an administrative prerogative. In the colonial college the president or his representative, usually called a proctor, enforced the rules. The faculty were happy to leave this task to him. By the mid-nineteenth century, there was a dean responsible for students, who took over the enforcement function. As coeducation emerged, there was a dean of women and a dean of men. It was not until the early twentieth century that campus police officers emerged, usually retired policemen who worked with their former colleagues at the line of the town/gown relationship. The revolution of the 1960s changed the enforcement patterns. The large-scale student protests brought the police on campus in a way that created more problems than it solved. In the 1970s, the campuses developed their own police forces to deal with civil disturbance and to cope with the problems of the complex societies that many campuses had become. The intervention of the courts forced campuses to give students due process rights and signaled the death of the tradition of *in loco parentis* that had structured the student/institution relationship previously.

Students and Faculty: Evolving Cultures

During the colonial and Revolutionary War periods, students were mainly young regionals en route to the professions. Student culture did not value academic achievement. The primary goal was to study as little as possible to graduate and to have as much fun as possible. The faculty were seen as adversaries.

The faculty during the first seventy-five years of the new country were small in number and endured quite low status. Their employment was at the mercy of the president and the board, both of which often fired faculty simply because they, or the parents on which the institution depended for funds, did not like them. At the same time, the faculty were poorly paid. They were often young graduates of the same institution, teaching for a period before going on to another profession that paid better and had more prestige.

The faculty member's role during the period leading up to the Civil War was one of both teacher of skills and knowledge, on the one hand, and moral tutor imposing personal discipline, on the other. In addition, at many religious institutions, the teacher had some obligations for the student's soul. Although, for the most part, college teachers had excelled in their own studies, they were not hired for their accomplishment in a specified area of learning, but for their ability to deal with vigorous adolescents who did not wish to play by the rules or commit much effort to learning. From the beginning, neither faculty nor students had much affection for each other.

There was an important evolutionary change in the structure of student-faculty relations that took American higher education away from its British roots. In Britain, as in the early American colleges, teaching and testing were separate. But by the early part of the nineteenth century, the current structure of distinct courses, being taught and tested by the same faculty person, had emerged. This gave new power to the teacher over the taught: he not only instructed, but he also vouched for the competence of the student to the world. By the end of the nineteenth century, with President Eliot's initiation of the elective system at Harvard, the course unit system, with its individual classes added together to qualify for a degree, had clearly emerged. This structure gave an individual professor more power to teach what he wished; it also gave students some power to choose. At the end of the nineteenth century, one finds the roots of market-driven higher education that increasingly has characterized the twentieth century.

As American colleges transformed themselves into research universities during the last third of the nineteenth century, the relationship between faculty and students changed even more. One contributing factor was the development of a universal secondary school system that allowed colleges and universities to set minimum entry standards to insure adequate prior preparation. This also moved the age of admission forward to eighteen and connected age to accomplishment.[24] The ladder of entry and progress became uniform and colleges and universities controlled the work of the secondary schools. Some midwestern universities, such as the University of Wisconsin, established high school graduation standards by their entry requirements. More students came to college better prepared; more faculty came from graduate schools trained to value research.

During the first two decades of the twentieth century, the preparation of public school students improved but, still, that preparation did not meet the standards of the private schools. As colleges and universities admitted students from diverse religious and economic backgrounds, they revised their curricula to include the common core of knowledge about Western Civilization that public school students lacked. At the non-elite institutions, students and faculty continued to have very different views of the purpose of undergraduate education. However, the evolving meritocracy meant that students did have to do some academic work to leave with a degree. The diversity of types of colleges meant that every student with economic means and a high school diploma could attend college, but it did not mean that all degrees were created equal. The hierarchy of institutions that, during the nineteenth century, had been based on social status, became one based upon faculty publication.

By 1940, the faculty had moved from being a small band of teachers (5,553 in 1870) to an eclectic cadre of 146,929, divided between teachers and scholars. The number of students had increased substantially, to 1,494,203, mostly through the growth of public universities. By the 1930s, the public sector had started its rapid ascent at the expense of the private institutions. This meant that the faculty-student relationship began to be affected by the size of the institution. Lecture classes grew much larger.

The out-of-classroom moral tutor role that had been part of the job description of faculty in the nineteenth century had actually started its decline on the eve of the twentieth century. It was the expansion of the 1920s and the rise of the land grant universities that subverted the dual role. Yet, before World War II, universities still viewed an important part of their mission to be the socialization of the young. As the years passed, the demands of research grew greater, and the faculty grew disinterested in the primacy of teaching because there was more prestige associated with research scholarship. By the early 1920s, students had moved from the center of faculty attention to the periphery.

During the period between the two World Wars, the faculty organized nationally to guarantee their status. After the president of Stanford fired a faculty member because his wife did not like him, a group of elite easterners organized the American Association of University Professors (AAUP), in 1915, to create a public organization to protect faculty from such arbitrary treatment. After twenty-five years of protest and cajoling, in 1940 the AAUP finally convinced the elite institutions to agree to a codified system of tenure and economic security for faculty in a joint statement with university representatives.[25] In future years, this codified system spread throughout the country. Since tenure was awarded primarily for publication, not teaching, this meant that both good teachers and bad teachers henceforth could secure their future in academe, provided they published. This reward structure created the conditions necessary for the research mission.

By the 1950s, the division between teaching colleges and research universities had become quite set. The elite research institutions became the stars, and the rest were aspiring actors. The launching of Sputnik helped the research institutions get richer and also brought to these elite university campuses a new breed of meritocrat: bright students with financial need who received federal student aid. However, most of higher education remained the home of students who were there to enjoy adolescence at a time when faculty were increasingly research oriented.

The 1960s were years of great expansion, with the creation of hundreds of new campuses for the baby boomers. Most of these campuses were part of large public systems. Many were two-year community colleges. The quick expansion of the system brought thousands of new faculty who developed great mobility and little attachment to particular campuses. Within the faculty ranks there developed two class divisions—the "cosmopolitans" who were researchers moving from promotion to promotion and campus to campus, and the "locals" left behind to teach students who were coming to campus by the thousands, many with weak preparation. The divergence between faculty aspirations and student quality became exacerbated in the 1960s and 1970s.

By the end of the 1960s, the first wave of minority students hit American campuses with fanfare. Diversity brought new problems. Although the 1960s had already seen an influx of students lacking the high standards of preparation of the earlier generations, it was the coming of African-American students from segregated high schools, who had even weaker preparation, that brought new needs for remediation as part of the college program. The distance of these new students from the experiences of the white instructional staff created new tension between faculty and students.

At the same time that the 1960s brought new challenges to the teacher-student relationship, they brought, for some, a new camaraderie. The politically active students found comrades among the liberal faculty. Together, they took on the American political system and many college administrations. This bonding was time limited, but it was a reality of the moment of the Age of Aquarius for many faculty and students.

As the Vietnam War wound down in the 1970s and the United States grew more overtly conservative, the campuses grew quieter. But there had been important changes in campus life and student-faculty relationships. The quality of faculty life was diminishing. Faculty were teaching many more students, more of whom were underprepared. Inflation had outrun faculty salaries. Most cosmopolitans had become locals, unable to move up. The life of more and more faculty members became one of overwork and underpay.

Student careerism took an upswing. Political affinities between faculty and students waned and disappeared. Students had more power on campus, having won expanded rights in the course of the revolution of the 1960s. They could, for example, grieve against faculty members who did not give them the grades they felt they deserved. Increasingly, they evaluated faculty teaching. The Buckley Amendment gave them access to faculty's letters of recommendation.

Yet conflict was constrained. Both students and faculty tolerated each other. The faculty did not want the retrenchment that enrollment drops would entail, and the students wanted good grades and good recommendations, as well as the degree. The deal was cut for the 1980s.

Student Affairs Professionals

During the time between the Civil War and World War I, as faculty began to undertake specialized scholarship and research endeavors, and as coeducation made new demands on the university, the student affairs profession emerged. To free research-minded faculty from the work of student caretaking and of institutional management, colleges and universities began creating administrative posts such as registrars, vice-presidents, business officers, and deans. Harvard claims to have appointed the first dean of men in 1870. His duties were to attend to discipline and enrollment matters in addition to teaching. Women often referred to as matrons, principals, and wardens acted as the prototypes of deans of women in their roles as watchdogs in the new arena of coeducation.

From these initial appointments, deans and other student services professionals have evolved from disciplinarians to custodians of student culture to educators and, most recently, to integrators. William Rainey Harper, of the University of Chicago, said in 1899 that the "scientific study of the student" would be the next great research field in higher education. Following World War I, Harper's proclamations came true as the profession witnessed the development of new psychological theories including the psychology of the individual, the holistic approach, and John Dewey's progressive educational theories. As the tradition of moral tutor faded from the faculty culture, student services professionals faithfully maintained their commitment to educate the whole person. They further professionalized and diversified their own ranks, creating student health and counseling centers, testing services, and career counseling and placement services. Despite this expansion and professionalization, the number of student affairs administrators on campuses has remained relatively small and they have not achieved equal status with faculty.

This very brief *tour d'horizon* of the history of campus life allows us now to move on to the 1980s with some important insights. Surely, we have seen that history does not document a "paradise lost." Rather, it shows enduring tensions between centripetal and centrifugal forces. Colleges and universities have always struggled to create and maintain a sense of community of the whole; individuals and subgroups have always posed challenges. We have glimpsed both continuity and change. On the one hand, many of the features that characterize current faculty-student relations are variations on longstanding themes. On the other hand, the death of *in loco parentis* and the challenge to reassess the boundaries of authority between students and their institutions are relatively recent. So is the challenge to create truly pluralistic campuses, campuses where difference, especially racial, ethnic, and gender difference, is framed by the shared commitment of mutual understanding.

Part 2

Diversity and Community: Can They Coexist?

Introduction

Over the last twenty-five years, thanks to historically unprecedented access, American higher education has grown much more diverse and complex. There are more minority and women students, faculty, and administrators in our colleges and universities. Many have given voice to their beliefs and needs, prompting institutions to reevaluate their most basic assumptions and least attractive biases.

As we summarized earlier, we found that American student culture is essentially segregated in terms of racial and ethnic-group relations, but that many individuals have significant and friendly interaction. We found little evidence of overt or premeditated racism, but ample evidence of misunderstanding and insensitivity. African-American students experience significantly more alienation than do other minorities; therefore we have devoted more time to examining this tension. In regards to undergraduate women, we found that the climate on campus has improved substantially over the last decade. Nonetheless, sexual harassment, in its subtler and grosser forms, continues, and students rarely learn about the experiences and contributions of women in their courses.

In this section, we will explore racial and ethnic as well as gender differences on American campuses. These differences, sometimes problematic and troubling, challenge community of the whole at the same time that they enrich it. We will examine both the factors that separate individuals and groups and fragment community, and those that connect individuals and groups and strengthen community.

Racial and ethnic diversity is the greatest challenge facing campuses as they move into the 1990s. Many campuses have accomplished much in opening their doors to African-Americans, Hispanics, native Americans, and Asian-Americans, but many of these students still do not feel that they belong. Academic difficulties combine with varying degrees of cultural alienation to diminish the satisfaction of many minority students. White students, raised in our still substantially segregated society, can experience discomfort and demonstrate insensitivity when interacting with minorities. The frequency with which minority students continue to report personal experiences of racism testifies to the scope of the challenge facing higher education.

The differential treatment of individuals based on their sex seems to continue on American campuses. Undergraduate women appear to experience less sexism than women graduate students or faculty, and they express equal or greater satisfaction with their experience compared with their male counterparts. Still, as continuing reports of sexual harassment and assault point out most dramatically, traditional stereotypes of women, and men, persist. In a variety of ways, these stereotypes constrict personal and professional growth and diminish the potential for a just campus community.

Racial and ethnic differences as well as gender differences often significantly shape the climate on our campuses, both explicitly and implicitly. The architecture of racial and ethnic difference, especially, is one of informal and formal subgroups, significantly isolated from each other, ignorant of each other, and, for the most part, unconcerned about the disconnections. It is as much this ignorance and lack of interest as the more visible clash of different factions that detracts from the potential for community on campus. Grouping by special interest or need is natural and inevitable. We believe that belonging to some campus subcommunity is probably a prerequisite for connecting to the whole. But healthy community strikes a balance between the parts and the whole. And on today's campuses we did not find enough attention being paid to nourishing the centripetal forces, the common values and experiences, the common structure within which different subcommunities can coexist and interact.

CHAPTER 3

Race and Ethnicity

We are multicultural, but we are not the melting pot.

—Student at a community college in the Midwest
with a significant minority population

Introduction

"E Pluribus Unum. From Many One." The American experience has long been marked by tension between the dual aspiration for national unity and for cultural pluralism: the affirmation of community of the whole on the one hand, the pull of racial, ethnic, or religious identities on the other. The cultural myth of America as the melting pot reflects the anxiety of a nation of immigrants. By the early twentieth century, assimilation of difference had entered the field of fundamental American values. It kept the risks of pluralism in check. By the 1960s, however, racial and ethnic pride had become another value held by many Americans, one that conflicted with the mainstream. Old questions resurfaced with great urgency. What is the common ground that connects members of a pluralistic society? What are the responsibilities of the majority in regards to minority groups? To what extent is racial or ethnic separation normal and to what extent is it problematic?

On many campuses, such questions have been central for more than twenty years. They came to the fore when African-Americans began attending white campuses in increasing numbers. And, although they have accompanied the arrival and increased presence of individuals of Hispanic and Asian backgrounds and native Americans, they continue to be most pressing in regards to African-Americans, for progress toward connecting African-Americans to the higher education community has been the slowest.

Campuses, of course, do not exist independent of social reality. The National Research Council's comprehensive report on the status of African-Americans since the end of World War II, *A Common Destiny: Blacks and American Society,* documents the mixed record of America's efforts to operationalize the principle of equality in all areas. Although

29

the social status of American blacks has *on average* improved dramatically, both in absolute terms and relative to whites,...today [it] can be characterized as a glass that is half full—if measured by progress since 1939—or as a glass that is half empty—if measured by the persisting disparities between black and white Americans since the early 1970s.[1]

Whether the glass is half full or half empty is important for the campus as well. When *Newsweek* interviewed 516 undergraduates at one hundred campuses in 1986, it found the following answers to the question, "How would you describe relations between whites and minorities on your campus?": friendly but not close—56 percent; close and harmonious—27 percent; cooperative but not friendly—13 percent; aloof and hostile—1 percent.[2] On the one hand, these results are encouraging; only 1 percent of students found relations aloof and hostile. On the other hand, it is disappointing that fewer than a third of the respondents found relations close and harmonious.

The American Council on Education's recent survey of presidents evokes similar mixed feelings. It is encouraging that 79 percent of presidents at all institutions do not consider racial tensions or hostilities a problem on their campuses. It is disturbing that only 34 percent of the presidents of research institutions can make this statement.[3]

The hard facts are not as encouraging as the administrators' opinions suggest. Higher education has not met the aspirations of the 1960s. Minority enrollments as percentage of the minority population have been dropping; funding has decreased; there are inadequate numbers of minority faculty and administrators; weak high school preparation of minority students has not been overcome; and campus integration has not occurred. The attitudes resulting from centuries of systemic racism and segregation—ignorance of difference, fear of difference, and, in some cases continued racism—have proven more difficult to modify than reformers imagined. The potential of higher education to be the laboratory for social change has not been met.

There are those who argue that the ideological commitments of the Reagan administration have been the principal cause of the lack of progress, in society generally, and on campus particularly. One should not forget, however, that the majority of white Americans has never endorsed the implementation of racial equality. *A Common Destiny: Blacks and American Society* contains a chapter on the racial attitudes and behaviors of white Americans and African-Americans from 1940 to 1986. This research documents a longstanding lack of widespread support.[4] The authors focus on attitudinal surveys. In one table, they report eight questions asked under the category of implementation. They compare responses from the first year the questions were asked and the last year they were asked, usually about a decade apart. In five of the eight areas of implementation there was no significant change in response (6 percent or below). For example, only 38 percent of those surveyed endorsed federal job intervention in 1964, and 36 percent in 1974; 22 percent of respondents approved aid to minorities in 1970, and 18 percent in 1982. Support for open housing increased 12 percent from 1973 to 1983. Support for federal school intervention dropped 17 percent from 1964 to 1978, and support for accomodations intervention grew 22 percent from 1964 to 1974.[5]

The authors formulate a number of conclusions. The most relevant to our discussion of race and ethnicity on campus follow:

• There has been a steady increase in support among white Americans for principles of racial equality, but substantially less support for policies intended to implement principles of racial equality.
• Blacks also exhibit a gap between support for principles and support for policies intended to implement these principles, and blacks show recent decreases in support for policy implementation strategies....
• Measures of black alienation from white society suggest an increase in black alienation from the late 1960s into the 1980s.[6]

Of course, the resurgence of conservatism, already underway in the 1970s, has likely been an important factor in maintaining the status quo vis-à-vis the implementation of equality for African-Americans and other minorities. In the light of the attitudinal research, however, one can see that conservatives have been voicing and acting on attitudes widely held by white Americans. The Reagan policies, in fact, articulated these longstanding attitudes.

It is certainly clear that American campuses now must address their somewhat greater racial and ethnic diversity in a social and political context far more overtly conservative than the historical period that opened campuses up originally. Part and parcel of this more vocal conservatism is the expression of attitudes that many would define as racist. Since colleges and universities tend to be more liberal than mainstream America, the potential for tension with more conservative students and alumni is very real. At the same time, even liberal faculty and administrators may be unable to overcome the barriers the others have erected because of distrust and alienation that many of their minority students and colleagues experience.

In this section we will consider the challenge to community that racial and ethnic difference brings to colleges and universities. As we discuss the impact of race and ethnicity on individual interactions and on the interactions of organized subgroups, we will also explore factors that influence minority students' sense of belonging on campus, the ways in which minority and white students experience the tension between separation and integration, and the kinds of conflict that result from the coexistence of people from different races and ethnic groups on campus.

Understanding the impact of racial and ethnic diversity on campus requires confronting a multifaceted and emotionally charged reality. Stanford University's Committee on Minority Issues put it well in its comprehensive 1989 report:

> The complex relations between minority and white students at Stanford preclude easy characterization. Paradoxes abound. On the one hand, minorities and whites socialize together regularly and frequently, and they commonly form interracial friendships. On the other hand, they often demonstrate a lack of understanding between groups.[7]

The Committee on Minority Issues commissioned a study by SRI International, a major consulting firm, that provided more data on race relations than were available to us on any campus. The committee offered recommendations on all aspects of campus life: academic and cocurricular. Ninety-five percent of the African-Americans participating in the survey said they did not fit into the Stanford community. Yet, at the same time, 77 percent mostly or strongly agreed "that they would recommend Stanford as 'a good place to go to college.'"[8]

At the institutions we visited we recognized the complexities and paradoxes found by the Stanford committee members. Like them, we will consider separately relations between individuals and relations between groups. Since the experience of different racial and ethnic groups varies, as we report from interviews on our campuses we will always identify the racial or ethnic identity of the speaker. The nomenclature of race and ethnicity is complex, as different individuals and groups prefer different terms. At the request of our publisher, we use the term "African-American" to designate native-born blacks. We use the term "black" to designate individuals who are not American, or a mixed group of Americans and non-Americans. Of course, the use of the term "black" to designate Americans is very common, and we have used it in quotations, organization titles, and commonly used phrases, such as "historically black colleges."

Individual Interaction

We found that individual minority and white students interact substantially. Students have friends from other racial and ethnic backgrounds and most residence halls and organized extracurricular activities are integrated. At the small research university in the East that we visited, a recent apartheid protest involved both black and white students. At the research university in the Southwest, students of all racial and ethnic backgrounds came together to call for greater diversity on campus. At the comprehensive university in the South, only 10 percent of the 535 students responding to a 1988 survey disagreed with the statements "Relationships between white and minority students are generally friendly" and "I don't think participation in campus activities is limited by a student's race." At a mid-Atlantic flagship university, a minority student commented: "As individuals, we either don't associate at all or we associate and integrate well. It is either good or not at all." In our travels, we found modest integration of Greek social organizations. At two southern comprehensive universities, individual African-American students had achieved notable success in assuming leadership positions on their predominantly white campuses. At one school, an African-American coed was elected homecoming queen and an African-American male was elected president of the student government for the past two years. At the other, an African-American woman was elected president of a women's leadership program.

Relations in class were also presented as generally positive. At the small private comprehensive university, an African-American woman student said: "I am often the only black student in class. For the most part, I feel just fine. I don't find problems unless I look for them."

Despite this evidence of friendly interaction, we also found evidence of racist attitudes and substantial racial and ethnic separation. The African-American vice-president for student affairs at the small research university in the East noted: "the climate for persons of color is by definition difficult and tense." There was significant tension on one other campus and black/white polarization at another.

At one comprehensive university, there had been a fight between a white member of the wrestling team and an African-American student in the fall. At another comprehensive university in a city with a high proportion of African-Americans, African-American students referred to the institution as "the plantation." A number of minority students who spoke with us shared experiences of encounters with fellow students that they considered racist. The homecoming queen reported seeing racist graffiti attacking her in the women's restroom. An African-American candidate for a student government position said that a fellow white student he had asked to vote for him responded: "Is the other candidate on your ticket a Nigger too?"

As our visits confirmed, African-American students, particularly, seem to be experiencing racism on American campuses. However, other minority students have reported incidents as well. Chicano students interviewed in *Change* reported similar encounters: "I've been stereotyped out the wazoo," said Jake Foley, a twenty-two–year-old Mexican-American accounting student at the University of Texas. "People will joke around—at least I hope they are joking—and say, 'Oh, he's Mexican, hide your wallet.' Or, 'Do you have a switchblade?'"[9]

Minority students often think white students view them as exceptions to the admissions standards of their colleges: "We carry a stigma in a sense....

When I first came here as a freshman, a white undergraduate said to me, 'You're here and my friend, who is better qualified, is not.'" (Chicana student.)[10] At MIT, an African-American alumnus reported:

> I was in a class where we needed to do a group project. All of the groups formed without me, so the professor was forced to assign me. They tried to delegate the important tasks to themselves and tried to give me the trivial assignments. I set them straight, though. Any activity that required group work was a tremendous strain due to prejudicial attitudes.[11]

A certain number of white students do question the justification for affirmative action in student admissions, faculty hiring, and in society generally. At our flagship research campus in the Southwest, an assistant dean of students commented: "Most white students don't understand why white applicants are being left out. Black students are asked, 'did you get in here because you are black?'" The campus "sweetheart" was quoted in the newspaper as opposing affirmative action in faculty hiring: "I don't think they [referring to the law school] should hire someone because they are black, because if we start doing things like that, it's not the university's reputation for having the best around. [sic]" A professor in the business school of a large midwestern flagship campus we visited reported that white students talking about a recent Supreme Court decision in a class on business law rejected affirmative action strategies: "This was an honors course for seniors and juniors, and none of them supported anything more than equal opportunity."

Student-faculty relations, as well as student-student relations, can be influenced by racial and ethnic difference. On our campuses, on the whole, students and faculty reported positive relationships between minority students and their overwhelmingly white faculty. The exception was a comprehensive, urban university in the East where many African-American students and white faculty felt uncomfortable with one another. At our historically black college, the small minority of white students and faculty felt completely welcome.

We received little systematic information from our schools regarding the impact of race and ethnicity on faculty-student relations. One institution had been carrying on a longitudinal study that included comparisons of African-American and white students. Results reported in 1988 showed that approximately two-thirds of the African-American respondents in their freshman, sophomore, and junior years agreed or were neutral that "instructors acted as if they cared for students." Even where relationships were generally good, there were occasional reports of racist encounters. For example, an African-American student at our urban comprehensive university in the South reported that a professor in his speech class told him not to major in communications, a comment that he interpreted as racist.

For residential minority students, there is some evidence that living in an integrated or a separate residence hall influences students' experience of race relations. The MIT African-American student experience of separate and integrated living as documented in a survey of African-American alumni helps explain why many African-American students feel more comfortable in separate living arrangements:

> Three-quarters of those who lived in predominantly white living-group settings described their experiences there in generally negative or mixed terms, while those who lived in predominantly black living-group settings (approximately one-third of the respondents) were unanimously positive about their experience there.[12]

The black/white tension at Stanford's Ujamaa House arose out of Stanford's commitment not to have completely separate living areas for minorities.

At the institutions we visited, students' experience of race relations on campus depended, in part, on whether they lived in residence halls or commuted. A number of commuter students expressed the sentiment that living off campus provided a buffer. It may be that students at primarily commuter institutions experience less tension since most of the racial interaction is either in a structured classroom setting or in a self-selected extracurricular program. Interestingly, commuting can create other tensions. An African-American student at a comprehensive urban institution said that the fact he went home everyday also exposed him to a different sort of pressure: "My black friends at home say that I am an Oreo because I go to a white institution."

It is certainly plausible, especially at primarily commuting campuses, that there is a connection between the state of race relations in the immediate community and the experience of students on campus. In a southwestern metropolitan community college, there were no individual experiences of racism reported to us, in part, we suspect, because of the multi-ethnic community surrounding the college. This western city is known for its good race relations. "We don't have racial problems, we get along very well," said a foreign student from Mexico. "We're our own little world," said a Mexican-American engineering student. "We're unique in that we have people from all walks of life; we don't identify people by ethnicity." "This is the only place where it doesn't matter who you are," said a white woman student. "We're all struggling, we're all in this together. We're too mixed to have racial problems."

Misunderstanding and insensitivity appear to be common sources of the behavior labeled racist. As we went about our exploration of the impact of racial and ethnic diversity on campus community we were reminded how little the larger society has addressed the issue of educating students to understand and respect difference. The overwhelming majority of all students come to college having had little contact with other races and ethnicities before attending college; even fewer have had any education about difference. The lenses students use to decode behavior are the ones they have inherited from a profoundly imperfect past, perpetuating itself in the present. Unexamined conscious or unconscious stereotypes, ignorance, insensitivity, and hypersensitivity are the barriers that must be surmounted between and among even well-meaning individuals before comfortable interracial and interethnic relations can occur.

Misunderstanding occurs on both sides of interaction across races and ethnic groups. Ironically, much of what is experienced as racism arises out of the greater contact that has become commonplace on American campuses. Stanford's "black-Beethoven" incident, which drew national attention and was carefully examined by a campus team, helps illustrate how insensitivity and bad judgment create hurt and escalate into campus-wide issues.

Two white freshmen and an African-American sophomore had a debate about racial purity, the importance of race in accomplishment, and the influence of blacks on music in America. This debate was a continuation of a discussion among about ten students in the hall of Ujamaa House, the black-culture residential theme house. As part of that conversation, the African-American student asserted that Beethoven was a mulatto. However, the white students were skeptical and asked the African-American student to offer some evidence. He responded that he had read this in two different books. Later that day, the two white students, after they had been drinking, put a poster of Beethoven next to the African-American student's door. They had altered the poster to depict a stereotype of a black man. This was interpreted as a racist act and became the focus of a major black/white confrontation at Stanford. This incident was certainly experienced as racist by the African-American student and his fellow students and it appears to have prompted retaliations. The two white students described their intent as parody, satire, "since it showed the connection between racial pride and stereotyping."[13]

The issue of misunderstanding of behavior is not new. Professor Michael Moffatt, in his study of students at Rutgers, provides an example from a decade ago that reminds us of the stubborn nature of the problem. On a residence floor divided into a white wing and a black wing, at the first floor meeting of the year, a group of returning black students joined some white students new to the residence hall to plan programs. This was an event. The black students had boycotted the meetings the previous year. None of the white students knew this. Neither side participated in the conversation at first. After the resident assistant suggested a folksinger similar to James Taylor as music for a party, one black student laughed derisively and mocked, "James Taylor?" The meeting broke up shortly thereafter. The white students viewed the black participation as hostile and aggressive. The black students viewed themselves as making an affirmative friendly act by attending the meeting. Neither side left with positive feelings.[14]

An incident that occurred at our elite flagship institution in the West, and was reported as an example of racism to a state legislative investigating committee, further illustrates the possibility for hurt born of cultural ignorance. An African-American student residing in a residence hall was stopped by her resident assistant (R.A.) and questioned about the texture and length of her hair. "How did you do this?" asked the R.A. "Yesterday your hair was short, and today you have braids." This question was raised while other students, mostly Asian-American and white, were present. The student, feeling embarrassed, replied, "Didn't you know? Black people's hair grows just like a Barbie Doll. Every time we wash it we simply pull it from our scalp and it grows." Promising the R.A. that she would be washing her hair that evening, the African-American student left the residence hall. When she returned, nine students were waiting to observe her "Barbie Doll exhibition."

This example also illustrates the subjectivity of judgments about racist behavior. Although the African-American student experienced the exchange as racist, the other nine students who showed up to watch her wash her hair appear to have interpreted the exchange at face value.

To some extent, racism is in the eye of the beholder. We found frequent, and occasionally angry, disagreement about what constitutes racist behavior. For example, at a large, comprehensive urban institution in the East with no majority but with a sizable minority of black students, the day-student government (DSG) president's objection to the decision by the administration to ask black street merchants to leave campus after they had been invited by the DSG was quoted in the day-student paper: "They [the administration of the college] don't want the community to know what is happening here. This school is in a black community and the students are predominantly black, but it is being run by Jewish people." There ensued a public dispute, documented in letters to the editor, as to whether the statement was anti-Semitic. One student, after commenting on a clarifying conversation with the DSG president—"From what he said to me, he is simply objecting to having faculty members of the Jewish faith! Does he realize the gravity of what he is saying?"—concluded: "I don't believe that [DSG president] had or has malicious intentions, but I do believe that he is ignorant of many facts and has been terribly misguided." Another student asserted her belief that the remark was racist:

> I expected further elaboration of this assertion, but there was none. Since the administration representative involved in the dispute is black, the president of the college is black, and the dean is black, [the DSG president] clearly reveals his own racism with this statement.

An anecdote from another of our campuses demonstrates how what might have begun as a clash of personalities can quickly be interpreted as and transformed into a racial incident. At a small, comprehensive institution in the East with a majority white population but a significant African-American minority, a white wrestler and an African-American student engaged in a fight at the student, nonalcoholic nightclub. This fight escalated into a brawl between African-American and white students. Our campus visitor talked with both African-American and white students present at the fight. None of these students believed that the incident was initially racially motivated.

Separate racially or ethnically based organizations, too, are interpreted differently by different students. To some, they are intrinsically racist; to others they are not. On one of our campuses, a small liberal arts college in the East, a number of white students suggested that the mere existence of a black student union polarized students by race. An officer of the black student union responded that if African-American students were inclined toward separation, they never would have chosen to attend a predominantly white institution. One of his fellow officers agreed and explained why African-Americans need the support of separate organizations:

> I got here and soon found out that I was one of twelve black people in the freshman class. I did not expect that to be a problem. I was wrong.... As the semester progressed, I realized that many people on the campus were not making the effort that I was to continue relationships. At this time, I realized that the 'black separatists' on campus were the only people who took me at face value, and at the same time, were themselves with me.... I still have white friends at this institution of higher learning but they are the exceptions that take me for what I am.... Basically, we 'black separatists' have set ourselves apart, on one level, because we were forced to do so.

An African-American student at an elite private research university in the East took a diametrically opposed position: "I get a lot of flack because I don't belong to the black student union. I think its stupid to have a Drama Association and a *Black* Drama Association."

We found renewed efforts to define racist behavior on campus. Institutions have been reviewing or creating racial harassment codes. It is certainly an institutional responsibility to help individuals and the campus as a whole to articulate explicitly the standards of conduct in regard to racial and ethnic relations, to determine principled ways to interpret and judge behavior, and principled ways to enforce the rules. However, this is not an easy task. Neither society nor campuses have codified "racist" behavior in any detail. And, given the spectrum of behaviors possible, disagreements can occur over whether any given behavior constitutes bigotry. Moreover, decisions about whether behavior is racist must take into account complex variables such as context and intent.

The university counsel of our midwestern flagship evoked some of the problems when he warned against labeling someone who made an offensive remark a racist when his intentions were not racially motivated: "If you say 'you're a racist' to someone because of something he said, you have just taken a person who could be on your side and turned him around." An associate dean added: "If we assume it's all malicious, we might polarize the campus."

Interaction of Organized Groups

"Minority students tend to all come together, they are so small in number," said the leader of the black student union at an elite, private research university in the East. He continued:

> Black students just don't feel welcome. Everything is separate for us. We have a totally different idea of what a party is. We don't get together with whites. It's kind of hard when you don't see anyone who can really understand you. But we don't get harassed here because we're black. We haven't had any open racial problems here.

Informal and formal subcommunities based on race and ethnicity are strong points of identification and participation for minority students on campus. These students spend substantial time together, organize their own clubs and activities, and, on occasion, actively promote their subcommunity identity and interests. All campuses have black, Hispanic, and Asian student groups. In recent years, other organizations, both American and foreign student, have appeared: Jewish student unions, Polish, Italian, Muslim, Arab, Vietnamese and Haitian student associations, and, at Temple University, a white student union.

The fraternity and sorority systems, too, are overwhelmingly separate. On most campuses, there are black fraternities and sororities as well as white ones. Occasionally there is a Hispanic-Greek society. On some campuses they are all part of one Interfraternity and/or Panhellenic system, on others there are separate umbrella organizations as well. At our flagship university in the Southwest, sororities had only recently signed a nondiscrimination clause and become affiliated with the institution, but this was an exception.

Do minority students separate by choice or by necessity? The answer depends on with whom you speak. On most of our campuses, segregation did not appear to be imposed by the majority population; it seemed to be chosen by the minorities, especially the African-American students, as part of their racial or ethnic identification. Those individual minority students who did not choose this path often felt pressure from their peers. For example, an African-American student who was a campus student government leader indicated that he did not want to be a "Blacktivist." He made this choice because he wanted "to get ahead" and did not find voluntary segregation to be the best road toward that goal. Some of his peers did not endorse that judgment.

Because part of the function of these organized groups is to promote racial and ethnic identity, they can emphasize the points of dispute between and among the groups and become the focus of tension and conflict. On two of our campuses, black/white disagreements emerged around speaker/performer invitations. At one flagship university, the black student union had invited Louis Farrakhan, the controversial black Muslim who has verbally attacked Zionism and Judaism. He is viewed by many as an anti-Semite but by African-American students as an advocate of self-help. The Jewish student union and a number of state legislators opposed the use of student fees to pay a "black racist" to come to campus to speak. They also opposed using state money to provide substantial security in response to threats to disrupt the speech. The university said that freedom of speech gave the students the right to invite a speaker of their choice, regardless of his views, and the threat of external disruption should not abridge free speech on a university campus. The event occurred without disruption.

The Jewish student union at the same university invited the late Rabbi Meier Kahane, who attacked black leaders because of their criticism of Zionism, and who advocated the expulsion of Arabs from Israel and the occupied territories. In both cases, the African-American and Jewish student groups opposed the invitation to the offending speaker and picketed the event. The groups then publicly attacked each other and created angry feelings. At another university we visited, an African-American student group had chosen not to invite Farrakhan for fear of offending Jewish students.

The second campus on which conflict occurred around a speaker or performer is a comprehensive public institution in the East with a history of tense race relations and where a 1986 presidential initiative to create a multicultural focus for the campus continued to be a source of tensions. Here, a white dean had allowed the drama department to invite an African-American actress to bring a one-woman show called N*gg*r Cafe to campus so that students could see how to deal with difficult racial issues through drama. The play had been presented on other college campuses and in Baltimore without incident. A long-time African-American faculty member and the black student union vigorously opposed the invitation, because of the title of the play, although they indicated they had never seen or read the play. The provost vigorously supported the invitation. But the pressure against the performance became so great that the dean, in consultation with the department chairs, withdrew the invitation.

Both of these incidents display the conflict that can occur at the institutional level between academic freedom or freedom of speech, on the one hand, and the prevention of racist speech on the other. There is great pressure from organized student groups, as well as organized racial and ethnic groups in the larger society, to control campus speech that aggravates racial and ethnic relations. Universities and colleges have quite mixed records in protecting free speech in these situations.

This issue also arose in the black-Beethoven case, where black students called for the expulsion of the white students who created the poster with the Beethoven caricature. Their position was voiced by student Sharon Gywn in a New York Times op-ed piece:

> Should the university uphold unlimited free speech? Or should it limit free speech, especially in incidents of group defamation?... Stanford must understand that unlimited free speech does not necessarily increase educational opportunities.... Promoting ideas of hatred, such as defamation against certain groups, is not permissible. University officials have said that they don't condone this type of behavior, but now it's time to say they will not condone it.[15]

Stanford, in its response, did not agree with Ms. Gywn and did not expel the white students, although it did discipline them.

The power of organized racial and ethnic groups and their leaders to create high-visibility campus tension is illustrated by the role of the leader of the black student union at a large and distinguished western flagship university we visited. Four years ago the president of the BSU claimed to have been the object of a range of incidents of harassment. The campus newspaper published all of the charges as he levied them. Each charge was investigated by relevant campus authorities, but there were never any witnesses and the student could never provide names of the harassers. Finally, the president of the BSU claimed that a group of students tried to push him out of a dormitory window. The president of the university called in the FBI to investigate. After a major investigation, no evidence was found to support the allegations. Still, even after four years, the allegations of the BSU leader continued to affect relations between African-American and white students on campus.

Politically conservative student groups also play a role in creating racial and ethnic conflict. The most visible case has been the activities of the *Dartmouth Review,* the publication that has attacked affirmative action, an African-American faculty member, and the Jewish president of the university. The challenge posed by this publication has created great tension on the Dartmouth campus, even though the *Review* itself is not a campus-based organization.

On several campuses we visitied, public confrontations had occurred between Arab student organizations and Jewish student organizations. This tension seemed to arise on campuses with large numbers of international students.

The degree of tension experienced between organized groups on our campuses seemed to vary according to the racial or ethnic identity of the groups. There is no doubt that the greatest conflict was between African-American and other organized student groups, especially Jewish groups. The various Hispanic groups on our campuses appeared to be less politically active. For example, at the southwestern flagship university, the leader of the

Mexican-American Student Leadership Council explained the absence of other members of his organization at a campus rally for increased diversity by saying they were attending class or at work. Asian-American students, too, seemed more inclined to organize for social activities than to engage in campus politics. The same was true for international students, with the exception of Arab students. For example, the large mid-Atlantic flagship institution with a subsantial international student population has a club for each ethnic group. The only tension we found was between the Arab student organization and the Jewish student union. We found similar examples at a large community college in the Midwest that has a large English-as-a-Second-Language (ESL) program.

On a few campuses, the organized groups had developed cooperative modes of interaction. At a small liberal arts college in the West and at the western community college, the ethnic student groups all had majority student members. At the small liberal arts college, which had only 1 percent African-American and 3 percent Hispanic enrollment, white students joined the ethnic student organizations so that they could have enough members to exist.

A major development of the late 1980s was the willingness of organized minority students to use public demonstrations and the take-over of buildings to assert political power. On balance, most of the protests accomplished their goals. In tactics reminiscent of the 1960s, during the spring of 1989, there were demonstrations and take-overs on a number of campuses. On National Black Student Action Day in April, 1989, African-American students were demonstrating at Duke, Penn State, Harvard, Barnard, and Columbia. At Wayne State, African-American students occupied the administration building for nine days, and the occupation did not end until the administration agreed to hire more African-American faculty and staff and to direct more resources to African-American studies.

The most striking demonstration of minority student power was the City University of New York student demonstrations in April and May, 1989. After students took over the administration building and halted classes at City College, the demonstration and occupation, which was in protest against a proposed tuition rise of $200 approved by the state legislature to compensate for cuts in the budget by the governor, spread to all CUNY campuses. Mark Torres, the leader of the students—who were overwhelmingly Hispanic and African-American—said: "These budget cuts only affect people of color and the working class. In the 60's our people rose up and were divided. We shall never be divided."[16] Governor Cuomo of New York then vetoed the bill that allowed the board to raise tuition and instead imposed a series of additional cuts on CUNY and SUNY campuses.

White students participated in a number of these protests. For example, on our eastern elite research campus, an anti-apartheid protest involved a mixed group of black and white students building a shanty to pressure the campus to sell stock in companies doing business with South Africa. At the College of Wooster, 150 students, mainly white, occupied the campus administration building to demand a commitment to hire an African-American psychologist and counselor.

Campus-Wide Initiatives

Racial and ethnic relations were campus-wide issues on many of the campuses we visited. On several they were the source of some tension, and on two there was substantial polarization and hostility. On most campuses, we found a variety of student and administration initiatives to understand and improve racial and ethnic relations. These initiatives include review of admissions policies, anti-harassment policies, programs to educate about racial and ethnic difference, and academic courses on race and ethnicity and non-Western cultures.

Admissions

Nationally there has been a continuing debate about the appropriateness of affirmative action policies informing the admissions process. This debate has been most visible at Berkeley, where the faculty adopted a new set of policies changing the campus's approach to maintaining diversity. Since 1986, the campus had used a complex set of procedures that admitted about 40 percent of the students strictly on grade point average and test scores and the remainder under a system tied to ethnic group.

This approach was challenged by Asian-Americans who believed that they were being discriminated against by the limitation on the number of students admitted strictly by grades and test scores. The protected racial and ethnic-group system was viewed as especially onerous. The Asian-American position is presented in a report to the Ford Foundation by Dr. Bob Suzuki of California State University, Northridge:

> In regard to the issue of maintaining the "ethnic diversity" of the student population, institutional officials appear to be taking the position that since Asian Americans constitute only 2.1 percent of the total U.S. population, they should be considered over-represented if their proportion of the student enrollment in an institution substantially exceeds this percentage....
>
> Such a position can be seriously questioned for at least two reasons. First, it presumes that Affirmative Action was instituted merely to maintain some sort of ethnic balance, when in fact it was actually implemented to overcome the effects of historic discrimination against certain groups in our society.... It was convenient and practi-

cal...to gauge the effectiveness of Affirmative Action efforts by determining the extent to which the proportion of minorities in institutions of higher education was increasing.... However, when that proportion for a given minority group reaches or exceeds their proportion in the general population,...it would seem reasonable to adopt a 'color blind' admissions policy and admit both Whites and members of that minority group on the same basis; i.e., using admissions criteria that do not discriminate against either group....

What has also bothered many Asian Americans are the claims of some college officials that they were forced to reduce Asian admissions in order to increase the admissions of Blacks and other minorities. Such an explanation, if accepted, could have the consequence of pitting Asians against other minorities in competing over admissions. However, as the studies cited earlier indicated, in institutions in which Asian admissions have declined, they have declined proportionally far more than white admissions. Asian Americans would probably not complain if these reductions were comparable, but object to having to suffer a disproportionate cutback.[17]

The Asian-American challenge, along with the continuing concern of Berkeley faculty, prompted the Berkeley committee to change its approach and increase the number of students admitted strictly on academic criteria to 50 percent. An elaborate system of "secondary review" was then established, based on flexible targets according to classifications, such as students with special talents, and a category of students who come from socioeconomically disadvantaged backgrounds regardless of race and ethnicity. No racial or ethnic group would have protected status. This is a change, although Berkeley expects the targets to mirror recent patterns of admissions of each ethnic group. This change reflects the tensions of addressing affirmative action in a zero-sum game of admissions to an elite university with a rapidly expanding population pool. In a non-elite institution, the admissions game would not be zero sum. However, once admitted students would face equally fierce competition for financial aid. The Berkeley experience in the next few years will test the viability of eliminating race and ethnicity as criteria for admission to competitive institutions, especially those located in areas where there is no clear single majority, but rather competing minorities.

On the campuses we visited, there was greater concern about competition in major fields than in admissions to the institutions themselves. At the flagship university in the Southwest, this competition was particularly fierce. At the Midwest flagship university, few African-American students have qualified for entrance to the Business School. An attempt in 1989 by the school's administration to alter the admissions policy in a way that would probably raise the enrollment of African-Americans caused a rift in the business faculty. The dean called for a voice vote and declared the proposal passed, avoiding the customary show of hands for fear that it might have indicated defeat. In our travels, we did not find much evidence of affirmative action policies that assured the fair access of racial and ethnic minority students to competitive majors.

Racial Harassment Codes

Racist attitudes and behavior are not new on campus. Nor are efforts to eliminate them. However, in the recent past, a number of institutions, including several we visited, have been reviewing or creating racial harassment codes in an effort to define and regulate racist behavior. As we mentioned earlier in this chapter, defining racist behavior raises complex conceptual questions. Regulating racist behavior poses serious ethical and legal questions stemming from the need to balance respect for difference and the First Amendment rights of freedom of expression and academic freedom. We discuss the critical issue of regulating racist behavior in Chapter 7, "Harassment and Free Speech."

Educating About Racial and Ethnic Difference

It appears, from our visits, that colleges and universities are increasing their educational programming in regards to racial and ethnic difference. Most of the initiatives we encountered were quite recent. For example, many of the activities of the Commission on Racial Understanding at the midwestern flagship university we visited were new: race-awareness training for faculty, staff, and students, an annual race-awareness retreat, an orientation program on racism and cultural diversity, among others. At one urban comprehensive university, student leaders had organized a Committee on Racial Awareness two years ago, holding Friday afternoon sessions to which every member of the university has been invited. This group has sponsored a number of prejudice-reduction workshops. The mid-Atlantic flagship university began "Diversity Management" initiatives in 1986, providing programming, primarily workshops, for one thousand students in 1988–89. For two years, the Human Relations staff, which reports directly to the president, had offered some programming to employees as well. Freshmen orientation includes programming to educate parents of students assigned roommates of different racial or ethnic backgrounds. At our small liberal arts college in the East, faculty and administrators were just beginning to examine the climate for minorities. In a recent retreat, department heads and deans decided the issue was one of the two top priorities for the college. At another small liberal arts college, the vice-president for student affairs expressed concern about the climate for minority students, but did not indicate there was any programming currently available. The University of Delaware, Smith College, and UC Santa Barbara are other institutions that provide programs to increase racial and ethnic awareness.

Curriculum

Some of our campuses were discussing how the curriculum should contribute to racial and ethnic understanding. A very few had taken or were about to take action. The urban comprehensive university in the East had recently instituted a substantial core curriculum that includes the history and literatures of many of the cultures from which its students come. One flagship university has a cultural studies requirement of two courses in the study of a single culture different from the dominant American culture.

At another public comprehensive institution, the president appointed a committee to create a campus plan for a multicultural institution in 1986. This campus draws students from major metropolitan areas in the state and has a history of tense race relations. This presidential initiative focused on curricular change. The report of the president's committee was significantly modified by the faculty who moved it away from multiculturalism to a world cultures focus. The faculty felt estranged from the presidential recommendation and uncommitted to the multicultural campus, which they seemed to feel was artificial given its setting in white suburbia. The African-American students and faculty felt that they were being rejected by the faculty action. The outcome of curricular change here is still unclear.

At our community college in the Midwest, a Multicultural Task Force Subcommittee had just submitted a proposal for a multicultural graduation requirement that could be met through coursework or supervised field placements. The liberal arts college in the West was planning a faculty seminar in 1989–90 to explore implementing an ethnic studies program at the college.

A small number of other institutions across the country already require a course or courses in multiculturalism for graduation. For many years, the University of Minnesota has had a pluralism requirement. Students take at least two courses where the primary focus is on any of four American cultures. Courses focus on significant factors in those cultures such as class, gender, age, and sexuality, and on the concepts of race, ethnicity, sexism, and racism. Mount Holyoke and Tufts University also have requirements.

In 1989, both Berkeley and Michigan debated requirements concerning studying other cultures. At Berkeley the faculty senate passed a proposal for an American cultures breadth requirement that requires every undergraduate to take one of several courses for graduation. These courses should "substantially consider at least three of the five main racial/cultural groups in American society: African-American, American Indian, Asian-American, Chicano/Latino, and European American."[18] This proposal passed after the earlier defeat of a requirement that students take a course that would "emphasize the cultural and political experiences and contributions of racial minority groups."[19] A proposal at the University of Michigan that would have established a requirement to take a course on racism was defeated by the Faculty of Letters, Sciences, and Arts by a vote of 140 to 120.[20]

In most of these examples, minority students and faculty proposed ethnic studies requirements. The large institutional response has been to broaden the proposal and make it into a requirement for the study of different American cultures in a comparative context. Proposals for ethnic studies or courses on racism, for the most part, are viewed by the institutions as lacking intellectual integrity. However, the broader courses are now helping the curriculum on many campuses better mirror the diversity of both the surrounding society and the campus community.

Conclusion

A seeming proliferation of racial incidents on campus has captured attention locally, regionally, and nationally.[21] The violence after the World Series at Amherst, the use of racial epithets on the radio station at the University of Michigan, the challenge of the election of a Chicano to the student government presidency at UCLA by white students that led to a second ballot and the election of a white, and the investigation of alleged discrimination in the admissions of Asian students to Berkeley are a few of the best-known examples.

The widespread concern of both educators and the general public that racial and ethnic relations have been deteriorating over the last few years was one important impetus for our study of community on campus. In our research, consultations, and site visits, we have found inadequate data to substantiate the view of those who assert that racist behavior and separation and polarization by race and ethnicity are increasing. More study of this fundamental and complex issue is imperative. However, it is clear that higher education has made insufficient progress toward eliminating attitudinal barriers that impede the development of common ground. Although there is greater racial and ethnic diversity on campus today than twenty years ago, there does not appear to be a greater degree of integration and understanding.

Although we found generally positive interaction between individuals of different races and ethnicities on our campuses, as did the Stanford and Brown reports,[22] we found on our campuses, and in reports from other campuses, that minority students, particularly African-Americans, do not feel that they belong in the way that white students do. The sense of loneliness and isolation that many minority students report affects their academic performance and how they relate to others on campus. It separates them from community of the whole.

The individual loneliness and isolation also help explain the development of group segregation that we found. Many minority students spend much of their time with others from their racial or ethnic background. This is a source of concern to many white students, who see it as detracting from the goal of integration. People vary in how much they attribute such separation to choice or to necessity born of societal racism. This is a critical question for community on campus and one that evades easy answers. Healthy community, of course, encompasses subcommunities, but subcommunities that are freely chosen by members who also connect to the community of the whole. If minority students feel the need to protect and support themselves in an alien environment or if they feel strong pressure from students of the same background not to interact with whites, then they are not choosing freely and campus community is gravely impaired.

Racist incidents have prompted campus-wide review and initiatives on many campuses across the country. Brown, MIT, Michigan, and Wisconsin have in recent years undertaken campus-wide studies of racial and ethnic relations on campus. The Stanford report was the most thorough and comprehensive we found. In our travels, we saw good faith efforts to increase student diversity and to provide a setting where diverse students feel at home and can pursue a constructive education. We saw institutions making efforts to engage minority students in campus community both by providing resources for minority subcommunities and by encouraging participation in other subcommunities.

Nonetheless, there is so much more to be done. Colleges and universities still must commit more seriously to building bridges across the existing chasm of ignorance, misunderstanding, and racism, bridges that connect individuals and connect campus subcommunities. Justice and respect for difference are principles that bind individuals and groups to the community of the whole. This glue of principle is especially important where there is so often strong emotion and actual conflict. For the glue to stick and hold the parts together, the whole must acknowledge the right for parts to participate in subcommunities whose primary source of common ground is race or ethnicity. This requires a new understanding of diversity and pluralism.

Increasing ethnic diversity has brought many changes to American campuses. One of the most significant changes—a real commitment to respect for difference—has only just begun.

> The challenge of diversity is not simply successful affirmative action programs, recruiting, and retention—that is—access, which is, of course, essential. Rather, the challenge of diversity is the challenge of pluralism, of building academic communities in which people learn to respect and value one another for their differences, yet, at the same time, are drawn together by certain fundamental values that they share in common as scholars and as citizens.[23]

Cultural pluralism is a concept that is both old and new to American higher education. Certainly since the end of the nineteenth century American campuses have been admitting new groups of students. But it has only been in the last twenty years that this challenge has focused upon a redefinition of pluralism. The issues posed in this task of redefinition have been well articulated in *The American University and the Pluralist Ideal,* a report to Brown University. The majority of the visiting committee wrote:

> The ideal of pluralism toward which we would have the University strive is one that can only be realized when a spirit of civility and mutual respect abounds, when all groups feel equally well placed and secure within the community because all participate in that spirit. By contrast to the ideal of diversity, which gives primary regard to the mere presence of multiple ethnic and racial groups within the community, pluralism asks of the members of all groups to explore, understand, and try to appreciate one another's cultural experiences and heritage. It asks a leap of imagination as well as a growth of knowledge. It asks for a most difficult outcome: cultural self-transcendence.
>
> One can say that the assimilationist ideal already asked that much from members of minority groups. But that was precisely the problem. Assimilation asked of minority students not only that they appreciate the majority culture and its values, but that they embrace that culture as their own and detach themselves from their roots in the process. By contrast, a pluralist approach to the multi-racial reality of modern university life would ask that members of both majority and minority groups step beyond their respective cultural and intellectual boundaries. It would also demand that cultural self-transcendence not be misinterpreted as the betrayal of one's own heritage.[24]

This analysis clearly focuses upon the reciprocity of understanding that the goal of cultural pluralism requires. The distinction between the ideal of diversity and that of pluralism is the committment of all to study and understand each other. The distinction between the assimilationist ideal and pluralism is that the demand for self-transcendence is equally shared by majority and minority.

The Brown report focuses attention upon the challenge of pluralism—deciding how much colleges and universities are going to accept, and indeed celebrate, subcommunities based upon racial and ethnic identification, and how much they are going to ask these subcommunities to endorse shared values and collaborate with each other in the life of the community as a whole. Enhancing the subcommunities while asking that they contribute to a new whole is the vision that will allow campuses to make pluralism concrete.

This commitment to pluralism will require rethinking both the subcommunities and community of the whole. Common ground will not derive from cultural assimilation but from mutual accommodation based on a compact for a pluralistic community (see chapter 13, pp. 155–164). In assessing the responsibilities of the various subcommunities, the haves will have to shoulder more of the burdens than the have-nots. The community of the whole will have to respect the needs of subcommunities that feel new to the whole while reasserting that there is, indeed, a whole.

Racial and ethnic pluralism is the greatest challenge the higher education community faces. Past accomplishments are real; the glass is half full. But the future is what matters now and, in that light, the glass is half empty. Real commitment to pluralistic community requires more minority students, faculty, and staff, more support for interracial and interethnic activities of all kinds, curricular change, more interracial-awareness education for individuals and groups, especially in residence halls. It requires money, lots of it. It requires patience, lots of it, and it requires partnership, trust, and courage.

CHAPTER 4

The Climate for Women

> My professor (an Anglo male) told me I should not be an engineer because I am Hispanic and a woman. I went home and cried. Then, I decided not to complain. I'd get my degree and show him.
>
> —Adult woman, community college in the Southwest

> Milder, but distressing occurrences [of negative fraternity group mentality] include: 'rating' female party guests at the door by writing numbers on their hands; 'No Fat Chicks' parties; Derby Day, when fraternity team captains get extra points by putting their letters on the back of women's shorts; derisive or harassing attitudes towards women identified with feminist causes and women's studies courses; telling advisors that alcohol is an important ingredient at fraternity parties '...so that we can get the women drunk enough to have sex with us'; etc.
>
> —Student affairs administrator reporting to the Greek Life Task Force of a small private university in the East

Introduction

In the late 1960s and 1970s, thanks to the combined efforts of feminist scholars and activists, higher education began to ask itself questions about its treatment of women students, faculty, and staff. Issues included women's health and safety, sexual harassment, the scarcity and lower status of women faculty and administrators, and the absence of women and women's perspectives in the curriculum. Nationally and locally, often-heated discussions occurred; there were self-studies. In the end, few could deny that sexism was alive and well in academe. Women on campus were still the second sex.

Affirmative action legal obligations put demands on institutions. National organizations such as The Project on the Status and Education of Women at the Association of American Colleges (AAC) and the Commission on Women in Higher Education of the American Council on Education (ACE) began to advocate, educate, and shape the debate. The National Women's Studies Association was founded in 1977 to connect and support the growing number of women's studies programs. In 1981, the National Council for Research on Women was created with funding from the Ford Foundation and the Carnegie Corporation. In the 1980s, also, the Mellon and Ford Foundations and the National Endowment for the Humanities supported curriculum integration projects. The number of women's studies programs grew from two in 1970 to over four hundred fifty in 1985. Feminist scholars in a wide range of disciplines have produced a wealth of new knowledge and uncovered old knowledge about the impact of women on society. Debates over the existence and causes of feminine specificity have been common on campus. But despite twenty years of efforts to improve the education of undergraduate women, there is still more to do to assure completely equal treatment.

The great majority of female undergraduates, at least white female undergraduates, are probably closer to being the equals of male undergraduates than they have ever been. There is more publicity and education about sexual assault and harassment, better safety on campus, more women faculty to serve as role models, more access to traditionally male fields such as business, more teaching about women. Compared with women graduate students and faculty, they appear to be more satisfied and less alienated.

Alexander Astin's 1985 follow-up survey of 1981 freshmen and freshwomen found female undergraduates in four-year institutions somewhat more satisfied with their college experience than their male counterparts in almost all areas he explored. Women at two-year institutions, however, were less satisfied than men with their overall college experience: 63.3 percent of women compared to 78.9 percent of men ranked it satisfactory or very satisfactory. Fewer women expressed satisfaction with courses in their major (69.1 percent versus 79.2 percent) and with job placement services (37.2 percent versus 47.6 percent).[1]

There are a number of challenges that face colleges and universities willing to commit to assuring equal treatment of men and women undergraduates. The widespread ignorance of or lack of interest in the issues among undergraduates themselves, including most women, is a significant concern. As one administrator, who had been at an urban comprehensive institution for fourteen years, lamented: "I get the feeling that students just don't care about sexual assault and harassment issues."

In this section we will consider the challenge to community that gender difference brings to colleges and universities. We will consider sexual assault, sexual harassment, the climate on campus more generally, the degree to which women are integrated into the curriculum, and the dilemma that a largely silent, uninformed yet satisfied, majority of undergraduate women represents. When appropriate, we will compare the dynamics and problematics of racial and ethnic difference with those of gender difference.

Awareness of Difference

On the campuses we visited, we did not encounter or hear about many alienated or isolated undergraduate women. Unlike numerical minorities, most white women did not appear uncomfortable on campus, and did not strongly identify themselves as women-different-from-men. Feminist consciousness was rare, particularly among traditional-age women, most of whom were not aware of having experienced sex discrimination. As Astin's freshmen survey data have shown, the traditional-age freshwoman of the mid-1980s has a higher intellectual and social self-concept and sense of leadership ability than ever before. She has identical degree aspirations to freshmen and her most frequent career choices (business manager, nurse, lawyer, doctor, dentist, computer programmer) are much closer to men's choices than in the past.[2] So it seems that there is less and less in the personal experiences of younger women that would contribute to a sense of difference and discrimination.

The role of sororities in promoting women's interests and personal development appeared ambiguous. On the one hand, we heard language appealing to liberated future careerwomen—that sororities offer leadership opportunities and eventual career networking. On the other hand, we found traditional male-centered values and behavior—social life revolved around and was subordinate to fraternity activities.

Except where there were substantial numbers of returning women, organizations and programs run by and for women did not appear to stimulate great interest. These older women did, on some campuses, feel rather out of place and marginalized. In some cases, they joined together for group support as a conscious minority. We rarely encountered a political agenda among these women on the campuses we visited, however.

As the 1980s moved into the 1990s, abortion became a central political issue. The intense national debate continues to affect campuses. Students Organizing Students, a new organization devoted to protecting reproductive rights, has chapters on one hundred campuses. Astin's 1985 follow-up survey of 1983 freshwomen reports that 62.1 percent in four-year institutions agree strongly or somewhat that abortion should be legalized; 54 percent in two-year institutions take this position. Of 1981 freshwomen, 66.6 percent at four-year institutions indicated they agree strongly or somewhat that abortion should be legalized compared to 58.5 percent at two-year institutions. Unlike child care, also a national conversation, abortion legislation affects women students of all ages and may repoliticize campuses around women's issues yet again.

There was one exception to the low profile of women and women's issues on the undergraduate landscape of our travels. At a small comprehensive university in the South, women undergraduates still expressed allegiance to the women's college, founded over seventy years ago, that is part of the larger university. There was a sense of pride in being a woman there. Indeed, the male undergraduates expressed some consternation and some envy at the women's sense of community as well as their higher academic achievements. The women had traditions, we were told by both sexes—a tree-planting ceremony, a ceremony to mark the signing of the honor code, several dances, a spring ceremony honoring leaders in the senior class—that the men did not. The women had an established leadership program; the men did not. With the encouragement of the dean of men, the men were making conscious efforts to create traditions, playing catch up. They had recently begun the tradition of an annual senior/alumni dinner and a canoe race.

The campus still reflects the earlier single-sex arrangements, with a women's campus and a men's campus separated by a lake. Despite the presence of a dining commons on the women's side and a beautiful student center bridging the lake, there is the sense of a women's space and a men's space. Interestingly, while we were visiting, there was debate on campus around a student-generated proposal to integrate the residence halls. Apparently the great majority of men supported it; a significant number of women felt no need to change.

Rape

In our visits, the most prevalent sense of gender difference was that of greater physical vulnerability. When it came to focusing on women, sexual assault, especially rape, was the topic about which there was the broadest awareness and concern among students, faculty, and administrators—that is, women as victims and potential victims. Institutions had recently created educational programs about date rape and safety awareness, improved security on campus including escort services such as "Women's Wheels," and developed or revised their sexual harassment policy. Although there was student participation in prevention and education, in most cases the initiative clearly had come from the institution.

On campuses, we found a variety of women students' attitudes toward the emphasis on safety and rape prevention. Most endorsed it; on several occasions, it appears that women students themselves initiated improvements. Some students seemed disengaged. Some worried about rape, others did not. There had been recent reported rapes on five campuses we visited and a widely publicized fraternity gang rape of a woman who was not a student the year earlier at a sixth. On three campuses, administrators noted an increase in reports of rape, especially date rape, to members of counseling staffs.

It is impossible to determine what the actual incidence of rape on campus is. Adequate national data are not available. There are bits and pieces of the puzzle. *USA Today* reported that its survey of 698 campuses turned up 653 reported rapes in 1987.[3] Another survey of over six thousand students from 32 colleges reported that one in six female students reported having been a victim of rape or attempted rape during the preceding year, and that one in fifteen male college students reported committing rape or attempting to commit rape during that same period.[4] At a public comprehensive university we visited, 21.5 percent of the women recently surveyed reported having had unwanted intercourse while students; 61 percent of these were nonromantic acquaintances.

There is general consensus that rapes and attempted rapes are substantially underreported. Some say as many as 90 percent are not reported. Vice-presidents of student affairs at National Association of Student Personnel Administrators (NASPA) member institutions, responding to a survey conducted by Towson State, estimated a two-thirds underreporting.[5]

Is the incidence of rape on campus nationally on the rise, as some people purport? No one really knows. There are inadequate data to provide comparisons. In addition, society has been redefining rape. Not long ago, date rape was not even recognized by victims or assailants. Violence against women is so ubiquitous in our society that it is rarely labelled rape. "When men are asked if there is any likelihood they would force a woman to have sex against her will if they could get away with it about half say they would," says Dr. Neil Malamuth, a psychologist at UCLA. "But if you ask them if they would rape a woman if they knew they could get away with it, only about 15 percent say they would."[6]

Events at Syracuse University in the fall of 1989 may signal important changes in gender relations on campus. Six rapes were *reported* within two months. All six women were eighteen or younger; in five instances, the women believed their assailants to be classmates or students visiting from another school. The dean of student relations indicated that all involved were believed to have been drinking heavily before the incidents occurred. The dean attributed the increased number of reported assaults to an increased awareness of acquaintance rape.[7] These events highlight the prevalence of violence against women *within* academe and the pressing need to educate all students, men and women, about their respective responsibilities.

Fifty-five percent of all the presidents surveyed by the Carnegie Foundation and the American Council on Education in 1989 indicated that rape and sexual assault were not a problem on their campus. However, only 17 percent of presidents of research institutions indicated they were not a problem.[8] Of student affairs vice-presidents surveyed by ACE and NASPA, 39 percent of those at all institutions indicated rape and sexual assault were not a problem; 50 percent considered them to be the same degree of problem or less of a problem than five years ago. Only 10 percent considered rape and sexual assault to be a greater problem than five years ago. Again though, at research institutions, only 3 percent said these were not a problem; 73 percent said they were the same or less of a problem, and 23 percent said they were a greater problem than five years ago.[9]

Sexual Harassment

In the wake of the 1986 Supreme Court decision in *Meritor Saving Bank, FSB v. Vinson,* which ruled sexual harassment to be sex discrimination and illegal under Title VII of the Civil Rights Act, sexual harassment has moved to center stage on many campus administrators' agendas. Most institutions have instituted policies or reviewed existing ones.

The Carnegie/ACE and ACE/NASPA surveys indicate a greater concern among top administrators about sexual harassment than rape and assault. Only 29 percent of presidents at all institutions do *not* consider sexual harassment to be a problem (55 percent for rape/assault); only 4 percent of presidents at research institutions responded thus (17 percent for rape/assault).[10] Twenty-six percent of vice-presidents for student affairs at all institutions indicated sexual harassment was not a problem (39 percent for rape/assault); only 2 percent at research institutions responded thus (3 percent for rape/assault).[11]

Everywhere we went there was significant concern about harassment, especially among administrators. But the relationship to the problem varied. On some campuses, sexual harassment was not a new issue; on others it was presented as the next important challenge to address. Generally, sexual harassment did not appear to be as highly visible a public issue on the campuses we visited as was racial harassment.

There is no way to accurately gauge the prevalence of sexual harassment on campus. To date, there have been only limited efforts to quantify incidents, and these have yielded a wide range of results. Mary Leonard and Brenda Alpert Sigall assert that in a 1983 study by Bogart and Truax 40 percent of undergraduate women all over the country report experiencing harassment.[12] The Association of American Colleges' *On Campus with Women* reported a survey at Harvard where 34 percent of women undergraduates reported sexual harassment from a person in authority.[13] A study at Michigan State found that 25.1 percent of female respondents to the questionnaire said they had experienced one or more of the following types of behavior in the recent past: jokes about women's anatomy; physical touching of breasts, buttocks, or pubic area; propositions of sex in exchange for a grade, an assistantship, or a recommendation; and sexual assault. One hundred and ten of the 147 reported incidents were jokes; 16 were incidents of touching; 2 were propositions; 15 were sexual assault.[14]

We need to be cautious in our interpretation of survey results. Like racial harassment, sexual harassment is difficult to define[15] and these efforts to quantify incidents run into the same methodological problems that efforts to quantify incidents of racial harassment do: lack of common standards for reporting and the danger of overgeneralization.

Many campus definitions of sexual harassment begin with the guidelines of the Equal Employment Opportunity Commission (EEOC). The EEOC defines sexual harassment as:

> unwelcome sexual advances, requests for sexual favors, and other verbal or physical conduct of a sexual nature...when (1) submission to such conduct is made either explicitly or implicitly a term or condition of an individual's employment,...(2) submission to or rejection of such conduct by the individual is used as the basis for employment decisions affecting such individual...or (3) such conduct has the purpose or effect of unreasonably interfering with an individual's work performance or creating an intimidating, hostile, or offensive working environment....[16]

The EEOC guidelines were developed for the workplace, a carefully circumscribed context where unequal power relations are ubiquitous. Campuses have had to adapt the EEOC definition to a broader context, one that includes peer relations in both the "work" and social environments. Different campuses have defined harassment quite differently. Some policies limit it to continuing or repeated conduct, others include one-time occurrences.

Overly broad definitions of sexual harassment run the risk of violating the First Amendment right of freedom of expression. The 1989 court decision striking down the University of Michigan's harassment policy as unconstitutional is instructive.[17] In the fall of 1989, Tufts voluntarily repealed its new harassment policy, which had been promulgated in the wake of protests over a T-shirt that was offensive to women. The policy forbade "expression which harasses or injures others" in public areas such as dormitory lounges and the library.[18] Regulating incivil, even bigoted expression has its limits in a democracy. Although intolerance of difference is a central challenge to our campuses, as it is to society generally, in the last analysis, the primary tool must be education and visible role models, not regulations.

Chilly Climate

Whether or not behaviors of male faculty, staff, and peers qualify as sexual harassment, they are often a source of distress and discouragement for women students, especially minorities, older women, and graduate students. There is no doubt that sexist behavior persists and affects the educational and social climate of women students, even undergraduates. As in society at large, women are still not perceived to be the equals of men. Colleges and universities have a special responsibility to work toward including women as full partners of the academic community.

On most campuses we visited, there were individual undergraduate women who shared with us their experience of sexist behavior from faculty, staff, and peers. We heard a number of examples of sexist behavior by faculty. The Hispanic woman at a community college in the Southwest provided the most striking example when she said that a faculty member told her she should not study engineering. There were also indications that institutional sexism is not dead, even for undergraduates. A traditional-age woman in an elite university in the Northeast shared that: "My professor told me not to bother to apply for the Business School's combined BA/MBA program because they never take women." At this same institution, another woman undergraduate reported that when she registered for an upper-level calculus course the male instructor asked her: "This is an advanced course. Why are you taking it?"

There were several complaints about service employees at various institutions. At a comprehensive university in the East, a female work-study student who assisted maintenance workers complained that they had put up offensive pictures of naked women in the maintenance lunchroom. Following her complaint, the pictures came down. At the same institution, we were told, a worker at the campus snack bar was suspended after the student newspaper published complaints from female students that he had made sexually offensive remarks. At a community college in the Southwest, we were told that female students complained about campus gardners making lewd remarks to them.

In regards to undergraduate life, the treatment of women by their male peers was the subject of greatest concern on almost all the campuses we visited, especially sexism in social interaction that ran the gammut from sexual assault to off-color jokes. At a small university in the East, one sophomore woman reported that members of the women's caucus "get insults shouted at them" when they hold programs and demonstrations. At a southern flagship university, the managing editor of the newspaper complained about T-shirts reading "ten reasons why beer is better than women." At a small comprehensive university in the South, many women students felt fraternity parties, the main feature of campus social life, were objectionable. A student member of the board of trustees said they were degrading to women. She indicated that male-female relations are a big issue on campus. The criticism of fraternities for sexist behavior was quite commonplace during our travels.

Sexist attitudes still seem much less a taboo than racist ones. The offhand comment of a physics professor at a small research university in the East, while complaining to us about the lack of student interest in interacting with faculty, illustrates their continued pervasiveness. He joked: "I will run office hours for three hours a week with a freshman class and have no one show up. Other than seducing girls, I don't know what to do."

Unconscious attitudes, poor taste, insensitivity, and ingrained stereotypes are the most pervasive form of sexism undergraduate women encounter. These can be so subtle and so much a part of an individual's conventions that they are not recognized. There have been some efforts to document the existence of differential treatment by sex in the college classroom, mostly in four-year colleges and universities, but the results have been inconclusive to date. Researchers exploring the presence of micro-inequities in the classroom deleterious to the experience of women students can't be sure whether their survey results, which often show little or no difference between men and women students' experience of their professors, discount the theory of "chilly classroom climate for women" or confirm the extent to which individuals are socialized to experience differential treatment of women as normal.

The power of nonverbal and paraverbal behavior, generally, however, has been amply documented over the years. Researchers such as E. T. Hall,[19] Ray Birdwhistell,[20] and many others have shown that myriad subtle nonverbal cues are the main sources of communication.[21] Robin Lakoff, Nancy Henley, and a host of subsequent researchers have studied the differences in the way in which women and men express themselves.[22] The excellent pamphlets of the Project on the Status and Education of Women at the Association of American Colleges summarize the complexities of everyday interaction—frequency of eye contact and responsive gestures, use of silence, calling on men more often than women, use of the generic "he," responding less positively to the more qualified and personalized speech of many women than to the more assertive and abstract speech of many men, etc.—that may have a negative impact on women both in and out of class. These pamphlets provide guidance on establishing educational programming that will be the key to enhancing the understanding of and respect for gender difference on campus.[23]

Education and Prevention

We found programming to address the most blatant forms of sexism on campus everywhere we went. However, many were relatively new, as was the case for programming that addressed racism. On most campuses, we found concerned and energetic administrators. However, on several the climate for women was not a high priority. Most programs appeared to be institutional responses to the *Meritor v. Vinson* ruling, and the prodding of women faculty and administrators, more than responses to student demand on campus. It seems that minority students have played a more active role in initiating educational programs about difference than have white women students.

White women have always been less sensitized to marginality and discriminatory behavior than racial and ethnic minorities. Moreover, feminism has not been part of the experience of today's traditional-age undergraduates. Unless they are educated to understand sexism, these women often do not recognize it, even in the more blatant forms of harassment and date rape. The importance of educating everyone cannot be underestimated.

The most common programs we found were those that focused on preventing violence against women. These programs educated women about campus safety and educated women and men about date/acquaintance rape. At the small southern comprehensive, for example, students, with the collaboration of campus police, had for three years presented skits at freshmen orientation designed to address what they called the Triple Whammy—drugs, sex, alcohol. Freshmen men, we were told, were the main offenders. However, the program is mandatory for all freshmen. A midwestern flagship university also ran workshops, run by peer presenters, on date rape, relationship skills, and communication. The Office of Women's Affairs had just gotten approval for a mandatory rape workshop for all six hundred athletes for the next academic year. At a small liberal arts college in the West, security education was a primary focus. The college offered free self-defense classes for women and provided them whistles. At a private university in the East, where the climate for women seemed particularly chilly, the Greek Life Task Force had just recommended the creation of a committee on gender relations. The committee would design more effective educational programs on alcohol abuse, sexism, and violence against women—programs that would extend beyond orientation and include follow-up procedures.

Women's Groups

Women have not relied as heavily on organized groups to affirm their identity as have minority students, for they have been less conscious of their difference. The success of the women's movement has been one reason for the waning of feminist consciousness in the 1980s. A number of faculty and administrators with whom we spoke reiterated the common theme that most of today's traditional-age students arriving on campus take for granted recent gains and show little or no interest in exploring continuing social and political inequalities. A recent poll conducted for Time/CNN found that 77 percent of the women polled thought the women's movement had made life better, but 76 percent said they themselves paid little or no attention to the women's movement.[24] A recent New York Times poll of 1,025 women seems to indicate that age does play a role in world view. Women between eighteen and twenty-nine were substantially more optimistic about their options and opportunities than women over thirty.[25]

We did find a number of support groups for women undergraduates on every campus, although few were issue oriented. The largest were institutionally sponsored women's centers. These went by different titles and offered different services and educational programming depending upon the campus. Services ranged from sexual harassment workshops to career planning sessions to single parenting discussions. Counseling centers also organized support groups for victims of sexual assault.

There were a number of leadership programs for women also. The most ambitious one, created by the faculty at a small private southern comprehensive, spanned four years and combined some academic coursework and an internship with personal discovery opportunities and cocurricular programs. Participants spoke warmly of the program as a place where they experienced community.

We found a modest number of student-initiated groups. At one small liberal arts college, the Feminist Collective had 150 members. This was the same institution where women students demanded improved safety measures. At another liberal arts school we were told that there had been an active women's group five to seven years ago, but that it had lost much of its steam. At a large private urban comprehensive institution, there was a small group called Women's Space, with fifteen to twenty active members, all of whom were upperclasswomen.

Sororities continue to be important social communities for traditional-age women on campus. Members of sororities, like their male equivalents, often report somewhat greater satisfaction with their college experience. At a public comprehensive university in the Northeast, a student affairs administrator had interviewed twenty senior women, and every one of them reported that it was her sorority affiliation that kept her from transferring or dropping out. On several campuses, however, people gave voice to the theme of the dual role of sororities: to provide "handmaidens" to men but also to provide leadership opportunities for women that are scarce on coeducational campuses. At a small liberal arts college, we heard that "sororities have come under fire from feminists on campus who claim they confirm and maintain the old stereotypes." The Greek report of a private small university found it "especially disappointing that sororities do not use their considerable organizational expertise to combat sexism and violence against women on campus generally, and among their Greek 'brothers' in particular." It is logical to look to sororities to be one focal point of advocacy for gender equality. At the same time, institutions may need to provide substantial support and education to sensitize these traditional-age women to the nature and scope of the problems.

All in all, we found a range of opportunities for undergraduate women to belong to a subcommunity of women. It is our sense that very few women sought out these opportunities, but that for those who did, they were centrally important to their campus experience. With the exception of women's studies (see below), most programs and groups primarily addressed the interests and needs of traditional-age students, although we usually found some group or program that focused on the adult/returning student. Also, most educational programming about gender difference rarely ventured very far beyond the arena of sexual assault and harassment into the broader topic of gender differences in moral development, learning, and leadership, for example.

The Learning Community: Women in the Curriculum

During our visits, many people shared with us their concern about sexual assault. Many fewer spoke with us about the need for more teaching and learning about women. There was comparatively less energy exhibited around the educational and intellectual challenge that the current absolute majority of women on campus represents or that the question of a women's way of knowing raises. There was little conversation about the need to include the new scholarship about women in the knowledge base of the academy. And yet, women remain underrepresented in the curriculum across the country.

Women's studies has made impressive progress in the last twenty years. Scholars of women have produced a wealth of new knowledge in all disciplines and across disciplines. There are now more than five hundred programs nationwide. Many of these programs are staffed with a small full-time core and much larger numbers of part-time and affiliate faculty. Few have departmental status and substantial budgets of their own. These programs have provided a crucial place of intellectual, emotional, and, to some extent, political community to women faculty and students.

The integration of women into the curriculum has been a topic of debate both nationally and on individual campuses for at least a decade. Advocates argue that the current curriculum continues to exclude the experience and perspectives of women; when they are present, it is usually as object, not speaking subject. Much of the new research on women calls into question the epistemology and pedagogy that are the foundation of the academy as it now exists. Women, it contends, may see the world differently from men; there may be significant gender differences in values, learning styles, and modes of interacting. Thus, without systemic change, the curriculum and those who teach it will continue to marginalize and subordinate women in the learning community.

The National Endowment for the Humanities and the Fund for the Improvement of Post-Secondary Education, as well as the Ford, Lilly, Mellon, and Rockefeller Foundations have funded integration projects. The University of Arizona, the University of Delaware, Hunter, the University of Maine, Orono, Montana State University, Rutgers, Smith, Spelman, Towson State, Wellesley, Wheaton, and Yale, for example, have instituted instructional development projects to integrate the new scholarship on women.

Almost all of the institutions we visited had some course offerings in women's studies, although not necessarily a major. Two of our huge flagship universities did not offer a major. A very small core faculty supplemented by part-time and affiliated faculty was the most common program structure. Usually, these programs drew their vitality from the devoted attention of a small number of women faculty.

At an urban comprehensive, women's studies had been a small master's program for fifteen years. An undergraduate minor had just been approved. At a small southern private comprehensive, the women's studies program, which did offer a major, grew out of a women's leadership program created by the faculty. At one liberal arts college, a self-designed women's studies major was available; at another, there was a minor that had been formalized only in the last year and had had twenty participants.

On one of the flagship campuses, the core women's studies faculty was only two full-time equivalents. There were also several part-timers, and about thirty affiliated faculty from other departments. The Committee on Undergraduate Women's Education reported that some departments did not value scholarship and teaching about women and made life for affiliates in the program difficult.

Few of the institutions we visited had taken steps to integrate women into the curriculum. A private urban comprehensive university had recently received foundation funding to begin to integrate minority women into the liberal arts undergraduate curriculum. At one flagship university, the administration had recently allocated some funds for summer workshops to allow fifteen men and women faculty to revise important courses to include women. During our visit, a number of senior male faculty expressed their strong concern that they, too, would be forced to integrate women into their courses, that there would be a "Big Sister" looking over their shoulder, or that radical feminists would take over the campus.

Our visits confirm that, for the most part, men are still the educational norm against which women are evaluated. The curriculum has remained substantially unchanged. In both content and pedagogy, learning continues to reflect the experience and assumptions of white males. Both men and women students learn about a truncated reality that confirms societal stereotypes disadvantageous to women.

On one of the flagship universities we visited, a Committee on Undergraduate Women's Education had submitted its report in 1988. The committee had found a number of programs that supported women students—a program on sexual assault, a coordinating task force on rape and security, an active Women's Commission, a program for returning women students, and a women's studies program. However, with the exception of the women's studies program, the committee found little systematic attention given to the educational and intellectual development of women students. It advocated three long-range goals that should be the goals of all colleges and universities:

1. transforming the curriculum to infuse it with the new scholarship on women and to be sure that course offerings truly reflect the full range of human experience and are not limited to the perspectives of white males;

2. improving the classroom climate for women students by encouraging more equitable treatment of women and men students in classroom interactions; and

3. encouraging more women to prepare for and pursue majors and careers in nontraditional fields, such as the sciences and engineering.

Conclusion

Differential treatment of undergraduates on the basis of sex as well as race and ethnicity is common on the nation's campuses, both in and out of the classroom. Like racism, sexism is often the result of ignorance and misunderstanding. The frequency of physical violence toward women (rape and sexual assault) may well exceed the frequency of violence against minorities on campus. Unlike minorities, however, who have a social and often political context in which to situate discriminatory behavior, most undergraduate women do not. Part of educating for community in regard to gender difference, then, is assisting women, as well as men, to recognize bigoted behavior and attitudes. Much has been done; much remains to be done. As the head of the Panhellenic Council at a small university we visited noted: "The climate for women is getting better, but it's still a male-dominated campus."

We are particularly concerned that higher education systematically address the issue of what it teaches about women and how it teaches it. Colleges and universities must revise their curricula and pedagogy to reflect not only the pluralism of race and ethnicity but also the differences that gender brings to a full understanding of the world. The campus learning community must engage with this multifaceted reality that is a reflection of its true self.

Part 3

The Boundaries of Authority:
Regulating and Educating for Community

Introduction

To explore community on campus is to explore the rules that govern individuals and groups, the ways in which these rules are formulated and enforced, and the nature and scope of opportunities to educate members of the community about appropriate behavior. In this section we consider the difficult problems that provide the major out-of-classroom challenges to community for most American campuses: alcohol abuse; Greek life, most particularly fraternity excesses; racial and sexual harassment as they relate to freedom of speech; and crime. When we began our campus visits, some of our colleagues expected to find distress and uncertainty among undergraduates and administrators about how to regulate these areas of student life. What we found, in most cases, was a considered, systematic, and competent approach to meeting these challenges. However, we are concerned that institutions must make greater efforts to protect freedom of speech.

Although the justification for the rules changed in the 1960s with the decline and fall of *in loco parentis,*[1] college and university students, especially residential students, still live in a dense forest of regulations. Over the last decade, institutions have reestablished most of the rules they abolished during the upheavals of the late 1960s. The only area where students are less regulated now is that of sexual expression.

However, the campus has remained "democratized." Students are still active in self-governance and institutional governance. In academic matters, students play a mainly advisory role. The faculty as a whole establishes the rules; and the faculty and the administration enforce them. On many campuses, student judiciaries do handle cases of academic cheating. Outside of the classroom—in the residence halls, in student organizations, in Greek life, and on the parking lot—students play a much larger role in the formulation and enforcement of the rules. Indeed, much of the responsibility for enforcement now lies in students' hands, whether they be resident assistants or members of the student judiciary.

In our visits, we heard few students complain of overregulation; more often, we heard support for the rules and for the role of students in creating and enforcing them. By encouraging and supporting student participation in self-governance and institutional governance, colleges and universities are educating for community in the strongest sense. It takes courage, commitment, and patience to make the campus such an educational laboratory.

Perhaps the most significant changes that have affected colleges' and universities' relations with their students have originated off campus. Federal and state legislation, such as that changing the drinking age and prohibiting certain hazing practices, have forced institutions to review and redraft their own policies. Court rulings have increased institutional liability for students on campus and have prompted change as well. Americans now live in the most litigious society in the world, and students and parents of students regularly sue colleges and universities; often they win. The traditional approach to regulating community on campus, where complaints are handled internally and some degree of trust undergirds authority, has eroded substantially. Often, we have a formal, legalistic approach, where outsiders adjudicate and there is no bond of group solidarity.

Colleges and universities today, then, face a legal dilemma of the first order. As soon as some "special relationship" beyond mere enrollment exists, institutions may be held liable for injuries caused by or to their students. Since legislation sometimes mandates this special relationship (for example the requirement to recognize student organizations), and since high standards of social responsibility argue in favor of doing more, not less, for students, risk is virtually inescapable. Institutions, caught between a rock and a hard place, have cause to feel vulnerable.

In the last few years, institutions have placed increased emphasis on educating more broadly for community. Everywhere we visited, student affairs staff and students themselves had recently created or were about to create new programs and initiatives intended to make students more responsible members of the campus community and, hopefully, more competent adults in society. Among these programs are alcohol- and drug-awareness workshops, workshops and presentations on ethnic relations and gender relations, programs on personal and group safety, and a variety of public service opportunities both on campus and off campus. Students play important roles as organizers, consultants, and teachers. By choice or by necessity, institutions are recognizing their responsibility not only to explain the what and why of the rules, but also to foster the growth of the whole student. There has been a move away from primary reliance on regulation and enforcement to influence student behavior to a balanced approach of regulation, enforcement, and education. Progress is encouraging, but we have much farther to go in this important arena.

As we view the horizon of regulatory challenges, we must keep in mind that each and every one has both legal and ethical parameters. Campuses must meet their legal obligations, but such a standard does not decide the ethics of the issues. In regard to harassment and free speech, for example, the lawyers are quite divided. This means that campus communities must come to their own conclusions based on ethics and educational goals rather than law. Even where the law seems to be clear, as is the case with alcohol use, the more important educational questions still remain; in this case the question is how can we best educate underage drinkers to drink responsibly since we know they *will* drink? A campus community must make decisions based on educational as well as legal standards. As we proceed we will note our understanding of the law where it is relevant, but we will be more interested in the ethical and educational issues that these matters pose for campus policy makers.

We have noted that *in loco parentis,* the theory that the institution is in the role of parent for students, is no longer the operative legal or ethical theory justifying campus rules. In its place in law are two sources of obligation. One is constitutional and is based upon the rights of citizens. The other arises from both common law and legislation and is based upon a contract between consumer and provider.[2] The constitutional frame for analysis looks to the First, Fifth, and Fourteenth Amendments to justify student rights in the arenas of free speech, privacy, protection against self-incrimination, and due process. The consumer-contract perspective looks to the standard of care that the university owes the student and the right of the student to delivery of services to which he or she is entitled.

To our knowledge, neither of these legal theories has been articulated in the framework of a general ethical theory to guide regulatory policy making on campus. We believe that both can be subsumed in the framework of a compact between and among faculty, students, and administrators, very much as our democratic and constitutional system is based on a social theory of contract. In chapter 13, we discuss an explicit compact for a reinvigorated campus community.

CHAPTER 5

Alcohol Abuse

Introduction: A Double Shot on the Rocks

During the past decade, higher education has been served a double shot on the rocks to help it deal with student alcohol use. That is to say that administrators have seen a double dose of change, change in societal attitudes toward drinking and change in laws governing its use, poured over a student culture whose drinking habits have remained virtually the same. As one might suspect, this concoction gets mixed reviews. While everywhere we visited campus officials were pleased by the decrease in public drinking on campus, they remained deeply concerned about off-campus drinking and the continuing student psychology that condones alcohol abuse.

That the environment surrounding student alcohol use has changed and grown more complex is one statement about which we find consensus. We will explore the nature of these changes and complexities and look at different institutional and student responses. We will explore the impact of new laws and campus regulations on student drinking. We will note significant court cases affecting liability issues facing institutions and their students. Finally, we will look at the development of campus awareness and prevention programs and intracampus cooperative initiatives that focus on education and responsible drinking.

A Decade of Change

Societal attitudes about drinking have undergone dramatic shifts in the past decade. Citizen outrage over alcohol-related traffic fatalities prompted federal legislation to make federal highway aid dependent upon increasing the legal drinking age. Those same fatalities, along with scores of alcohol-related injuries, opened a national debate centered on the legal liability of those who provide and consume alcohol. States responded to changing attitudes and federal pressure by raising the minimum legal drinking age to twenty-one and, in some cases, enacting blue laws, prohibiting happy hours, and strengthening drunk-driving penalties. None of this has altered the drinking habits of college and university students. According to a 1988 survey by Campus Alcohol Consultants, student drinking habits have remained virtually unchanged despite the efforts of federal, state, and institutional governing bodies to curb alcohol consumption and abuse on campus.[1]

Given what we know about student drinking habits, it is not surprising that 45 percent of the presidents responding to an open-ended question on the Carnegie/ACE survey listed alcohol abuse as one of the three campus life issues of greatest concern. Similarly, 67 percent indicated alcohol abuse to be among problems that are moderate to major in intensity.[2] In Carnegie's faculty survey, 33.2 percent of all faculty said that there was more alcohol abuse among today's undergraduates than five years ago, while more than half were neutral about this judgment. Forty-one percent of faculty in liberal arts colleges thought there was currently more drinking.[3] Thirty-one percent of all chief student affairs officers in the ACE/NASPA survey thought alcohol abuse was now a greater problem, while 40 percent thought there had been no change. Forty-eight percent of chief student affairs officers at research institutions thought the problem had increased.[4]

It is clear from these surveys that a significant minority of campus leaders think alcohol abuse is a serious problem. The Campus Alcohol Consultants survey, however, reports no significant change since 1979 in the proportion of schools that allow the legal consumption of beer (78 percent) and hard liquor (71 percent) on campus.[5] Although some campuses have responded to the heightened concern about alcohol abuse and illegal drinking by banning alcohol altogether, most have gone to great lengths to regulate and prevent underage drinking while, at the same time, teaching and counseling students more in its responsible use.

Today's student party culture reflects this increased regulation of individuals and organizations. Open beer bashes have become a thing of the past as many institutions have suspended alcohol consumption in public areas such as campus quadrangles and lounges. Similarly, regulations have been promulgated to prohibit ad hoc alcoholic parties. Many campuses now require individuals and organizations to hold parties in private rooms or halls and to register parties—that is to provide time, place, and guest list—if alcohol is to be consumed. Such registration is used by some institutions to determine the amount of alcohol that can be provided to party-goers and the number of security officers or chaperons that must be present. Some campuses now require students to wear wrist bands or badges to identify those of legal age and some go even farther by issuing drink tickets to party-goers to limit consumption. Many institutions also require nonalcoholic drinks and food to be served as well.

All of these measures have increased the cost, both in time and money, of holding a party. There is also greater risk of legal liability when alcohol is involved. Student groups unable to pay for extra security and chaperons, food, alternative beverages, and other trappings, or unwilling to shoulder the added responsibility, have opted for "dry" celebrations or activities where no alcohol is served.

These changes prompted positive reactions by students on two of our campuses. At a northeastern comprehensive university, the head of the Inter-Greek Council recalled that alcohol use was virtually unrestricted when she first came to campus. Now, following the increase in the drinking age and the restriction of alcohol use in the residence halls, she believed the campus has "cleaned up and gotten people more involved in campus activities." A student active in intramurals agreed. The alcohol restriction has "improved the school's image," he said. "It used to be that [our school] was thought of as a party school, but no longer. I feel better about this place now."

Similarly, students at a southern community college that neighbors the state flagship were happy about the lack of alcohol abuse on their campus:

> I don't see a problem with drugs and alcohol at [our school]. Let [our neighbor] be the party school. We project something else. Most of the students in four-year colleges are out on their own for the first time. Most people here are living with their parents or are older. The mix is good. Older students have a sobering effect on the younger ones.

Cooperative educational measures such as those we have described have allowed alcohol consumption to remain a part of campus life for those of legal drinking age who are willing to abide by new "responsible use" guidelines. On residential campuses, we found the greatest concern. On community colleges and substantially commuter campuses, student social life, with its accompanying drinking, occurs off campus. Institutional responsibility and liability is extremely limited. These campuses still engage actively in educational efforts. What remains unsolved, however, is the question of regulation and supervision of and liability for those students who don't drink by the rules.

"Displaced Drinking"

History has taught us that prohibition does not work. Underage students are going to drink if they so desire. Legal-age students are going to have beer bashes without all the trappings of a "campus-sponsored" event. Greek letter organizations, which often take much of the blame for campus alcohol abuses, may take their alcohol-soaked rituals underground. To a disturbing degree, laws and regulations designed to curb and/or prohibit drinking and its abuses have merely changed its time and place. This has led to a new phenomenon: "displaced drinking."

Displaced drinking refers to the movement of student alcohol consumption out of sight or perceived reach of institutional regulation. For instance, underage students and students unwilling to obey campus alcohol restrictions increasingly go off campus to private residences and bars to drink. If students can no longer drink legally in public because they are underage, they acquire false identification cards or drink privately in their dorm room or other residences. In fact, students in a northeastern school reported that false IDs are easy to obtain and that many students under twenty-one go to the local bars.

These behaviors have forced campuses to reexamine the limits of their authority and responsibility. One of the most telling examples of the dilemmas raised by displaced drinking occurred in 1984 at a private research university in the Southwest. After a rash of fraternity problems related to alcohol, the institution placed a moratorium on alcohol consumption. Not long after the moratorium was imposed, students responded in a manner the administration called blackmail. The student message was clear: "If you're not going to allow us to drink on campus, we'll drive drunk." The school lifted that moratorium, but only after imposing a new rule that required a uniformed police officer and four non-drinking upperclassmen or alumni to be present at all parties where alcohol is served.

As mentioned above, institutions are also concerned about illegal drinking in residence halls. Alcohol consumption, if allowed at all in residence halls, is usually restricted to private rooms. Of course, many occupants in campus residence halls are underage. Residence hall administrators on one of our large urban campuses reported an increase in alcohol abuse, especially contraband in the freshman dorm. None of the campuses in our sample search students and their bags as they enter the halls. Thus, alcohol can be carried into buildings with relative ease, consumed in private rooms, and go undetected unless students are overtly inebriated.

Such maneuvers will remain troublesome for campuses as administrators weigh a student's right to privacy against an institutional duty to prevent abuse. Unfortunately, this is merely one dilemma in the growing labyrinth of liability concerns for institutions of higher education.

Liability

Courts, legislatures, and the public have launched an increasingly vigorous attack on alcohol abuse in recent years. Subsequently, there has also been an increase in people seeking compensation for alcohol-related injuries. Colleges and universities have historically been responsible for the actions of their students under the doctrine of *in loco parentis*. As many courts have responded to increased societal outrage by spreading legal responsibility to third parties, institutions of higher education have become acutely concerned.

In response to this increase in concern for liability, campuses must come to a realistic understanding of their student and administrative cultures and match them accordingly to the emerging legal realities. Campuses that banned alcohol completely or that have promulgated strict and unrealistic rules for alcohol use can actually invite greater legal liability than those that promote reasonable and enforceable standards. Although no analysis can provide a foolproof formula to safeguard against legal liability, an understanding of risks can minimize an institution's exposure to litigation.

Areas of particular concern for institutions include the school's role as a seller of alcohol, the school's role as a social host, and the school's role as proprietor. Perhaps the most global and greatest concern for many institutions and their students is the school's role as a supervisor of student conduct. While, in the past, courts have held institutions of higher education liable under the doctrine of *in loco parentis,* modern judicial thinking has eroded this principle. Currently most courts hold that the student-college relationship in and of itself does not make a school liable for the conduct of its students, although, as we note in the introduction to this section, many features of the student-college relationship can create special institutional responsibilities. Several leading cases hold that colleges and universities have no inherent duty nor any realistic ability to control students who are acting in their personal capacities.[6]

In *Bradshaw v. Rawlings,*[7] the plaintiff suffered injuries as a passenger in a car driven by an intoxicated student. The two were returning from a sophomore class picnic, an annual event that a faculty advisor helped to plan. Class funds had been used to buy beer for the picnic and campus advertisements for the event had featured beer mugs. The court held that "the college was obliged neither to control the conduct of the student driver nor to protect students traveling to and from the off-campus picnic."[8]

Endorsing the *Bradshaw* decision, the Supreme Court of Utah in deciding *Beach v. University of Utah* declared that "colleges must not be saddled with unrealistic, unenforceable duties of supervision that undermine the educational goals of a college education."[9] In *Beach,* a twenty-year-old student was severely injured during a geology field trip. The student fell off a cliff while others in the party slept. The faculty advisors for the trip knew the student had been drinking before the accident and, in fact, had consumed alcohol themselves. The court held that "neither the university nor the faculty members breached any tort duty by failing to supervise the student's conduct, to enforce laws and school rules against underage drinking, or to refrain from drinking themselves."[10]

The court went on to say:

It would be unrealistic to impose upon an institution of higher education the additional role of custodian over its adult students.... Fulfilling this charge would require the institution to babysit each student, a task beyond the resources of any school. But more importantly, such measures would be inconsistent with the nature of the relationship between the student and the institution, for it would produce a repressive and inhospitable environment, largely inconsistent with the objectives of a modern college education.[11]

These cases forcefully demarcate the limits of responsibility of colleges and universities in regard to their students' private conduct. It is important to note that the facts of these cases both involve events that occurred off campus and the rulings do contain a number of qualifications that suggest caution in generalizing from them. Also, the law in regard to institutional tort liability is a matter of state precedent and legislation. What is unequivocally clear, however, is that the rejection of *in loco parentis* by most state courts has given birth to new opportunities to educate students as responsible citizens.

Alcohol Awareness and Abuse Prevention: Campus Cooperation

What have emerged from the woes of abuse and fear of litigation are national alcohol-awareness programs and organizations. Campus Alcohol Consultants report in their 1988 survey that 97 percent of schools now have alcohol education and prevention programs, and 77 percent have special task forces on alcohol education and substance abuse prevention.[12] Many of the campuses we visited organize alcohol-awareness weeks in conjunction with national observances and conduct special programming during orientation and in the residence halls. Similarly, many of our campuses now have full-time health center staff and counselors to deal with alcohol-related problems. In fact, the student health service at a large southern flagship university has developed substance abuse peer education programs in which students can receive academic credit for learning about substance abuse and then conducting awareness programs for other students.

At a national level, organizations such as SADD (Students Against Drunk Driving) and BACCHUS (Boost Alcohol Consciousness Concerning the Health of University Students) have begun chapters on campuses across the country and a new network of institutions that wish to fight substance abuse has been created by the U.S. Department of Education. This network of Colleges and Universities Committed to the Elimination of Drug and Alcohol Abuse banded together in 1987 to: (1) collect and disseminate research and practice-based knowledge about successful programs; (2) provide a forum and mechanism for continuing communication and collaboration among institutions of higher education; and (3) identify areas and problems for further research and development.[13] The network has developed standards for membership that have been endorsed by the American Council for Education board of directors and the Higher Education secretariat.

One of the most promising developments we found on our campuses is a new cooperative spirit among students, student affairs staff, and campus police in regard to the regulation of alcohol. Students have joined campus professionals in drafting new alcohol policies and, on one southern campus we visited, fraternity members now hire off-duty campus policemen for every weekend party. In an interview on health and security issues, the campus police chief stated that his officers are now viewed in a more positive light and not as the enemy by students. "We made it our business to get to know the students as individuals. It helped a lot that the university hired a Greek advisor around that time. There has been great improvement. I can call [the Provost] anytime and he'll listen. All the way down the line, we have a good working relationship."

Indiana University offers an excellent example of these new initiatives. Each April, IU holds its famous bike race, the Little 500. This is the big social weekend of the year, both for IU and for Bloomington. In 1988, the event culminated in a drunken riot at an apartment complex off campus where many students live, and the Bloomington police made arrests after rocks and bottles were flung at their cruisers.

For the 1989 festivities, planning began long before the annual weekend to dampen the likelihood of an encore. Extra entertainment events were scheduled to keep students busy and away from their bottles and flasks. Also, student organizations sponsored extensive free bus service so that students, including those who drink, would not have to use cars. Local bar owners also participated by offering free nonalcoholic beverages to designated drivers. Students exchanged their keys for a cup imprinted with a special logo and distributed by IU student organizations to local establishments. Students, administrators and civic leaders worked together.

"The more things change, the more they stay the same." This French saying aptly describes the dilemma on our campuses concerning student drinking. More rules have not assured compliance. We must hope that the improvements in prevention, education, and cross-constituency cooperation will begin to modify student behavior positively.

CHAPTER 6

The Greeks

Introduction: Mixed Blessings

Greek social organizations are among the most visible and cohesive sub-communities on today's campuses. After a decline in popularity during the 1960s and early 1970s, fraternities and sororities are again popular. The National Interfraternity Conference estimates its membership has almost doubled in the last fifteen years, reaching 400,000 men in 1989. We have no firm data on the level of increase in the number of women in sororities. This growth has created substantial ambivalence on the part of faculty and administrators, for the legal and ethical issues raised by these private social clubs are complex. Greek societies have the potential both to enhance and undermine the quality of community on campus. In the 1980s, hazing deaths, rapes, and other assaults, usually associated with heavy drinking, focused public attention on fraternities. During our visits we found that every institution had reexamined or was reexamining the role Greeks do and should play on its campus.

In this chapter, we will explore continuity and change in the relationship between Greek organizations and their host institutions. We will also examine the paradoxical nature of fraternities and sororities, which can both foster and weaken community, and we will review how institutions are handling this challenge.

Continuity and Change

Despite the growth in numbers, the power the Greek system exercised on campus up to the 1950s has not returned.[1] For one thing, the traditional-age population that Greek organizations serve is a much smaller percentage of the whole. At community colleges, the fastest growing sector of higher education for the last two decades, Greek organizations are virtually nonexistent. Although Greeks may still dominate the extracurriculum on some campuses, on others they are scarcely involved, and the importance of the extracurriculum to the average student everywhere has waned. Perhaps this

79

is why we found little tension between Greeks and "Independents." On one of our campuses, a small private research institution where the percentage of Greeks had increased from 11 percent in 1982 to 26 percent in 1989, administrators speculated that the increase was primarily due to the change in the drinking age and the scarcity of residential housing, rather than the desire to participate in Greek life per se. Still, their Greek students reported greater satisfaction with student life generally than their independents.

There are other theories as to why, after more than a decade of decline, Greek organizations are growing. Some people see it as part and parcel of the increased social conservatism of the 1980s. Others point to greater pragmatic careerism among students, who desire to establish solid professional networks as early as possible. In addition, many campuses today are larger and more impersonal than they used to be. Perhaps the need for the community that Greek societies provide is greater. We have been unable to find data on the number of commuter students who are Greek. It would be interesting to see if fraternities and sororities play an important role in connecting commuters to their campus. Whatever the reasons for joining may be, there is no doubt that, for students who participate, Greek life is central to their collegiate life and is experienced as overwhelmingly positive.

Changes in the law have affected the relationship between the Greek societies and their institutions. The most important one is the externally imposed legislation raising the drinking age, which has reshaped campus life more generally. Since the Greeks, especially fraternities, are a focal point for student drinking, the institutional efforts to enforce legal drinking that we described in the preceding chapter have been directed substantially at fraternities. However, there has also been an increase in the number of states that have enacted anti-hazing laws, up from six in 1978 to more than twenty-five in 1989.[2] Court rulings influencing the degree of institutional liability have also played a role.

As we mentioned earlier in this section, the courts are increasingly finding institutions legally responsible for student safety when some "special relationship" beyond mere enrollment exists. Greeks are a particularly thorny instance of the larger dilemma: to intervene is to demonstrate and confirm a special relationship and potentially increase liability; laissez faire does not completely protect against risk and, for many, violates the ethical responsibilities of colleges and universities to guide and shape the behavior of members of their communities. Three of the campuses we visited had recently confronted this predicament. One chose to "derecognize" Greek societies. The other two opted to intervene.

A large research institution in the Southwest hired a Greek advisor despite advice not to do so because it would increase liability. In so doing, the university was implementing several of the twenty-one recommendations made by its 1987 Presidential Commission on Fraternal Organizations. It is interesting to note that, although fraternities at the university had a national reputation for hazing violence and alcohol abuse, the commission focused less on regulatory recommendations, per se, to improve the situation than on increased education and collaboration with the Greek societies.

In 1988, a small private research institution in the Northeast that was part of our sample was shaken by a fraternity gang rape. The administration suspended the fraternity and removed it from its building on campus for ten years. There is nearly unanimous feeling on campus that the administration acted properly in this case. However, the fraternity members brought suit against the university, claiming it failed to follow due process. This example illustrates compellingly the difficult task institutions now face in seeking to exercise authority in our increasingly litigious society.

The Greeks and Community: The Exemplary Paradox

The Greek presence on campus has long raised fundamental questions about the role of cohesive subgroups in the life of the campus community as a whole. Greek societies have long been associated with elitism and discriminatory practices. In the 1950s, in response to the civil rights movement, a number of institutions put pressure on Greek societies to sign antidiscrimination agreements. Nonetheless, de facto segregation still remains the rule. Today, when college and university administrators are so acutely concerned about the health of community on their campuses, they are taking a hard look at the advantages and disadvantages of Greek life. In 1988, Franklin and Marshall and Gustavus Adolphus withdrew institutional recognition from Greek organizations, joining Williams, Amherst, and Colby. In our travels, we found a broad spectrum of opinions regarding Greeks, from strong disapproval to enthusiastic endorsement.

At one liberal arts college that is 30 percent Greek, the faculty had several times recommended disaffiliation to the board of trustees, citing the use and sale of drugs and alcohol abuse by fraternities as cause. On the other hand, a small private comprehensive university in the South that has a significant Greek presence and a large public research institution in the Midwest that is 20 percent Greek are both encouraging additional national chapters to colonize their campuses. On a fourth campus, a public comprehensive university in the Northeast that is 5 percent Greek, there was consensus that the Greek organizations, both fraternities and sororities, are a positive force. Indeed, administrators identified their work with Greek organizations as a concerted initiative to build community on campus.

Most institutions, even those faced with egregious fraternity behavior, acknowledged the positive attributes of Greek life, particularly sororities. Clearly, Greek organizations provide their members, both residential and commuter, with a sense of belonging, a structure where friendship and activities develop. As the head of the Panhellenic Council at our small private research university in the Northeast put it: "Greeks form a sense of community for themselves. The freshmen who rush want a place to belong. I joined a sorority because I had no girlfriends. I wanted some friends." This university's recent Greek Life Task Force reported that fraternity and sorority members express significantly greater happiness with their housing situation and student life generally than other students and their alumni contribute more money to the institution than other graduates. At a public comprehensive in the Northeast, both students and administrators indicated that membership in Greek societies helps students bond to the institution. For example, the assistant vice-president for student affairs interviewed twenty senior women and every one reported it was her sorority affiliation that kept her from transferring or dropping out. We found numerous examples of campus leadership and public service by fraternities and sororities as well.

The drawbacks of Greek organizations and the deeply troubling dark side of fraternities were represented in our sample also, often side by side with the positive features. On a number of the campuses we visited, students, both Greek and non-Greek, perceived fraternities, and to a lesser degree, sororities, to be the sole source of social life. For whatever reason, these students did not feel alternatives were readily available. Providing these alternatives is part of the current wisdom among student life professionals and we found efforts to create them. But there may well be limits to what institutions can do to entertain students. After studying traditional-age students at Rutgers, anthropologist Michael Moffatt expressed such reservations.[3] The private comprehensive university we visited in the South had gone to considerable expense to create a nonalcoholic nightclub on weekends, as yet with little student patronage. Given the interests of today's youth culture, the appeal of Greek parties may remain unbeatable.

The two campuses we visited that had done studies of their Greek students found them very self-contained. At these research institutions both task forces concluded that the amount of time required for Greek activities was so great that it precluded significant participation in other student organizations. These findings go counter to conventional wisdom about broad Greek involvement in the extracurriculum.

On several of our campuses we found concern among administrators, faculty, and non-Greek students about the homogeneity of Greek societies. The practice of "like choosing like" is at the heart of fraternity and sorority selection. To some this is discrimination; to others it is the right to affective association. The most obvious, and, for many, the most troubling aspect of "like choosing like" is the continuing racial segregation of Greek organizations, which we found everywhere. On one flagship university campus, white sororities had only recently become recognized by the university because they had refused for years to sign the required antidiscrimination clause.

At five of the eighteen institutions visited—two liberal arts colleges and three research institutions—fraternities had been the scene of repeated and serious antisocial behavior, including abusive drinking, hazing violence, and violence against women. We could not help but be concerned by such a high percentage. It is widely believed that such dysfunctional behavior is increasing. Even President Loring of the National Interfraternity Conference, a confederation of fifty-nine fraternities, in his 1988 message to members, evoked images of moral decline: "Chapters that have gone undisciplined for years now resent our discussion of basic standards and expectations. They cannot begin to relate to our dialogues about the 'values and ethics' of fraternity membership."[4] However, we could find no reliable data to substantiate the commonly held opinion that things are actually worse than they used to be. As we will see in the chapter on crime, these data may not exist.

Mr. Loring's message includes also a call to action by fraternities themselves, a call for self-regulation and self-education, and an endorsement of strong college and university involvement. Institutions, by choice or by necessity, are monitoring Greek life more carefully. Many have enacted new regulations of their own. Examples include the following: Greek societies must be recognized student organizations; they must have an adult advisor; they must have dry rushes; their officers who are members of Interfraternity Councils on campus must participate in leadership retreats and educational programs; in order to serve alcohol, officers must attend university-run alcohol-awareness sessions each semester. Even more institutions have increased their advisory and educational services, designed to encourage greater civility and community involvement. On occasion, relations between Greeks and administrators have become more strained. Often, though, the result has been more and closer collaboration in enforcement and education.

Although social pathologies attract attention like the squeaky wheel, they are only the most obvious part of the total challenge fraternities and sororities present to campus community. Much of what is intrinsically appealing about the Greek social organizations—small-group loyalty, like-mindedness, affective associations—is at odds with the openness and pluralism the larger college and university community endorses. At the same time, fraternities and sororities provide just the sense of belonging and shared purpose so lacking on our campuses. Finding the ways best to balance the needs of these small groups and the needs of the campus as a whole is a difficult task. It is not a new one, but the resurgence of Greek societies brings it to the fore. The past, where there was little regulation, education, and collaboration, provides inadequate guidance.

CHAPTER 7

Harassment and Free Speech

> It is an unfortunate fact of our constitutional system that
> the ideals of freedom and equality are often in conflict.
> The difficult and sometimes painful task of our political
> and legal institutions is to mediate the appropriate balance
> between these two competing values.
>
> —Judge Avnor Cohen,
> *John Doe v. University of Michigan*

We have seen in our review of ethnic and gender relations on our campuses that, although individual students from different racial and ethnic backgrounds and individual men and women coexist in relative harmony, there is still incivility and even harassment. These occasional acts of incivility and harassment often generate major policy initiatives, especially when organized racial, ethnic, political, or gender-based groups mobilize around such incidents. Legitimate concern about examples of incivility and cases of discriminatory action have led many campuses across the country to enact broad codes of regulation that govern harassment, both racial and sexual.

In this chapter, we briefly discuss how a number of colleges and universities have been addressing one of the most difficult issues facing them: How does an organization whose lifeblood is both justice and free speech control verbal behavior that may be construed by some as harassing while protecting the right of free speech? We also express our belief that many campuses, as they respond to legitimate concerns about sexual and racial harassment, chill the climate for free speech and public debate. They confront the constitutional dilemma Judge Cohen articulated by underestimating the claims of free speech, because there is no organized political constituency clamoring for it.

The difficulty of balancing these regulatory and free speech interests is illustrated by examples of policies we have examined. The task in constructing policies for sexual and racial harassment is to draft the language narrowly enough to proscribe clearly objectionable conduct directed at particular persons without limiting expressions of opinion and fact generally. In evaluating examples of policies, it is useful to consider: (1) the types of speech and conduct included, and (2) the sensitivity of the policy to appropriate speech and action for different contexts.

For example, a prestigious private university in the South has promulgated a "Policy Statement on Discriminatory Harassment" that has two common shortcomings. First, the policy's definition of conduct is so broad that it prohibits speech that is not accompanied by discriminatory action. Second, it does not distinguish different standards for different contexts:

> Discriminatory harassment includes conduct (oral, written, graphic or physical) directed against any person or group of persons because of their race, color, national origin, religion, sex, sexual orientation, age, handicap, or veteran's status and that has the purpose or reasonable foreseeable effect of creating an offensive, demeaning, intimidating, or hostile environment for that person or group of persons. Such conduct includes, but is not limited to, objectionable epithets, demeaning depictions or treatment, and threatened or actual abuse or harm.

The definition of discriminatory conduct—"objectionable epithets, demeaning depictions or treatment..."—could preclude a public debate about the College Board scores of African-Americans or the low math scores of women. Also, there is inadequate language specifying the importance of context—classroom, dorm room, or plaza. An offensive poster criticizing affirmative action could be equally precluded in the plaza, in the classroom, or tacked on the door of an African-American student, whereas one could argue its appropriateness as a political statement in the plaza, or in a class where the topic under discussion was American social policy in the 1980s. The qualification in the policy statement—"Nothing in this policy statement is intended to limit the scholarly content of written or oral presentations"— helps define standards for academic freedom but does not protect speech that is not academic in nature.

Tufts University initially approved a policy that prohibited any form of expression that could be viewed as harassment in its residence halls. The impetus for this policy was the appearance on campus of a T-shirt that was demeaning to women. Apparently, under the rule, a student could not wear that T-shirt in a lounge in the dorms. One can argue that there should be a distinction between public space and private space. A student wearing the T-shirt should not have the right to enter another student's dorm room if that student finds the T-shirt offensive. Lounges, however, are public space even within a residence hall. Yet there seemed to be no free speech right for students in any part of the residence halls. Students demonstrated against the rule by dividing the campus with chalk lines into free speech and speech-free zones. The president of Tufts withdrew the policy.

The University of Michigan, whose policy was enjoined by the decision quoted at the beginning of this chapter, enacted what was, in fact, a relatively clear set of guidelines that differentiated among public, educational, and residential settings. However, the guidelines did not spell out the standards to apply in residence halls, where the rights of speech were severely constrained. And the actual enforcement practices described in the decision offer a bone-chilling example of the risks of these codes to free speech. Two incidents cited in the decision clearly illustrate how risks become realities:

1. A student in class stated his belief that homosexuality is a disease and that he intended to develop a counseling plan to help gay clients become straight. After heated discussions, one classmate filed a charge of sexual harassment and sexual orientation harassment against him. The hearing panel on the case unanimously found that the student had violated the sexual harassment policy but it did not convict him. The court wrote:

> Although the student was not sanctioned over the allegations of sexual orientation harassment, the fact remains that Policy Administrator—the authoritative voice of the University on these matters—saw no First Amendment problem in forcing the student to a hearing to answer for allegedly harassing statements made in the course of academic discussion and research. Moreover, there is no indication that had the hearing panel convicted rather than acquitted the student, the University would have interceded to protect the interests of academic freedom and freedom of speech.[1]

2. In a pre-dentistry class, known for its difficulty, a white student stated that "he had heard that minorities had a difficult time in the course and that he had heard that they were not treated fairly." Apparently, he had heard these comments from his roommate, an African-American former dentistry student. The African-American professor teaching the course filed a complaint that the comment was unfair and hurt her chances for tenure. The student was then "counseled" to write a letter apologizing for making the comments.

The Court concluded about all of the incidents it reviewed that they

> demonstrated that the University considered serious comments made in the context of classroom discussion to be sanctionable under the Policy....The Administrator generally failed to consider whether a comment was protected by the First Amendment before informing the accused student that a complaint had been filed.... There is no evidence in the record that the Administrator ever declined to pursue a complaint through attempted mediation because the alleged harassing conduct was protected by the First Amendment.... The University could not seriously argue that the policy was never interpreted to reach protected conduct. It is clear that the policy was overbroad both on its face and as applied.[2]

We have quoted at some length from the *Michigan* case for two reasons: (1) on its face it was one of the better campus policies we read, but still it clearly constituted a major limitation on academic freedom and free speech, and (2) the court decision report on implementation shows how difficult it is to respect free expression rights when the pressures are on from various individuals and/or groups to "prosecute."

The university setting brings with it the cultural norm of academic freedom and freedom of speech. Overly broad policies that restrict free speech represent a form of censorship that would be legally and ethically unacceptable in many other settings and especially so in a university or college where freedom of speech is part of academic freedom.

The best policy statement we have read is Stanford's, adopted after eighteen months of heated debate, following the black-Beethoven incident reported in chapter 3. Stanford's free expression and discriminatory harassment policy carefully circumscribes the limitations on free expression in an interpretation of Stanford's Fundamental Standard, the policy that frames all student policies and regulations.

The Fundamental Standard states: "Students at Stanford are expected to show both within and without the University such respect for order, morality, personal honor and the rights of others as is demanded of good citizens. Failure to do this will be sufficient cause for removal from the University."[3]

After reiterating Stanford's commitment to the principles of free inquiry and free expression, as well as equal opportunity and nondiscrimination, the Interpretation of the Fundamental Standard states:

> 3. ...Prohibited harassment includes discriminatory intimidation by threats of violence, and also includes personal vilification of students on the basis of their sex, race, color, handicap, religion, sexual orientation, or national and ethnic origin.
>
> 4. Speech or other expression constitutes harassment by personal vilification if it:
>
>> a) is intended to insult or stigmatize an individual or a small number of individuals on the basis of their sex, race, color, handicap, religion, sexual orientation, or national and ethnic origin; and
>>
>> b) is addressed directly to the individual or individuals whom it insults or stigmatizes; and
>>
>> c) makes use of insulting or "fighting" words or non-verbal symbols.[4]

The Stanford Interpretation of the Fundamental Standard delimits the types of speech and conduct prohibited by focusing upon the use of insulting or "fighting" words or nonverbal symbols. The Supreme Court, in defining this language as that which will inflict injury or tend to incite an immediate breach of the peace, has used objective standards, not the subjective feelings of the aggrieved. The interpretation further specifies that these words or symbols must be "commonly understood to convey direct and visceral hatred or contempt" (gutter epithets, for example).[5] The interpretation also includes the critical point that the originator(s) of the act must intend to insult or stigmatize an individual or small number of individuals. This focus on intent assures that thoughtlessness, poor judgment, or ignorance will not be sanctionable and that the offended party will not define sanctionable acts. The Stanford policy does not use the context private space versus public space (dorm room, classroom, public plaza) as a factor in distinguishing prohibited from allowable acts. Rather, it distinguishes "personal vilification" from "group defamation" in public debate. Apparently, if one candidate for president of the student body called another by a gutter epithet in a public debate, this would constitute a sanctionable act. We believe the distinction between public and private contexts affords clearer constitutional protection of free speech. Even with this limitation, however, the Stanford policy is a model for other universities.

This brief consideration of harassment policies illustrates how difficult it is to define harassment adequately. As we explore the difficult issue of balancing the ideals of freedom and equality, we must remember the framework of our democratic society. According to our laws, there are very few instances where speech alone can constitute sanctionable behavior. Yet, the potential of overgeneralizing is very real, as we have already seen. Another example of such overgeneralizing can be found in the National Institute Against Prejudice and Violence's 1987 report, *Ethnoviolence on Campus*.[6]

The report presents the results of a survey of 347 university students, 35 of whom "reported they had been victimized by an ethnoviolent act during the school year."[7] Ten examples of "ethnoviolence" reported by students are given. Among them are: "I was playing basketball and blocked a shot, I was called a nigger" (African-American male); "A group of people in the library poked fun at me and my friends" (Chinese female); "In discussion, a person mentioned that Jews had control of the economy. I was insulted" (Jewish female); "An issue was raised in a predominantly white class about the nature of Black men and the instructor and the class seemed to take the matter very lightly" (African-American male). Only one of the ten examples cited could qualify for sanction under the guidelines we have just sketched out: "In biology lab, an instructor labelled one of my questions as being dumb and said that those kinds of questions are to be expected from a Black person" (African-American female). Yet, all are lumped together and categorized as examples of "ethnoviolence"; the respondents are all called "victims." It could be easy to justify regulating "violence" and protecting "victims" when we would not regulate speech. We are concerned that such overgeneralizing may signal to colleges and universities that they need not distinguish among harassment, incivility, and thoughtlessness.

Derek Bok, then president of Harvard University, in response to a lewd, insulting, grossly demeaning letter about women distributed by a Harvard club, eloquently identified the issues posed by the approaches to legislating speech that are becoming ubiquitous in American higher education:

> Although such statements are deplorable, they are presumed to be protected under the Constitution and should be equally so on the campus as well. Why? The critical question is: Whom will we trust to censor communications and decide which ones are "too offensive" or "too inflammatory" or too devoid of intellectual content?... As a former president of the University of California once said: "The University is not engaged in making ideas safe for students. It is engaged in making students safe for ideas."[8]

The justification for allowing bigots to be uncivil, in public and in private, is that the very rules that a society might draft to control them could be used by them to control society. The Supreme Court has, in fact, allowed certain limitations on free speech, but only where the exercise of speech is likely to cause substantial harm, and the limitation must be very narrowly construed: fire in the theater or "fighting words" that might provoke a melee.

The harassment codes on many campuses are, in part, a response to a 1986 decision of the Supreme Court, in *Meritor Savings Bank, FSB v. Vinson*.[9] In this decision, the Supreme Court used the "fighting words" rationale to determine that an offensive sexual environment constitutes sexual harassment under Title VII of the Civil Rights Act of 1964 as amended, 42 USC s2000e-2, in terms of the relationship between employer and employee. The facts of the case included a pattern of overt sexual relationship between a supervisor and an employee and the subsequent firing of the employee. This case and others under Title VII only apply to the employee/employer relationship, not to the student/institution relationship. Neither the facts nor the judgment would seem to support the broad harassment policies on many campuses, even if Title VII applied to students.

These harassment policies pose the question whether anyone, the majority or a minority, can limit a constitutional right of another minority, because of displeasure with the exercise of the constitutional right, in this case, free speech. In the historic *Cooper v. Aaron*,[10] the Supreme Court took the position that the negative reaction of an audience to the exercise of constitutional rights is not a justification for limiting these constitutional rights. The threat of riot in Little Rock was not sufficient to justify limiting the constitutional right of African-American students to attend desegregated schools because segregationists were opposed.

The challenge to universities and colleges in balancing the two values of free expression and equal rights in the arena of verbal harassment is to understand the values encapsulated in the Constitution and inherent in the nature of the university. Since the 1960s it has been settled law and practice that campuses can regulate the time, place, and manner (where manner is volume, not tone of voice) of speech but that they cannot regulate content. Those who disagree with or are offended by the free expression of others can themselves respond publicly and vigorously.

Derek Bok responded to the derogatory letter at Harvard with a strong and public denunciation of the letter and its authors. He justified this action:

> The wording of the letter was so extreme and derogatory to women that I wanted to communicate my disapproval publicly, if only to make sure that no one could gain the false impression that the Harvard administration harbored any sympathy or complacency toward the tone and substance of the letter. Such action does not infringe on free speech. Indeed, statements of disagreement are part and parcel of the open debate that freedom of speech is meant to encourage; the right to condemn a point of view is as protected as the right to express it.[11]

We, too, urge restraint in regulating speech in the protection of women and racial and ethnic minorities from offensive language, yet strongly endorse the importance of vigorous denunciation of harassment or incivility by campus leaders (presidents, faculty senates, student governments, and newspapers). Challenging bigotry forcefully and thoughtfully constitutes an essential opportunity to teach by example. It is equally, if not more, important that institutions acknowledge the existence of bigotry and ignorance in our society and take serious steps to educate members of the campus community to understand and respect both diversity and the constitutional principles that frame interaction in a pluralistic democracy.

CHAPTER 8

Crime

Introduction

In the last several years, crime on campus has become a common topic of debate, speculation, and controversy. In a time of increasing public scrutiny, a number of violent crimes have focused attention on colleges and universities and fueled sharp criticisms of rising crime, inadequate security, and cover-ups. Alarmist headlines, justified outrage, overgeneralizations, and grossly incomplete data combine to cloud observers' views. As yet, no one has succeeded in presenting an adequate and accurate picture of the reality of campus crime.

In this section, we will lay out the different realities we have encountered. We will review the history of crime reporting and examine various data sources. We will hear the voices from our campus visits and share how these institutions were dealing with crime. We will review institutional liability concerns and note significant changes in campuses' response to crime.

Obstacles to Understanding

Of course, assault, rape, and even murder do not stop at college gates. However, news reports, including those in widely read publications, portray our campuses as patently dangerous. In October, 1988, *USA Today* printed a special supplement which focused on crime on campus and concluded in its cover story headlines that: "Schools fail safety test...Sad truth is 'serious crime is rampant.'"[1] Unfortunately, neither Gannett nor anyone else has compiled adequately comprehensive and representative data to support such generalizations.

Since 1930, the Federal Bureau of Investigation has been compiling crime statistics for the United States based on reports given voluntarily by city and state law enforcement agencies. Not until 1971 were college and university crime statistics included in the digest known as the *Uniform Crime Reports*. In 1971, only 34 campuses supplied statistics and only thirteen states had initiated central collection systems to conform with Uniform

Crime Reporting Standards. In 1987, only 354 campuses reported, barely 10 percent of the 3,340 institutions of higher education listed in the *Statistical Abstract of the United States;* forty-one states had central collecting systems by 1989.[2] Federal legislation passed in 1990 now requires all colleges and universities that accept federal aid to contribute annually to the *Uniform Crime Reports* (UCR). These new data should provide a much clearer picture of campus crime.

The Center for the Study and Prevention of Campus Violence at Towson State University in Maryland has reported since 1985 on statistics it has collected nationally from student affairs, security, and residence halls professionals from member schools of the National Association of Student Personnel Administrators. In 1986, 321 student affairs officers responded; in 1987, 367; and in 1988, 368, that is, 9.6 percent, 10.99 percent and 11 percent of all institutions respectively.[3] This is a small sample, and one that is not representative of American higher education, since the average student attends a much larger institution (the average campus size each year in this study has been about 3859 students). The Gannett-*USA Today* team obtained responses from 698 schools nationwide, a larger sample than the FBI or Towson State, although still only 21 percent of the total. This study focused on four-year colleges with on-campus residences and at least two thousand students, so it provides no information about community colleges, where 38 percent of undergraduates were enrolled in 1987.[4]

Sample size is not the only problem. Because of the unreliability of most data about crime on campus, the opportunity for misinterpretation is ubiquitous. The Uniform Crime Reporting Standards are not widely used, so even the basic definitions of crimes counted vary. In addition, different studies count different categories altogether. It is extremely difficult, then, to obtain comparability across studies, and rarely do people attempt it. So the reader is often faced with the apples and oranges dilemma. The *USA Today* special supplement, for example, made no efforts to compare crime on campus and crime in surrounding neighborhoods, nor did it compare its results with national FBI statistics. The supplement reported thirty-one murders and murder/suicides on American campuses in 1987 and made much of this. If one were to compare this sample with national statistics, though, one would have to translate the thirty-one murders and suicides out of over fifteen million students, faculty, and staff into crimes per 100,000 of population, which turns out to be 0.20 murders/100,000. The national average for 1986 was 8.6 murders/100,000.[5] Likewise, the paper claims 1 of every 500 students had experienced "violent crime." National statistics for 1987 indicate that 617.3 people/100,000 experienced violent crime, that is, a rate three times as high. From this national standpoint, then, campuses appear to be very much safer in regard to violent crime than society at large. This is not mentioned in the *USA Today* piece.

Another useful approach would have been to compare the campus statistics for each crime per 100,000 of population with similar statistics for the immediately neighboring reporting areas. Michael Clay Smith reports work by Fox and Hellman comparing the campus crime figures at 175 colleges and universities with those of cities and towns in which the campuses were located. Fox and Hellman found that in 1979,

> on the average, the campus crime rate was only about half that of the adjoining cities and towns (the correlation was 0.58). On the safest campus, the rate was only one percent of the community; at the other extreme, the most dangerous school had a rate three times that of the community. Only twenty of the 175 campuses [11.4 percent] had rates that exceeded those of the community.[6]

The dangers of incomplete data reports and their use for comparison are illustrated in a law review note, where the author summarizes the Fox and Hellman study and then asserts that the Gannett figures confirm that "incidents of crime on campus have risen dramatically in the last decade."[7] There is simply no evidence in the Gannett sample to support this judgment. Such loose use of noncomparable and incomplete data is what creates alarm on campus and off. It does a great disservice to all those seriously confronting crime on campus.

A small research university in our sample participated in the *USA Today* survey. As a result of its participation, the school earned the distinction of having one of the highest crime rates in the nation. The head of the campus police force told us that he provided *USA Today* with complete crime statistics, including petty theft and minor incidents. He claims other schools did not make such full disclosures and that the report grossly distorts his school's situation regarding serious crime. "I caught more grief about [our school] having [one of the highest] crime rate[s] because we count every broken window," he said. It is no wonder many campuses worry about bad publicity from reporting.

At the end of its 1988 table entitled, "Number of Offenses Known to Police," the FBI warns that

> caution should be exercised in making any inter-campus comparison or ranking schools, as university/college crime statistics are affected by a variety of factors. These include: demographic characteristics of the surrounding community, ratio of male to female students, number of on-campus residents, accessibility of outside visitors, size of enrollment, etc.[8]

The FBI has the good sense to warn that comparisons could mislead and result in the kind of unfair and undeserved distinction received by the aforementioned campus.

The reality about crime on American campuses is that no one really knows what the reality is. Misinformation has led to the commonly held opinion that crime is epidemic on campus. It certainly has increased in the United States as a whole. The FBI's national statistics show an increase in violent crime, up 8.1 percent, and a decrease in property crime, down 3.4 percent between 1982 and 1986. From 1977 to 1986 violent crime increased 29.7 percent; property crime increased 5.7 percent.[9] However, the FBI does not have per capita data over time for the campuses that report. Nor does anyone else, as far as we know. Higher education needs more information and less alarmism.

Our Campuses

Speaking with students, faculty, and staff on the eighteen campuses we visited, we found no sense of crisis and, for the most part, a feeling that there was less crime now than five years ago, even taking into account the under-reporting of crime that everyone acknowledges. One liberal arts commuter college did report a 27 percent increase in case reports in the last year. At another liberal arts residential college, moving about campus at night was deemed unsafe. At most institutions, however, most people felt safe going about their business both day and night. Women were more concerned about their safety than men. There was a high awareness of the possibility of rape, and on several campuses there had been a reported rape in the last year or two. As a faculty member at an urban community college in the Southwest put it: "I lock my office when I leave. There have been rapes or attempted rapes. They're rare enough so that I'm not terrified, however."

In our travels, police and administrators attributed the majority of campus crime to students themselves. The Towson results for 1988 corroborate this; student affairs officers estimated that 78 percent of sexual assaults, 52 percent of physical assaults, 66.7 percent of strong-arm robberies, 91.5 percent of arsons, and 85.5 percent of incidents of vandalism were perpetrated by students.[10] Many of our campuses noted a high correlation between alcohol abuse and crime on campus. One reported that 80 percent of all cases heard by the student judiciary were alcohol related. Another attributed the recent increase in vandalism to increased drinking.

On all of our campuses we found improved security—institutions had increased or upgraded their exterior lighting, added emergency phones, increased the number of police officers, improved their equipment. Some institutions had done this recently, others as much as a decade ago. Everywhere there were escort services, substantially student run, and programs to educate students and staff about personal safety. Students understood that the campus was just like the real world and, therefore, they had to take appropriate precautions.

While crimes against persons occur on campus, we found that the overwhelming majority of campus crime is against property. For example, on two flagship campuses, property crime was 96 percent and 99.1 percent of total reported crime. Theft and larceny headed the list. Comparing 1985 data from the seven campuses we visited that are included in the UCR to the national UCR data, we found the rate of property crime is fairly similar to larger societal trends. In four instances, our campuses had a somewhat higher frequency of property crime than the national aggregate.

These data corroborate the sentiments we heard from campus police and administrators that students tend to be lax in protecting their property. For instance, at a small college in the Mountain states, students are admonished to lock their dorm rooms. Still, it was estimated that of all the unoccupied rooms in the residence halls at any given time of day, 80 percent of the men's and 50 percent of the women's rooms are not locked. Housing officials at other institutions spoke of different offenses. Many residence halls now have outside doors which automatically lock when closed. Some officials reported that students prop those doors open so they do not have to carry their keys, leaving the building accessible to any passerby. Internal safeguards are also breached by students. Many residence halls require guests to be accompanied by a resident at all times. Often students let unknown visitors into buildings and allow them to wander freely.

The Campus Environment: Institutional Responsibility?

Criminal activity may prompt victims to file negligence lawsuits against colleges and universities. In most cases, plaintiffs claim that an institution was careless or failed to protect the victim properly and adequately against foreseeable campus crime. The courts have been slow to find campuses liable for crime on campus.

However, in addition to legal liability, crime on campus has become a major political liability. In 1986, Jeanne Clery was raped and strangled in her dorm room at Lehigh University. Her parents settled out of court with Lehigh, which agreed to invest $1 million in lights and other security precautions. Her parents also lobbied the state legislature, and Pennsylvania lawmakers enacted a bill requiring all the state's colleges to publish crime rates for the previous three years. The law that took effect November 1, 1988, is the first of its kind. Eight more states have been considering similar legislation: California, Illinois, Indiana, Massachusetts, Missouri, New Jersey, New York, and Washington. Recent federal legislation requiring the reporting of campus crime makes it clear that the publicity and public pressure have made crime on campus a political issue.

Awareness and Prevention

Perhaps the most notable efforts to prevent crime on campus have come from the professionalization of campus security forces. From their inception, campus security posts seemed to be havens for retired police chiefs who sought to supplement their pensions while enforcing parking regulations and quelling occasional panty raids. But modern campus security officials face a much different world, one that can include assuring the integrity of computer systems and protecting against terrorist attacks. While some campuses still deploy only unarmed security personnel, many now employ sworn law enforcement officials. The campus police are today professional law enforcement officers, who know how to work in their unique environment. One mid-Atlantic research institution has created a state-certified police academy on its campus where it trains its own recruits, many of whom are recent graduates of its criminal justice program. Another institution is a candidate for accreditation as a police force by the national quality control panel for metropolitan police forces.

New technologies are also playing an important role in campus security. For example, the campus chief at our southern comprehensive university created a computerized dispatching and analysis system that allows him to deploy his forces to respond to changing patterns of crime by time and day. Many of our campuses had installed state of the art communications systems that allow all of the security officers to be in constant touch with home base no matter where they are on campus and to respond quickly to calls for assistance.

Campus police forces are diversifying quickly in terms of gender and ethnic groups. A continuing problem on some campuses is the relative pay of campus security officers and metropolitan police. As neighboring jurisdictions deal with shortages of officers, particularly women and minority groups, campuses are often hampered in this competition by their salary scales. The chief security officer of the private comprehensive institution in the South with a progressive police force said that much of his turnover came from recruitment raids by neighboring forces.

Although there are more and better-equipped police officers on campus and their jobs include protecting against the pathologies of the real world, campus security professionals face a much different charge in their duties than their municipal counterparts. As Michael Clay Smith points out:

> Local police departments aim primarily at catching and prosecuting criminals; campus security departments, on the other hand, should have crime prevention and avoidance as the paramount focus. A good campus reputation for safety and security is of far greater value to a college or university than efficiency in sending criminals to jail.[11]

This sentiment was echoed loudly on all of the campuses we visited. Schools in our sample were trying to dispel any notions of "us against them" in regard to their security personnel. They were including their security officers in the educational process by involving them in lectures, seminars, and other special programs on crime prevention for students and staff. The new president of an eastern liberal arts college told us that when interviewing candidates for the vacant director of security position he was put off by former police officers who proposed hard-nosed approaches toward students. "One of them even talked to me about how he wanted to assign some men to work undercover to look for drugs in the dorms among the students." The president hired a social worker, one of whose first steps as chief was to outfit security personnel in slacks and blazers instead of police uniforms. The students responded warmly to the changes.

The emphasis on prevention, cooperation, and education has led to heightened awareness of crime on campus. Freshmen now participate in crime awareness and prevention programs during their orientation. Residence halls offer similar programs on a regular basis. These programs range from education about harassment and date rape to self-defense instruction. Most campuses now provide escort services. Many have student-operated security patrols supervised by the campus police. One northeastern university has instituted an "Operation ID" program to mark and register personal property. As is the case with alcohol abuse prevention, campuses are linked formally and informally through national networks. One such network is provided through the National Crime Prevention Council's clearinghouse.

College and university campuses are not idyllic communities. But they are unquestionably safer than society in general, and, for the most part, are safer than their surrounding neighborhoods. They are communities whose members are mobilized and collaborating to maintain and improve security. The truth about crime on campus, insofar as we know any facts, is sad but not alarming; the truth about crime awareness and prevention is encouraging. Our nation's campuses deserve more credit than they have received.

CHAPTER 9

Enforcement

We began this chapter with an acknowledgment that even though *in loco parentis* is dead, regulation of both academics and student life is alive and well on college campuses. In the last decade, institutions have reinstated most of the rules eliminated in the late 1960s. Residential students and those who participate in campus organizations and activities are most affected. In this section, we will consider the extent to which students themselves participate in the process of regulating the campus community.

With the revolution of the late 1960s and early 1970s, students gained significant control over their own lives and a more substantial role in institutional governance. Student interest in "student power" waned in the 1970s, and substantial activism subsided, but throughout the 1980s, students played a continuing role in the creation and enforcement of rules governing their behavior.

The drafting and revision of codes of conduct have been usually collaborative and consultative processes, involving students, student affairs staff, the university lawyer, and, sometimes, faculty. Of course, the president and board of trustees have had to approve these codes. On a number of the campuses we visited such reviews were going on; at others, they had recently been completed. An exception to this collaboration has been the intervention by the state through laws regulating behavior, particularly alcohol use and fraternity hazing. The student role in regard to these external interventions is limited, although students do participate in adapting the law to the campus. They have little sense of ownership in the regulations imposed by external authorities.

Students we encountered had mixed reactions to the rules governing their behavior. In our travels, we heard few complaints. Criticism of excessive paternalism was most loudly voiced at a southwestern community college where there was little student involvement in decision making. The twenty-seven–year-old president of student government said: "We are older, we work, we pay our tuition, but they don't treat us that way. There is excessive regulation, too many rules, too many small rules." Although, clearly, many students simply break rules that they find constraining—witness underage drinking, and the propping open of residence hall doors at night for

101

convenience sake—on the great majority of the campuses we visited, discipline is less of a problem than it was five years ago. Nationally, chief student affairs officers surveyed concurred, agreeing that there had been no change or there had been a decrease in discipline problems by percentages ranging from 71 percent in relation to violation of campus rules in the residence halls to 81 percent in other campus settings.[1] On repeated occasions, students actually expressed the desire for more active regulation by the institution. The assistant dean of students at a large midwestern flagship university said, "Whereas students in the late 1960s said 'Hands off' to the administration, today's students have more of a consumer attitude. They are calling for services and protection and rules that are for their own good. They ask why we are not patrolling the residence halls at night to keep them safe." "Students don't want to put up with others who are on drugs, alcohol and the like. They turn to the university and ask us to intercede," said the director of student mental health services at a small private research university.

Most student affairs professionals we spoke with focused on the educational aspects of the student discipline function entrusted to them. The prevailing ethos is one of providing learning opportunities rather than imposing punishments. One vice-president coined the phrase "*in loco amitas*" to express his vision of collaboration with students.

The greater possibility of lawsuits has affected enforcement on campus as well as increased the number of rules. Lawyers play a larger role in judicial proceedings, both for the defendants and the institution. The increased external scrutiny of the campus enforcement process and the increased formalism it brings with it are at odds with both the traditional informal parental model, vestiges of which still remain, and the new collaborative and educational one.

We found that the degree of student involvement in enforcement varied greatly. Among their many duties, resident advisors, present on all residential campuses we visited, play the role of enforcer of the rules in the first instance, keeping the peace and reporting infractions. Often, students, collaborating with campus security, patrol the residence halls and the parking lots. On several campuses, students play the major role in judging and assigning punishment to student misconduct. "Now the students are the enforcers and the punishers," said the chancellor of a Midwest flagship institution. "They accept this responsibility very seriously." The student judiciaries are advised by student affairs professionals who guarantee procedural due process.

The most substantial student role in discipline appeared at a small liberal arts college in the Rockies and at a comprehensive private institution in the South. Both have student judiciaries. The university in the South has two judicial councils that enforce academic honor codes, one for the male college, one for the female college. The student role is so significant that, although a decision of a council can be appealed to the dean of the residential college, if the dean disagrees, he or she can only remand the case for review again by the judicial council, not overturn the decision.

At other institutions, both large and small, students work together with student affairs professionals and faculty to judge violations. The students have a very significant role at the Midwest flagship and mid-Atlantic flagship universities we visited. At a comprehensive commuter institution in the South, the dean of students plays an important initial role in resolving all disciplinary problems. In academic matters, a student can elect to have his or her alleged offense heard by a committee of four selected from a panel of fifteen students and fifteen faculty. The chair is a faculty person. Of the remaining three, at least one must be a faculty member and one a student. In nonacademic matters, students may be heard by three different panels, each with significant peer involvement, depending on the alleged offense. The student government provides advocates for students accused of violating rules. At a comprehensive university in the East, the hearing panel is a triumvirate, involving one faculty person, one student, and one administrator. Each panel is appointed by the president from lists submitted by the faculty and the student government. Panels hear complaints when they are not resolved by the judicial officer of the institution. At one of our community colleges, also, two students, two faculty members, and one student affairs officer make up the judicial council. They get little practice, however. The vice-president for student affairs remarked that, during some years, there is not one case to hear.

At a minority of the institutions we visited, students played no role in enforcing the community's rules. At the very large flagship university in the Southwest, student infractions of campus rules first go to the dean of student's office. If they cannot be resolved there, a student can request a formal hearing, where a faculty person, usually a lawyer, will hear the complaint against the student and render a judgment that is itself appealable to the president. A public liberal arts college with no student government has an administrative disciplinary system, in spite of the general spirit of laissez faire. Three of our four community colleges have a traditional administrative disciplinary system.

It is not clear that student involvement in the enforcement of rules has brought significant programs on all campuses to train students to participate in this regulatory activity. On most campuses with residential students, the largest cadre of student "enforcers" are the resident assistants. Resident assistant training programs usually educate students about the rules and how to use mediation and counseling skills to deal with most infractions informally. Some campuses have programs for training other student participants in the judicial process, although many treat students as members of juries of their peers who do not receive special training.

Large campuses with student judiciaries have extensive consultative resources for student judges. The student affairs officer in charge of the disciplinary process is often a lawyer. Indeed, at the large mid-Atlantic flagship university we visited, the student disciplinary process is coordinated by a lawyer who has developed a national reputation. On other campuses, such as our southwestern flagship, lawyers actually implement the formal procedures as hearing officers, so students do not play a significant role. The presence of lawyers in the student disciplinary process is now ubiquitous at large institutions and constrains student participation.

The student disciplinary process can be one that allows the participating students to experience the exercise of citizenship in a setting where he or she serves others and also makes decisions that affect the lives of fellow students, sometimes significantly. This experience allows the student to understand the responsibilities and opportunities of living in a community. The students who come before student disciplinary bodies to face charges encounter another form of learning: they are held responsible for their actions and must accept the judgment of a tribunal that includes their peers.

Regulatory activities, both in the creation of the rules and in their enforcement, establish the boundaries of authority that help define community. Participating in these regulatory activities is one of the most valuable learning opportunities open to students on American campuses.

Part 4

The Learning Community: Promises to Keep

Introduction

Among the various functions that higher education has served over the years in this country, the most endangered today is that of providing a learning community for students and faculty. Powerful forces are limiting both the nature and scope of students' learning and their experience of intellectual and civic community. In this section, we will explore how the expectations, attitudes, and behaviors of students and of faculty limit the potential for undergraduate learning.

The conjunction of learning with the experience of community is not self-evident on American campuses. Although the heart of the academy is teaching and learning, and although students and faculty have contact first, foremost, and often only, in the classroom, we have found that there is relatively little academic community or interest in building it on the part of either students or faculty.

One primary obstacle is the lack of interaction among students and professors. Many classes are large, but, even when they are not, they are overwhelmingly lecture based. Maintaining students in the passive role of recipients of information does not promote a sense of connecting to the professor, the other students, or the course content. Few students seek assistance or intellectual exchange outside of class and few faculty take proactive steps to increase it.

In addition to the obstacles created by our teaching and learning norms, the lack of intellectual common ground is another impediment to the experience of academic community. Consensus about the content of higher education weakened in the 1960s. Much ink has flowed in the debate over the legitimacy of core curricula in pluralistic America. Forty-seven percent of the faculty in Carnegie's 1989 survey endorsed a required common core at their institution.[1] Only 2 percent of American campuses currently have a common core.

The opening of colleges and universities to more diverse and less well-prepared students has also weakened the traditional common ground of the academy. Many of these students do not meet the expectations faculty have of threshold verbal and quantitative skills and substantive knowledge. Indeed, even traditional students are less well equipped than in the past. So, on two counts, the gap between faculty and students has widened.

In the following two chapters, we will explore the ways in which students, faculty, and their institutions limit learning and the experience of academic community. We will consider careerism, factors influencing the importance of academic work, satisfaction with teaching and learning, and the extent to which students experience being part of a learning community inside and outside of the classroom.

Careerism can contribute to students' sense of community when it connects them with their major department or program and creates shared interests with faculty. On the other hand, careerism can preclude interest in and connection to the broader goal of higher education: membership in the community of liberally educated Americans.

Academic work is not the primary concern for most of today's students. A number of factors influence the importance students attribute to academic work, among them (1) the demands and rewards of paid work; (2) the availability of the major of choice; (3) family responsibilities that claim adult students especially; and (4) the primacy of having fun, a tradition that is alive and well among traditional-age students. For faculty, too, other priorities compete with teaching, including research and departmental duties.

Both students and faculty appear to be quite satisfied with the status quo of teaching and learning. Since they have never been socialized to value intellectual community, most students do not expect or desire interaction with faculty and, therefore, do not regret its absence. Most faculty are concerned about lowering of academic standards and the weaker preparation of many students. But few take the time and expend the energy to create more interactive and demanding classes. There is little extrinsic reward for good teaching. Of faculty respondents to Carnegie's 1989 survey, 44.7 percent indicated that they are more enthusiastic about their work now than when they began their academic careers; 33.6 percent are as enthusiastic or less enthusiastic. Only 12.2 percent expressed strong lack of enthusiasm, and only 14.2 percent rated the quality of life at their institutions to be poor.[2]

Ironically, the lack of mutual engagement in intellectual community may facilitate this satisfaction. With minimal expectations and minimal investment of energy, there will be minimal frustration. Lack of relationship buffers both students and faculty from their differences and from the unmet potential for learning and connecting.

CHAPTER 10

Student Priorities and Opportunities

Credentialing: The Number One Goal

The strongest common denominator we found among students is the focus on obtaining a degree in a major that will assure them of a good job. From traditional-age freshmen in private liberal arts schools, to returning homemakers in community colleges, all put the highest educational priority on securing a credential.

Careerism, what has been referred to as "grim professionalism," has been amply documented in many studies. Observers of higher education note its resurgence after the 1960s, starting in the mid 1970s. This conclusion is dramatically illustrated by looking at the trend in degree majors from 1970–71 to 1985–86.[1] Overall, the number of degrees granted increased 18 percent (far less than the increase in enrollment during that time). In fifteen years, the number of degrees in foreign languages dropped 50 percent, letters dropped 46 percent, mathematics dropped 36 percent, and social sciences dropped 39 percent. At the same time, business majors increased by 107 percent, engineering majors by 69 percent, and health sciences majors by 56 percent. Interestingly, education, a vocational major, dropped by 51 percent. When one compares the absolute numbers, it is clear that business, by itself, absorbed most of the shifts from the arts, letters, some sciences, and education.

Alexander Astin has also documented a shift in student values toward greater materialism during this time. This helps explain the decrease in education degrees, a traditionally female and relatively low-paying occupation, as well as the rise in undergraduate business degrees.

In her book *Campus Life,* Helen Lefkowitz Horowitz laments the limiting of student horizons that careerism brings with it, targeting the 12 to 15 percent of undergraduates who go on for advanced professional degrees: "...when undergraduates perceive college as a mere preparation for professional school, they hold themselves in.... They have concentrated on the husks of grade-grubbing, ignorant that kernels of knowledge exist. In their competitive struggle for high grades, they do not allow themselves time or the risks necessary for personal growth."[2] Intellectual exploration and growth, through either liberal arts electives or required general education courses, rarely occurs. The cost of overly narrow careerism is paid not only by individuals, but by society. The community of liberally educated Americans is not growing as access to higher education increases. It is eroding.[3] Students have become novice technicians learning limited substance and modest skills, both of which are usually outdated by the time they graduate. They are not developing the broad perspective and analytical rigor that is the aspiration and often the outcome of a strong liberal education, where one is prepared not just for a job, but for a multifaceted life.

The increasing vocational emphasis among undergraduates has led them overwhelmingly to study business.[4] From 1970–71 to 1985–86 the increase in degrees granted was four times greater in business and management than in engineering. In 1985–86, three times as many individuals received degrees in business than in engineering.[5] There are about forty times as many business majors as philosophy and theology majors, although there is some evidence that liberal arts majors perform as well as, and in some cases better than, business majors as managers of corporations. AT&T, in its definitive study of liberal arts, engineering, and business majors concluded: "One overall conclusion from these data is that there is no need for liberal arts majors to lack confidence in approaching business careers. The humanities and social science majors, in particular, continue to make a strong showing in managerial skills and have experienced considerable business success."[6] The fact that liberal arts majors perform well in business testifies both to the strength of a liberal education and to the complexity of the requirements of modern business, where continuing learning is a must. Pursuing the average undergraduate business major actually may weaken overall performance in the corporate and small business environment.

Students too often choose courses that are narrow in their focus, and/or quite insubstantial. For example, a longitudinal study of 1972 high school graduates who went on to college found that 35 percent of those who earned more than ten credits in college studied no mathematics and another 30 percent percent took only remedial math. Almost 30 percent of the class took courses in aerobics, jogging, body-building, karate, yoga, and the care of athletic injuries.[7] In a recent study of transcripts of students at thirty colleges, Robert Zemsky concluded that science majors took few courses in the humanities and that humanities majors took few courses in the sciences; neither pursued subjects outside of their major field in any depth.[8]

It is easy to criticize students for their narrowness, but doesn't their professionalism respond to social reality? How often have we heard business people say they want to hire business majors? Liberal learning is in jeopardy in this country. Still, we can hardly expect students to come to its defense. Student protest in the 1960s was grounded in a large public consensus around the importance of civil rights and substantial questioning of the morality of the Vietnam War. Where is there similar support for the liberal arts, for a coherent and broad education? Even within the academy, there are few supporters. The problem is not exclusively that students' freedom of choice in course selection has decreased curricular breadth and depth and jeopardized the mathematical and scientific literacy of the country. Institutions bear responsibility too through their decisions about what to offer and what to require.

It is also simplistic to indict professionalism. On the campuses we visited, we found much vitality and enthusiasm associated with career-related activities, both academic and cocurricular. We found many professional students to be serious students, and they participated often in clubs, honor societies, and departmentally based activities like conferences. Quite a few experienced a sense of community with students in other majors and faculty members. Institutions can build on this sense of belonging while at the same time enriching the professional major to create a broader experience of community.

Academic Work: An Endangered Occupation?

The importance academic work has in student culture varies depending on various factors. One of these seems to be age. Traditional-age students have never placed academic achievement at the top of their priority list. Helen Lefkowitz Horowitz contends in her book *Campus Life* that increased competition, beginning in the 1970s, has changed students' attitudes, and she describes the students as grinds.[9] We did not find that traditional-age students study a great deal, nor that they place a higher priority on academics than on having fun. We found much more representative the attitude Michael Moffatt documents at Rutgers. During orientation at Rutgers, a student resident assistant provided clear advice to the new freshmen on her floor:

> Her first year at Rutgers, she said, she had been very upset by a preceptor (a grad student living in the dorms) who told her that she would be OK at Rutgers if she studies five hours a day. But this was nonsense, she told us: "You have to make up your mind what you want here. If you want to enjoy yourself, if you want to have a social life at all, two hours a day is plenty, one in the morning and one in the evening. A 'B' or a 'C' isn't a disaster. Of course," she amended, alluding to the great status divide among undergraduate majors, "you bio-sci people are different...."[10]

Students we spoke with were committed to having fun. A central component of having fun is partying. It begins Thursday night and runs through the weekend. Heavy drinking is the norm. Except at elite institutions, academics are completely back burnered until Monday morning. In our informal conversations with students about the amount of time spent on academic work we found few individuals who averaged twenty hours a week. One hour of study for each hour of class was the norm.

Data from the Astin follow-up study of students beginning college in 1981 through 1984 illustrate an annual decline in "studying or doing homework": in 1985, 32.8 percent of the students who entered in 1981 (most were seniors) said they spent sixteen or more hours a week studying or doing homework the previous year, whereas in 1988, only 23.1 percent of the students who entered in 1984 so reported. In 1985, 81.2 percent said they had spent six or more hours a week studying or doing homework the previous year. In 1988, 70.3 percent indicated that they had spent six or more hours.[11]

Curiously, in every category, students who had entered college in 1984 reported spending less time on activities than students who entered college in 1981. Of those who entered in 1981, 52.6 percent reported spending sixteen hours or more per week the previous year attending classes or lab session; of those who entered in 1984, only 42 percent reported sixteen hours or more per week the year before. There were drops also in time spent socializing with friends, watching television, participating in student clubs or groups, and working for pay.

Data collected by Professor Robert Pace at UCLA suggest that, even though students who spend more time on quality academic work do better academically than those who do not, the results may not warrant the effort required. Students who commit high-quality academic time of twenty hours or less are likely to have a grade point average of 3.0; those who more than double their hours to fifty per week increased their grade point only 20 percent to 3.6.[12] For a student who wishes to continue on to graduate or professional school, the difference between 3.0 and 3.6 may be the difference required for admission. But, if most students are studying less, it may be that they have made a rational decision about the lack of return on the time investment.

Traditional-age student culture rigorously distinguishes between intellectual activity and entertainment. Our experience indicated almost no intellectual content to activities undertaken outside the framework of the classroom. A conversation with a freshman at an aspiring private comprehensive institution in the South is illustrative. This disaffected young man said that friendship was completely isolated from the life of the mind. He had come to college expecting to learn in the classroom but also to learn in informal, intellectual conversation with his friends. He said that there was little of that experience at his institution. Most of this informal time was spent in kidding and friendly banter that did not meet his standards of learning through conversation. Evidence at large state universities and local community colleges suggests that his observation is quite accurate about non-elite universities and colleges.

Everywhere we visited, older students came across as more serious. As one younger student remarked to us at a comprehensive university: "They set the curve." Faculty too remarked on the difference. Older students were presented as more focused, more motivated, more disciplined, and, as a rule, more academically successful.

A second factor influencing the value placed on academic work is the choice of major field. On all our campuses, students in the sciences, engineering, and the allied health professions dedicated more time to their field than students in other majors. Whether students were biology majors at a small historically black college in the South or engineering students at a mid-Atlantic flagship university, they expressed the same experience: life revolved around academic work. Many students remarked on the bonding with other students, and sometimes with faculty, that grew out of this intensity.

A third factor that influences the value placed on academic work is the inability of many students to major in the field of their choice. Many students at research and comprehensive universities cannot pursue their top academic and vocational interests. This is because American universities have become like the German ones. They admit all who qualify (though in America, at most campuses, qualification is irrelevant) but they then limit the most desirable majors to only the best through quotas on majors. In business, engineering, computer science, and allied health professions, there are strict admissions standards to the major and very few of the students admitted to the university can actually pursue their first-choice major.

At many of our schools, students experienced great pressure and competition in qualifying for a major. At a large state university in the Southwest, for example, there were hundreds of applicants for the few places available in the business school. Those who did not get into the business school then enrolled in business-related social sciences disciplines like economics and political science. These majors are now bursting at the seams. The College of Arts and Sciences asked for the right to establish minimum entrance standards in order to reduce the teaching load and improve the quality of students. The president withheld the right of selection, because then students, unable to choose a relevant major, would drop out. Limiting access would have created a political firestorm on campus and in the legislature.

Thus, the student experience of academic opportunities is frequently one of scarcity and relegation to second and third choices. Where competition is most intense, relations with faculty become strained, particularly with those who are perceived as the gate keepers for the desirable majors. Ironically, these are not the faculty in those schools and departments, but faculty in arts and sciences who teach the general education courses. When one realizes how many students are barred from pursuing the degree of their choice, it is no wonder that there is not great interest in finding more time for academic work outside of the classroom. There is little interest in what is going on *inside* the classroom.

Last, but not least, student attitudes toward paid work may have an impact on the value they place on academic work. There is no doubt that, even among traditional-age students, a larger percentage are working than in the past. According to United States Department of Labor statistics, in 1972, 41.7 percent of students age sixteen to twenty-four were working. In 1988, this percentage had risen to 53.7 percent. In 1988, 10 percent of these students worked thirty-five hours or more per week; 53.5 percent worked fifteen to twenty-nine hours per week.[13] In its 1984 student survey, the Carnegie Foundation found that almost half of the sixteen- to twenty-four–year-old respondents reported working over twenty hours a week. Older students, of course, work even more. About 74 percent were employed in 1988, and, on average, they worked thirty-seven hours per week.[14]

Substantial work is an economic necessity for many students, especially adults. The 1989 student strike at City University of New York over a tuition increase of $200 highlights the financial constraints that frame the lives of so many adult students. However, paid work in the universe of traditional-age students may not be reducible to financial need. In her article "Students Who Work," Anne-Marie McCartan raises a number of interesting questions about the role of paid work on campuses today. Drawing on research on teenagers in high school, she suggests that, for traditional-age college students, acquiring discretionary income and having fun are two important functions of work. In addition, the concern to develop work experience for one's resume plays a role. She voices the concern that "when students have unfilled hours in the week, they simply fill those hours with more work."[15]

There is some research that indicates that students who work fifteen to twenty hours a week perform better academically than those who work more or not at all. We hope there will be ongoing concern to document the impact of paid work on student learning and to develop ways to integrate paid work with academic work. It is also important to explore how students perceive the demands and rewards of paid work in relation to academics. If there is, indeed, a higher priority given to paid work, as many faculty members suspect, higher education and society itself must come to grips with that reality. If students are unwilling or unable to meet the academic expectations of colleges and universities we had better take stock of the ramifications.

Attitudes About Learning and Teaching

Student attitudes about what constitutes learning and effective teaching frame and influence their entire academic experience. Information from a number of surveys indicating a high level of satisfaction with academic life suggests that student attitudes are quite consonant with the reality they encounter.

The Higher Education Research Institute's 1985 survey of student experience found that four years after entry, 83.8 percent of students polled were satisfied or very satisfied with courses in their major; 77.3 percent with overall quality of instruction; 73.3 percent with humanities courses; 68.5 percent with social science courses; 65.7 percent with science and math courses; 65 percent with lab facilities and equipment; 60.7 percent with amount of contact with faculty and administrators. Only 56.1 percent were satisfied or very satisfied with tutorial help or other academic assistance and 44 percent with academic advising.[16] The Center for Education Statistics' *High School and Beyond* study found that 88 percent of students polled four years out of high school were "satisfied" with the "ability, knowledge, and personal qualities of most teachers." Eighty-three percent were satisfied with the quality of instruction.[17] In 1986, a large, prestigious, public research institution in the West conducted a survey of students who received undergraduate degrees during the 1984–85 academic year and reported very similar results on the quality of instruction. Of the 56 percent who returned the questionnaire, 54.2 percent were "very satisfied" with the quality of faculty teaching and 33 percent were "satisfied"—a total of 87.2 percent. Teaching assistants fared less well (a total positive response of 69.1 percent).

Our campus visits seemed to corroborate these studies. Students we spoke with were generally satisfied with their academic experience and with their professors. Within our limited sample, almost all students felt they had adequate access to faculty, even students at comprehensive and research universities, where they seldom have contact with tenure-track faculty in settings other than large lecture courses until they are upperclassmen. Invariably, students said it was up to them to seek out the faculty member, and they acknowledged that few students take that initiative. If they did so, they received attention. They all agreed that some faculty were unavailable or uninterested in undergraduates… but that, on balance, most were accessible.

There were some angry voices at our research institutions. At a southwestern flagship, the campus was tense and students saw liberal arts faculty who teach the general education courses as gate-keeping adversaries. At a small private university, one student complained: "It seems they turn down all the professors the students like the most." And occasionally there was indifference. At a western flagship, one student said: "I don't care to know the faculty personally. They let me sink or swim. So far I've swum."

The picture was brightest at liberal arts and community colleges. Students expressed enthusiasm and appreciation for most of their faculty. At a midwestern community college, for example, the typical attitude expressed was: "We have access to talk to people. All faculty have an open door policy. They are personal and caring. There is a lot of one-on-one work." Large impersonal neighboring institutions were often negatively compared to the community college.

Although occasional student leaders criticized faculty for not supporting student organizations and activities—"They're too involved in their work, in tenure. We invite professors to attend our events, but they rarely show up"—most students seemed to have no expectation of contact with faculty outside the academic arena, and, even on liberal arts campuses, no great enthusiasm for it.

In sum, for the most part, students viewed faculty as supplying what is necessary for acquiring the credential, as part of a very specific transaction. They were not interested in more than this instrumental relationship. There was little sense of shared goals, destinies, or values with the faculty in general, or with particular professors. Many colleges and universities are not realizing the potential for creating academic learning communities for and with their students. And most students do not even realize what is missing. Nor can we expect them to without educating them first about what constitutes quality learning and teaching.

Intellectual Community: No There There

The classroom is the most logical, most visible, most ubiquitous, and most neglected place for community on campus. It is a lost opportunity of the first order. Few classes, now, are subcommunities. The commitment to recreating the classroom as the model and microcosm of connecting and collaborating on campus is one of the highest priorities for institutions committed to improving community.

Common interests, abilities, or needs can help create a sense of community in the classroom and beyond. In our visits, the students who expressed the strongest sense of community in class included business majors, nursing majors, engineering and chemistry majors, students in remedial programs, and students in honors programs.

Basic Skills Programs

Basic skills programs, designed to overcome the limits to learning imposed by inadequate academic preparation, have grown enormously in the last twenty years, as access to higher education has expanded. Such programs offer the potential for creating strong learning communities, whether the programs occur during the summer preceding freshman year, during the freshman year itself, or both. These programs are often called remedial or developmental education programs. They are sometimes reserved for minorities and low-income students. Other times they are services offered to everyone.

Professor Richard Richardson of Arizona State University has studied a number of basic skills programs in the course of his work on recruiting and keeping African-American students in American universities. He has concluded that successful forms of support are tied to appropriate recruitment strategies. An institution should recruit only those who fit its profile generally, but who have some relatively modest weakness when compared with its norm. Students in need of remedial assistance, then, still will be within the general frame of background, ability, and achievement of the typical students at the institution. The difference between students who can do the institution's level of work without remediation and those who need help cannot be great. The institution must provide targeted support services before accepted students begin their freshman year and while they are mastering the missing skills. Also, the programs that had the best minority retention were those that most actively supported minority identity.[18]

The pattern on many campuses that we visited was one of providing a panoply of services (academic advising, counseling, credit and noncredit courses, tutoring) to a large number of students using relatively few faculty and staff. For example, a midwestern community college offered free, noncredit study skills workshops through a number of centers. The college offered a first-year general studies credit course that taught survival strategies. The staff of the centers offered tutoring and small mini-classes in most academic subjects, as well as conversational English for foreign students. In addition, the college offered more specialized support services for displaced homemakers. There were also some large-scale programs. One was a mathematics skills program that operated with a budget of $644,000, where twenty to twenty-five faculty, twenty to twenty-five staff, and an administrator taught more than fifteen hundred students.

Another community college, this time in the East, offered special support services, including tutoring and advising, but also had created special space in order to facilitate community. The students in the program had a kitchen and a study room. An elite private research institution took a different approach to remedial support. It identified each student who was at risk and then recruited a faculty member to be that student's mentor. In 1989, sixteen faculty mentored sixty-one students. A large public flagship university campus in the Southwest had twelve professional staff and ninety peer tutors to tutor eleven thousand students who came to its center and to offer tutoring services in the field to about fourteen thousand more. This learning center had contact with the students they served only a few hours per term. No community developed among the students who used these services. An elite western flagship university structured new opportunities for minority students to study together as a way of creating support systems for learning.

Our campuses varied widely in their ability to retain minority students, and in the efforts made to create community within basic skills programs. We also found variety in the ways in which students, themselves, took advantage of basic skills programs. Many, especially minorities, created their own communities within the program. Often, those who were successful and remained at the institutions relied on the supportive environment of the basic skills program to help them succeed in the academic mainstream. A sense of community, both in class and beyond it, appears an important factor in the success of basic skills programs.

Honors Programs

Honors programs, meant to provide challenging academic experiences for particularly talented students, have also grown steadily since the 1970s. An important part of the explicit mission of the honors program movement has been the creation of intellectual community. Some programs focus on freshmen and sophomores in general education courses; others focus on juniors and seniors within their majors. They range in size and scope from small programs that serve few students to freestanding colleges within large universities. Generally, the institutional investments in the programs are small. Few have dedicated meeting space; fewer still have residential accommodations. There is little discretionary program money. Rarely do they have their own faculty. Most faculty participate through release time from the departments or on overload. The director of such programs is usually a faculty person on part-time release.

Common features of such programs are small classes and more collaborative, student-centered pedagogies. Honors programs also usually try to connect intellectual community in the classroom and outside it. Often, faculty expect to interact with honors students more intensively outside of the classroom than they do with other students. Some programs sponsor weekend "Sleeping Bag" seminars, organized by students, where discussions carry on into the wee hours of the morning.

A number of our campuses had formal honors programs. At an eastern comprehensive campus, the departmentally based honors program has had great difficulty attracting students. It seems that this is because it competes with an integrated multidisciplinary program based on a team-teaching and a mentoring model that has attracted a stable number of students over almost two decades and has built a strong sense of community among them. At a southern comprehensive campus the honors program was strong. The latter was departmentally based and gained strength from the departmental identification with it. At the mid-Atlantic landgrant university, a separate Honors College was part of the plan to improve the university's academic standing by attracting better undergraduates. Many campuses use the honors option to attract students who would otherwise attend more elite private or public national institutions.

Occasionally, we heard that students do not want to join an honors program because they do not want to set themselves apart. It is clear, however, that honors programs provide important opportunities for intellectual community for bright and motivated students who move in a broader student culture that does not highly prize the life of the mind. Those who do participate find great value in the program.

"Learning Communities"

Curricular specialization and fragmentation impose serious limits on learning that the general education and interdisciplinary studies movements have been trying to counteract. Some institutions have combined their concern for greater curricular coherence with a concern for increasing students' sense of community by created programs where students take a number of courses together in the same cohort.

Washington State has a network of learning communities administered through the Washington Center for Undergraduate Education at the Evergreen State College. The center coordinates public and private universities and also community colleges where various forms of collaborative learning have become institutional realities.

Among the institutions we visited, several had "learning communities." On two campuses, the honors program included this learning community format. On one, the freshman seminar programs used this structure. On another of our campuses, the whole curriculum was structured around team-taught coordinated programs where faculty had more than one hundred students for the semester or for the year. The learning experience was built on collaboration between and among students and the professors to explore a multidisciplinary topic. On most campuses, however, learning communities served small numbers of students. Generally, these students were very enthusiastic about them.

We found few campuses where even 5 percent of the students chose to participate in programs that seek to foster academic community, whether in departments or in multidisciplinary programs. Basic skills programs are not, for the most part, self-selected. Most of the honors programs or learning communities are, and they enrolled between 100 and 350 students in institutions ranging in size from five thousand to thirty thousand students. Some of these programs were actually having difficulty recruiting students, while others just maintained current size. Nowhere did we find student demand unmet. This reality seems to be part of the overall pattern of lack of student interest in academic experiences that require additional commitment of time and energy or that take them too far from the major department.

Class Size

Class size appears to have an impact on learning. Although the research on class size is quite mixed in its conclusions, Professor Wilber McKeachie of Michigan has summarized the results: "If one takes these more basic outcomes of retention, problem solving, and attitude differentiation as criteria of learning, the weight of the evidence clearly favors small classes."[19] It is unclear whether students, themselves, actually prefer small classes, however. One study, at the University of Washington, found that students preferred classes with enrollments of seventy-five or more. Indeed, these students concluded that in regard to the instructor's effectiveness, the best large classes were as good as or better than the best small classes.[20] This is surely good news for administrators at research and comprehensive universities. The dean of undergraduate education at a mid-Atlantic flagship told us that the best one could hope for in terms of reducing class size at her institution was to offer each student one class of fewer than forty taught by a tenure-track professor every semester.

However, another study of 2571 students at a flagship university we visited reported that "students have a definite preference for classes with sixteen to thirty students in them." Those with one hundred or more ranked lowest. The main reasons students gave for disliking large classes were: "they get less feedback from the instructor on their progress/learning; they don't feel comfortable participating in classes that large; they feel distant from the instructor; and they think the course can be taught more effectively in smaller groups."

Common sense would indicate that large classes are an obstacle to the creation of an experience of intellectual community between faculty and students and among students. Academic community requires sustained interaction, an occasional reality in smaller classes that can only be a dream in large lectures. Despite the lacunae in the research, and the relatively small samples in most studies, there are people on campus concerned with decreasing class size. Some of them are students. Among these is a group organized by students at Syracuse University, Undergraduates for Better Education. In 1989, these students convened peers from thirteen campuses to talk about the impact on students of "publish or perish" and large lecture classes. Kara Kinney, the organization's president, said: "Students are paying good money for courses, but getting cheated out of a good education by professors who are too busy with their research projects. I'm not denying the importance of research, but it is more important for students to be taught by good professors."[21]

One approach to reducing class size has been the movement toward freshman seminars at a number of institutions. On the campuses we visited, we found freshman seminars at elite research universities and small liberal arts colleges. For example, our elite public flagship university in the West started a freshman seminar program that serves approximately one-third of the entering class. These seminars are intended to be multidisciplinary, to provide a close relationship between and among students around an academic interest, and to enhance the connection between students and faculty. A formative evaluation of the freshman seminar program at a public research university in the East suggests that the program there has not been completely successful in forging closer relationships between students and faculty. The report's conclusion raises interesting questions about what it takes to create connection: "Although the Freshman Seminars were designed to improve faculty feedback and mentoring, it is the area reported by faculty and students alike, to require the most attention.... Students gave, on average, their lowest scores to the question on faculty feedback and for all but the summary questions, the faculty did the same." Having a specific program with explicit intent and small classes does not guarantee student-faculty connection.

Honors programs, basic skills programs, writing-intensive courses, foreign language courses all lay claim to small classes. But the need is much greater. Smaller classes and continuing cohort groups are important but they are not enough, separately or together, to assure that the classroom becomes a community of learners. Even in small classes, even in classes held in residence halls, even in team-taught courses, faculty-centered pedagogy is still the norm. Students accept this norm—straight lecture and lecture with some discussion—and the underlying epistemology that says that knowledge exists outside the learner, in individual experts who convey it to others. For many students, for whom William Perry coined the label "dualists," this hierarchical conception corresponds to their intellectual level of development and thus is comfortable.[22] In addition, of course, faculty-centered pedagogy relieves students of the responsibility to prepare and study that participation requires. Collaborative learning takes hard work. In a world where time is scarce, expediency has its appeal. However, there is little in lecture-based pedagogy to enable students to develop either the critical thinking skills or the active community-building skills that a pluralistic democracy needs. Only a small number of students have the opportunity to participate collaboratively in learning, their own and others', as tutors, peer teachers, members of problem-solving groups, and as co-researchers.

Beyond the Classroom

Various sources estimate that fewer than 10 percent of today's undergraduates participate in the formal extracurriculum offerings on campus. In the arena of co-curricular activity—that is, those student activities that connect directly with learning in the classroom—evidence suggests an even smaller percentage.

Over the last thirty years, there has been an ebb and flow of experiments designed to connect the classroom with student activities. In the 1970s, a number of large institutions established multidisciplinary living/learning settings. The University of California created Santa Cruz as a collegiate university with residential colleges and departments. The departments now dominate the residential colleges, and the close connection between study and residence is lost. The State University of New York (SUNY) at Buffalo created in the 1970s one of the largest living/learning experiments, as a structure parallel to the academic departments: a system of colleges designed to provide credit courses and out-of-classroom learning opportunities for both residential and nonresidential students. These colleges ranged from a college for the arts, Black Mountain College, to Rachel Carson College for the study of the environment, to Women Studies College. By the mid-1980s, SUNYat Buffalo had completely dismantled its collegiate system. The large-scale experiments in living/learning have disappeared. In institutions dominated by departmental structure, they were too deviant. Modest living/learning dorms continue at Michigan and Michigan State.

On our campuses we found very circumscribed living/learning arrangements. At a small private liberal arts college in the East, there was an Arts House and a French House serving fewer than a dozen students each. At an elite private research university in the East, students could propose courses for their residential area. Also, there are "special interest centers" concentrated on a dorm floor, such as the Drama Center, Medieval House, Computer Interest Floor, and the International Living Center.

The largest residential program in living/learning was at a midwestern flagship university. Approximately five hundred students, out of more than twenty thousand, live in a dorm where the students initiate six courses each year. However, in recent years, these courses have rarely been taught by faculty; usually graduate students teach them. A half-time senior faculty member directs the house and another more junior faculty person lives across the street and is the faculty member in residence. Departments offer some introductory courses in the dorm, as they do in other dorms. There are also dinners where faculty come and give talks on topics of interest to the residents. Demand for space by students in the living/learning center has abated in recent years and there are often vacancies for male residents. One student who lived in another dorm described the residents in the living/learning center as "the 80s hippies, punksters, and granolas who march to a different drummer."

Another, and growing, approach to connecting the classroom with cocurricular activities is through the public service programs on a number of campuses, many of which are part of Campus Compact, a national coalition to promote public service headquartered at Brown University. For example, one of the largest programs is at Stanford, where more than a thousand students engage in public service activities ranging from tutoring in East Palo Alto to helping out in a clinic in San Francisco. This program is mainly noncredit but it does connect with a number of credit-bearing courses. On the campuses we visited, we found the volunteerism movement growing. At the private comprehensive in the South, there was a new organization encouraging students to engage in public service activity. Although it was not directly related to credit-bearing courses, its student participants used the voluntary activity to explore the application of their academic work to real-life problems.

Perhaps the most careful integration of the classroom with out-of-classroom activity in the past five years has occurred on campuses with leadership education initiatives. The best example of this undertaking is the Duke University leadership program that a trustee initiated. Two courses focusing on leadership incorporate a public service project by each student. The classroom core of the program involves reading important philosophical and literary texts, but the experiential center is public service. The Duke leadership program also offers summer internships, including "Interns in Conscience" who worked with migrant workers in Florida and the homeless in Washington, D.C. Although none of our campuses had such programs in place, one of our campuses was just beginning a major leadership education program.

Although there are many attempts to connect the classroom with out-of-classroom activities, we must conclude that on most campuses—and even small residential campuses—there is little energy and time committed to exploring academics outside of the classroom structure. Campuses themselves invest little money and faculty little energy in creating such complementary environments for students. Earlier, we observed that on many of our campuses students did participate in clubs associated with their majors, particularly in the pre-professional settings such as business and engineering schools. Even here, the percentages and absolute numbers of participants were small. Yet if campuses wish to create a culture of higher academic expectations, establishing new out-of-classroom learning opportunities offers an important strategy for creating a student culture that makes academic matters central to campus life.

Conclusion

As we have seen, today's undergraduates are satisfied with their college or university experience. From one point of view, this is good news. From another it is not. Derek Bok makes the point incisively:

> ...colleges work very hard to provide new facilities, useful services, and absorbing activities. In so doing, they make the undergraduate years a pleasant, even a memorable, experience for large majorities of their students. Nevertheless, they feel no necessity to make a sustained collaborative effort to discover how to help their students accomplish more in their academic work.[23]

Students settle for second best in terms of academic instruction. Not that one can blame them. Few have standards against which to gauge a quality curriculum or excellence in teaching. To some extent, they do not know what they are missing.

It is rare, also, for students to experience intellectual community on America's campuses. In part this is by choice. Students do not always choose learning opportunities that would enhance community available on their campus, whether it be a collaboratively run class, an honors program, a learning cluster, or a living/learning option. If the students in the University of Washington study are typical, for the vast majority of students, academic community is not an important goal. The students at the University of Washington identified the lack of student/teacher interaction as the worst aspect of large classes. Yet this did not keep them from endorsing large classes. Community is not required for obtaining a credential.

The potential for learning and for the experience of intellectual community that comes from engagement with the liberal arts and from substantial faculty-student and student-student interaction is rarely realized in this country. Students bear some responsibility for this. What responsibility do faculty have for the current state of affairs?

CHAPTER 11

Faculty Priorities and Opportunities

> Here you can make a difference with people. The student
> is always first. Everyone is here for that emphasis. It pulls
> the administration and faculty together. There is instant
> recognition of this on the part of transfer students. They
> think the services we offer are fabulous.
>
> —Chemistry professor at a rural southern
> community college

> I have a class in which the professor's lectures consist of
> outlining the chapters of the textbook on the chalkboard
> (worth the $500, isn't it?). After having a problem with the
> nature of one of the professor's exams, I confronted her
> with my feelings. Upon confrontation, the professor pro-
> ceeded to chastise me and tell me how much she hates
> teaching, is sick of students, and can't wait to leave the
> teaching realm of professorial life next semester. And trust
> me, her language was not as pleasant.
>
> —A senior at a major public research university
> in the Midwest

As the above quotes remind us, two very different faculty cultures have
evolved on American campuses: one that values teaching and one that values
research and publication. Although both coexist to some degree at all institutions, it is useful to think of a continuum with research universities at one
end and community colleges at the other. The Carnegie Foundation's 1989
faculty survey confirms yet again this well-documented split in the academy:
58.1 percent of faculty in research universities reported being more interested in research than in teaching, whereas 77.8 percent of faculty in comprehensive institutions, 83.7 percent in liberal arts colleges, and 92.9 percent in
community colleges reported being more interested in teaching than
research.[1]

In the course of visits to our eighteen campuses, we were forcefully reminded of the differences between faculty who live on opposite sides of this great divide, and of the far-reaching influence of the research model. Even at many comprehensive and liberal arts institutions, the reward systems now in place overwhelmingly favor research and publication. Thus, many faculty whose main interest is teaching work in settings where excellence in teaching and other contributions to the campus learning community are not rewarded as they should be.

Before turning to a more detailed consideration of the various ways in which institutions and the faculty in them limit learning, we'll briefly review the changes that most of today's faculty have faced over the past twenty years.

The Changing Environment for Faculty

Career Choice and Careerism

The last two decades have brought changes that have created greater and different demands, pressures, and problems for many faculty. One major change has been the shift in majors that has made a small number of faculty responsible for the education of a greatly increased percentage of the students and sometimes left others with few students. The spectacular growth in numbers of students who wish to enroll in business, combined with the precipitous decline in enrollment in education and some of the humanities, has created great disparity between and among departments. The "haves" get better students because they can be more selective, even in institutions which have open admission policies. The arts and sciences faculties have become, to some degree, service providers and gate keepers with large classes and few resources, whereas the professional schools, such as engineering and business, have seen dramatic enrollment increases, often without commensurate increases in resources. These reallocations have had an impact on faculty morale.

Increased careerism among students per se does not appear to be a significant source of discontent for faculty. Most professors consider career preparation to be a major goal of higher education. Almost 85 percent of the faculty surveyed by the Carnegie Foundation strongly agreed (37.6 percent) or agreed with reservations (45.9 percent) with the statement: "Undergraduates have become more careerist in their concerns since the late 1960s and early 1970s." However, they split quite evenly between those who prefer teaching students with a clear idea of the career they will be following (37.4 percent), those who are neutral (31.9 percent), and those who prefer students whose career goals are not clear (30.7 percent).[2]

Student Diversity

In the past two decades, the age, gender, and racial and ethnic distribution of the student body has changed, and there has been an increase in the number of part-time students. The mean age has moved to twenty-five. There are more women, especially older women, and there are also more minority students. Although there are fewer African-American males than twenty years ago, the increase in Hispanics and Asian-Americans has been substantial. This diversity has not been reflected in the demographics of the professoriate, which is still overwhelmingly white and two to one male.

Many teaching faculty view this diversity of students as a positive contribution to their experience as teachers, especially the increasing percentages of adult students. However, there is clear concern about academic standards. Of the faculty Carnegie surveyed, 62.6 percent strongly agreed or agreed with reservations to the statement: "Too many students ill-suited to academic life are now enrolling in colleges and universities"; 56.1 percent of faculty felt that undergraduate admissions standards at their institutions should be much higher or somewhat higher. The figures were 66 percent at comprehensives and 63.6 percent at liberal arts colleges.[3]

Relatively few faculty have learned how to adapt their teaching to this new population. For the most part, neither course content nor pedagogy has changed in proportion to the new mix of students. For example, the perspectives and experiences of American minorities and even of women, the numerical majority since 1979–80, have still not been integrated into the curriculum. On many campuses this is a continuing source of student dissatisfaction, particularly among African-American students, who often feel that white faculty have difficulty relating to them. Few faculty are familiar with the growing literature on adult learning; fewer still know how to implement the insights and suggestions born of this research. In addition, the continuing weakness in academic preparation of students, particularly minority students, has created a tremendous need for basic skills instruction. Yet, most regular faculty, with the exception of those in the community colleges, do not consider such instruction to be part of their job and do not teach in these programs. At one comprehensive university we visited, faculty are required to teach in the basic skills program. We were told that they do not enjoy the assignment and go to some length to avoid the task. For the most part, academically weak students interact with staff, not faculty.

Attitudes toward Teaching

Faculty have mixed feelings about teaching undergraduates. Most faculty prefer to teach upper-level courses rather than introductory ones. Many prefer older students to traditional-age students. Heavy teaching loads are most likely to dampen enthusiasm at comprehensive universities. Of Carnegie's survey respondents, 26.9 percent at comprehensives rated their teaching load as poor, twice as many as faculty at research institutions.[4] Perhaps the most critical factor affecting faculty attitudes and behavior is the nature of the institution in which they work.

Research Universities

Twenty-nine percent of American students, most of whom were undergraduates, attended doctorate-granting institutions in 1987.[5] The majority of professors at these institutions embrace a culture in which faculty are first and foremost researchers; their role is to advance knowledge and provide services through consulting to government and industry. Through graduate programs they educate the future professionals in their field.

In research institutions, undergraduates are sometimes seen as a distraction from the real work of faculty. Only 41.5 percent of faculty at research institutions polled in Carnegie's survey said their relationship with undergraduates is very important (compared to 60 percent at comprehensives; 71.7 percent at liberal arts colleges; and 68.9 percent at community colleges).[6] This does not mean, as Charles Sykes contends in his controversial *ProfScam,* that faculty loath undergraduates.[7] Carnegie's survey shows that a substantial minority of faculty teaching at research institutions (41 percent) say that their interests lie more in teaching than in research.[8]

But colleagues and administrators do not reward good teaching. Ninety-one percent of respondents to Carnegie's survey who teach at research universities said that the number of publications is important for granting tenure in their department, and 88 percent said the type of publication is important. Only 13 percent said syllabi for courses taught are important; 27 percent indicated that observations of teaching by colleagues and/or administrators are important; and 52 percent indicated that student evaluations of courses taught are important.[9]

During the first two years, it is rare for an undergraduate at a research institution to see a tenure-track faculty member in a setting other than a very large lecture class. At one of our most elite public universities, the average class size is 125. Teaching assistants take responsibility for most intellectual contact. At these institutions, only a minority of regular faculty puts substantial time and energy into the teaching task, a much smaller number than those who express interest in teaching. At a prestigious public university in the West, efforts to provide freshman seminars in order to enhance student-faculty relations were thwarted by the unwillingness of enough faculty to teach them. This has led to an administrative strategy of recalling emeriti professors to teach, for about $2,000 per semester.

At most research institutions, faculty are told, directly or indirectly, to devote their time to research and subordinate teaching and service. A faculty member at an elite public western institution reported hearing the provost address new faculty in the following terms: "Ignore your students. Students have nothing to do with your success here." At another research university the message was similar. A faculty member in psychology commented: "It is made very clear to us in our departments that there is a high cost to doing student things. If your teaching is awful it is harder to get tenure, but if you have grants you will get it anyhow. The people who are involved with students are senior and have been here a long time." On a number of occasions we heard how older, even emeriti faculty, are central to student-faculty interaction at research universities. Over a decade ago, Grant and Riesman advised institutions wishing to revitalize undergraduate teaching to look to their older faculty.[10] So it appears today.

Although a number of the research institutions we visited indicated that they now consider teaching when judging both tenure and merit pay, none claimed that outstanding teaching by itself would garner rewards in the way that outstanding research alone does.

Comprehensive Universities

Twenty-eight percent of American students, most of whom were undergraduates, attended comprehensive universities in 1987.[11] Although many of these comprehensive schools espouse the norms of research institutions, Carnegie's survey data indicate that 77.8 percent of faculty working at comprehensive colleges and universities are much more interested or somewhat more interested in teaching than in research.[12]

Burton Clark identified a central difficulty faced by faculty at comprehensive universities in this quote by one of his interviewees: "I think the most difficult thing about being at an institution like [this one] is that it has a difficult time coming to terms with itself.... Often you don't really have a clear idea of what the university is setting as its goals, as its standards." This is what Clark calls the "muddled imagery that often adheres to the second and third levels of the American institutional hierarchy."[13]

The comprehensive universities in our sample combined the two faculty cultures, and there was significant tension stemming from contradictory priorities. At the wealthy private liberal arts university in the South, at the very poor public institution in the South, and at the "average" school in the East overshadowed by neighboring research institutions, we, indeed, saw a preponderance of faculty who were mainly teachers, although they did some research as well. None of these institutions had teaching fellows, and faculty spoke of spending significant time with undergraduates. "People really teach here," they said. On two of the campuses we visited, faculty give students their home phone numbers and expect to be called.

At many comprehensive institutions, except the most aspiring, teaching appears to play a role in tenure decisions. We found evidence for this in our visits. At one institution, a professor in the health sciences had recently received tenure primarily on the basis of her teaching, and her work in creating a date rape video for use on campuses and in conducting date rape workshops in the dormitories. The vice-president for academic affairs there told us that in recent years most denials of tenure had been on the grounds of inadequate teaching. A recently tenured communications professor at another school asserted that teaching had played an important role in his case. However, at an aspiring small private comprehensive, the chair of the tenure and promotion committee told us that there is an unspoken policy favoring publishing.

At many comprehensive institutions, deans aspire to research fame and send out signals emphasizing research over teaching. One dean ventured that, at his institution, teaching probably counted 60 percent at the departmental level, but that the percentage decreased as the case went up the administrative ladder. Administrators seeking status and grants and contracts may be the most serious threat to the faculty culture that values teaching in comprehensive institutions.

Teaching Colleges

Forty-two percent of undergraduates in 1987 attended liberal arts colleges (5 percent) and community colleges (38 percent).[14] With the exception of the most elite liberal arts colleges, where the two cultures mix, faculty at these schools are committed to teaching and see themselves primarily as teachers. Carnegie's survey indicated that 83.7 percent of faculty in the liberal arts schools, and 92.9 percent of faculty in community colleges, have this perception.[15] With enrollments that have declined 15 percent since 1970, liberal arts colleges are becoming an endangered species. It is thus in community colleges, whose enrollments have doubled in the same time period, that the culture of teaching has the greatest chance of benefiting large numbers of students.

In our travels, we found that faculty at liberal arts and community colleges have a ubiquitous concern for helping students learn. For example, at a relatively rural community college near an elite research university, a faculty member commented: "We set deliberate traps to lure students into our offices. We always leave our doors open." He juxtaposed this attitude to the attitude toward students at the elite university, recounting the experience of a former philosophy major of his who transferred to the neighboring university. When the student went to a professor's office and said he "just wanted to talk about Camus," the professor was surprised and a bit disconcerted. Like community colleges, the small liberal arts colleges also attract faculty who value teaching, but here we found creeping concern about publication and research among the faculty. Nonetheless, there is strong evidence that faculty who teach at liberal arts colleges and community colleges, are, on the whole, happier about their lot and the roles they play than their colleagues in the other institutional environments.

Certainly there is less dissonance between their personal interests and institutional rewards. In Carnegie's survey, only about a third of faculty from liberal arts colleges indicated that the number or type of publication is important for granting tenure in their department, whereas 50 percent said course syllabi are important; 67 percent that observations of teaching by colleagues and/or administrators are important; and 87 percent that student evaluations of courses taught are important. About 10 percent of community college faculty indicated that number and type of publications are important for tenure; 44 percent said that course syllabi are important; 75 percent indicated that observations by colleagues and/or administrators are important; and 64 percent said student evaluations of courses taught are important.[16]

Departmental Power

Departments are the ever more powerful local representatives of a national and international faculty culture that, over the last twenty years, has become increasingly differentiated by discipline and subdiscipline. At most institutions, the power of departments to dispense and withhold rewards shapes the relationship between faculty and students in powerful ways. Since departments mediate continually between faculty and students, the role they play in creating and in limiting academic community is important to consider.

At their best, departments constitute academic subcommunities to which students, primarily majors, may belong. Many faculty enjoy teaching majors more than nonmajors, especially at the freshmen and sophomore level, since the greater knowledge and more focused interest of these young majors help diminish the intellectual gap. Making the most of this natural academic common ground is critical. We found quite a few examples of departmentally based academic subcommunities. At two of our research institutions, engineering students spoke of the esprit de corps in their department, where academics combined with picnics and softball games. At a community college, students and faculty spoke of the department of nursing as "tight knit." At a number of schools, business majors expressed a sense of connection with their department. Also, students frequently said they found community in disciplinary and professional clubs and honoraries affiliated with the major department.

The power of departments, however, is virtually complete. Thus, departments can impede, in various ways, the creation and maintenance of other programs such as ethnic studies, women's studies, honors programs, or freshman seminar programs that offer important alternative academic subcommunities to faculty and students. At the same time, they can hinder the creation and ongoing health of overarching programs designed to enhance community of the whole on campus, such as general education programs, and the much-discussed but rarely acted-on core curriculum.

Such programs, and the faculty who wish to teach in them, encounter common problems as they relate to departments. Financial independence is often impossible. Often these programs are a part of the budget of the academic dean or vice-president for academic affairs, not independent line item programs. This makes them more vulnerable to the vicissitudes of the budgeting process. At one fiscally strapped comprehensive, a faculty member gave voice to the siege mentality that had been abroad for several years: "Each department has braced itself and turned more inward in order to survive. We built our own forts." Staffing is a major problem. A faculty member's participation usually depends upon the department's willingness to release him or her from a departmental offering. Often, the faculty who wish to participate in these programs must do so on an overload basis. Even when a program can reimburse departments for faculty time, the departments forfeit full-time equivalent (FTE) credits. Academic legitimacy is another problem. Without departmental status, a program is suspect and automatically inferior. Evaluation of faculty for tenure and promotion is yet another problem. When faculty teach or teach and publish outside their department with any regularity, it usually becomes more difficult to evaluate them, since their work is outside the competence of departmental colleagues. Individuals also run the risk of appearing not to support their department, of not contributing as much as they could to their immediate colleagues and to their field.

General Education

The general education movement has attempted to affirm some minimal intellectual common ground at colleges and universities. Career-oriented students rarely take general education seriously. Even among faculty, however, general education is a stepchild. Few faculties have gone further than trimming down long lists of courses that fulfill distribution requirements. More structured general education programs, often interdisciplinary, serve only small numbers of students who elect them. Although 47.5 percent of all faculty responding to Carnegie's survey indicated that undergraduates should take a required common core, only 2 percent of our nation's campuses have some form of core curriculum.[17] Even at Columbia, where the core is a solid tradition, there is ferment around its staffing. Senior faculty are becoming less willing to participate and junior faculty perceive the effort required in teaching the courses as a diversion from the research necessary for tenure.

The campuses we visited seem to reflect national trends in general education, which is to say that there is more talk than action. At a large flagship university, there was much ado about a faculty report on general education. The report dealt with the current distribution requirement, where each of the distribution categories had more than one hundred courses. Although there was much rhetoric about raising the standards of courses in the general education curriculum, the "new" proposal essentially maintained the current cafeteria approach without any new coherence, and it did not propose to reduce class size. The hollowness of the university's commitment to general education was documented in this conclusion:

> Presently some sections of Distributive Studies courses have five hundred students and many have enrollments of 150 plus.... After months of consideration the committee decided not to recommend a ceiling on Distributive Studies and Advanced Studies course enrollments but to urge that academic unit heads, led by the provost to seek to ensure that class sizes are appropriate to allow effective teaching and active student learning.

Aspiration at this flagship in regard to general education stands in great contrast to its aspirations to become a leading research university.

At one of our comprehensive universities, there were modest efforts in the 1970s to introduce some common material, but these were shortlived. The chair of the chemistry department said: "In our hearts, we know something is wrong in a curriculum that allows a student to graduate without a course in literature or history, but faculty are afraid that a change might mean they will have to teach a new course."

At a small private aspiring comprehensive, the president characterized general education as "scatter gun." The chair of the curriculum committee said that there had been no attention paid to general education until three years ago, when the committee began considering some interdisciplinary courses. He said the faculty had had great difficulty agreeing on a plan, and he was not sanguine that the proposal the committee was soon to make would be well received.

At another comprehensive, the chancellor had initiated a proposal for a competency-based core curriculum to be implemented in individual courses and across the curriculum. We heard a wide range of faculty responses. Early in the process, about sixty faculty signed on to task forces. However, momentum seemed to be waning as disagreements over the nature of the program, concern for its impact on departments, and skepticism that the state would provide the necessary funding for faculty development and reduced class size continued. One professor commented: "We've had fist fights over it in our college."

We did encounter an exception that proves the rule. At an urban comprehensive university we visited, where there is much tension around a whole range of issues, the president took the initiative to create a new core curriculum. A faculty committee, led by the dean of sciences, then adopted the initiative as its own and, after much compromise, got a diverse faculty, dealing with even more diverse students, to agree on a core curriculum that included new core courses giving explicit attention to the cultural diversity reflected on campus. The faculty senate passed the core curriculum with only one dissenting vote. The core is now being governed by faculty elected by the senate and is being taught by all of the departments. The whole enterprise appeared collegial. In its third year, it involved more than seventy-five faculty. Here, faculty and administration cooperated, and the departmental structure was coopted rather than challenged.

Small, Nondepartmentally Based Programs

A number of institutions we visited are seeking to use small, nondepartmentally based academic programs to increase faculty-student connection and to foster a sense of community among their participants.

Several of the institutions in our sample have special programming for freshmen. The program at the small private university, which began in 1984, received funding from the National Endowment for the Humanities. About one hundred sixty students participate yearly, choosing from a selection of thematic clusters and then taking two to three coordinated courses. Thirty to forty faculty teach each year. The program coordinator said: "Faculty who are committed to undergraduate teaching are more than willing to sign up." But the departments are "somewhat understaffed," so there is some tension around staffing. At a small private comprehensive, a long-time faculty member told us their freshman colloquium was small and understaffed.

At one of our comprehensives, a program initiated in the early 1970s to allow better-prepared students to graduate in three years or to take an enriched fourth year, continues, serving about three hundred fifty students annually. It features a general education core and team-built, team-taught, interdisciplinary courses. Faculty, who usually commit to three years of service, do not teach overloads. When asked why the program has endured, the vice-president for academic affairs offered several explanations: during the years of severe retrenchment at the university, departments were more than happy to have faculty teach in the program. Now, when enrollments are up, the program serves as a more agreeable alternative to required participation in basic skills courses. Even today some underenrolled departments (e.g., anthropology) depend upon student credit hours earned through the program, which flow back to the department. But also, he added, the program has a strong faculty constituency and a solid tradition. The first dean was "a legendary curmudgeon."

The director explained that there used to be seven full positions allocated to the program. They have all disappeared, because faculty, who were originally hired jointly between the program and the departments, all chose to move their lines to the departments. Some of those faculty had difficulty getting tenure in their departments, but most succeeded. Now, the participating faculty, who number a modest fifteen, are drawn from senior professors, often departmental chairs, who are known to the dean, himself a long-time faculty member. There is a sense of academic community among those who participate in the multidisciplinary teaching.

Attempts to enhance learning and intellectual community through academic programs based outside the departments are certainly not new. More often than not, such efforts are the result of initiatives from presidents, provosts, or deans, not faculty. Their fate usually has depended on the amount of power and autonomy they have been able to acquire within their institution. Those that are most successful are endorsed by the faculties as a whole, and are led by a few politically astute faculty with a strong personal commitment to the curriculum as a place for building academic community between faculty and students.

The building block of the academy is the powerful discipline-based department. Like any strong subgroup in a larger group, departments play a dual role in regards to community. On the one hand, they have the potential to be a place of connection for both faculty and students. On the other hand, they can put up obstacles to curricular changes that expand and improve student learning and offer alternative ways to experience community—community of the whole and of the parts. The broad, connected learning and intellectual common ground that the best interdisciplinary and general education programs represent do not garner adequate faculty support. Programs and projects that respond to today's more pluralistic campus environment by educating about diversity also remain low priorities. By choice and by necessity, faculty bow too low before the alter of specialization housed in their departments. We need to strike more of a balance.

Taking Teaching Seriously

> That people can learn is an undeniable fact of life; that
> people can teach is an interesting hypothesis, but unsub-
> stantiated.
>
> —Leon Jakobovits

In the last twenty years, there has been substantial progress made in understanding the ways in which people of different ages learn. It is unclear, however, whether there has been any improvement in teaching on our campuses. Perhaps Jakobovits was right. Perhaps, rather, colleges and universities have made a grossly inadequate investment in teaching professors to teach.

There has long been a small minority of active practitioners, some isolated on campuses across the country, others connected through local, regional, and national networks, whose goal has been to create learning communities for colleagues wishing to improve their teaching. They are often the same faculty interested in curriculum reform, and in interdisciplinary studies. The American Association of Higher Education, Collaboration in Undergraduate Education (CUE), the Professional and Organizational Development Network in Higher Education (POD), the Washington Center in Washington State, and the consortium in Minnesota, North and South Dakota, funded by the Bush Foundation, are among the larger and more active of such efforts.

There has been some foundation funding of faculty development (e.g. Bush, Exxon Education, Ford, Mellon), some modest federal funding (the Fund for the Improvement of Post-Secondary Education, the National Endowment for the Humanities, and the National Science Foundation), and some state-supported teaching improvement (the creation of the New Jersey Institute for Collegiate Teaching and Learning, for example) over the years. But the efforts that are campus based are usually run on a shoe string. By contrast, the obstacles to quality learning and teaching are enormous: high student-faculty ratios, large classes, objective tests, machine-graded tests, ignorance of even the basics of good teaching.

Most faculty, of course, did not learn how to teach in graduate school. The movement to introduce a new terminal degree, the Doctor of Arts, has been an effort to honestly address this shocking absence of preparation. This logical reform has made little headway in the last twenty years despite the growing body of research on teaching and the ever increasing need for skillful teaching. The research Ph.D. simply reigns supreme.[18] A teaching handbook prepared for large-class instructors at a flagship university we visited bears witness to the low expectations of universities in regards to their faculty's ability to teach. The authors include such advice as: "Use an outline of the day's lecture on the board or overhead"; "Repeat major points several times"; "Put all assignments in writing"; "Don't re-teach the text"; "Give students time to copy what you have written"; "You must project an image of being a very accessible and concerned person."

Some experts believe that graduate students are now receiving some training. Still, the reality remains that if most faculty are to learn to teach, they must do so on the job. Yet, the inadequacy of teaching improvement efforts was clear at the great majority of institutions we visited.

At one of our huge flagship universities, a Center for Teaching Effectiveness, with a full-time staff of three, a half-time staff of four, and a total budget of $200,000, endeavors to provide services to 2500 faculty members and 3700 teaching assistants. These resources are 0.04 percent of the 1987–88 annual budget: $32.25 for each instructor. The center offers a fall seminar for new faculty to which only about 50 percent come. Only between

8 and 10 percent of the regular faculty attend their yearly winter conference. Most services are only available on request, and faculty must pay for resource materials provided. The center calls on about two hundred faculty who are willing to volunteer their time to stretch its meager resources.

At another prestigious flagship, the Office of Educational Development runs a somewhat more extensive and better-funded program. With a full-time staff of three professionals and four support personnel, a part-time staff of three graduate students and two undergraduates, and an operating budget of $265,000, the center serves 2400 faculty and 2400 teaching assistants. It runs a discussion series, a one-day orientation for new faculty, a mentor program that pairs new faculty with the winners of distinguished teaching awards, and individual consultations. Unfortunately, the office had no data on faculty participation. The office also administered $400,000 to $500,000 worth of teaching- and learning-related grants for which about three hundred faculty apply yearly.

At a third huge aspiring flagship, there was no such teaching improvement program at all. The report from the Ad Hoc Committee on Undergraduate Education had recommended the establishment of a center in 1987. The university, which had recently received increased state funding, was providing summer support to fifteen faculty to begin integrating scholarship on women into the undergraduate curriculum.

At one of the comprehensive universities, interested faculty had formed a Committee on Excellence in Teaching and had been coming together several times a year. They receive between $1500 and $2000 a year from the academic vice-president's office to help fund retreats, workshops, and invited speakers. Fiscal austerity was presented as an obstacle to increasing support. Another small comprehensive institution, this one better off financially, has a budget of $18,000 yearly to serve its faculty of two hundred. This is used primarily to sponsor two one-day teaching improvement workshops a year and to provide travel funds to faculty giving papers relating to teaching. Corporate funding secured fifteen years ago provides $12,000 annually for six teaching awards. The head of the curriculum committee, while criticizing the inability of his colleagues to renew the traditional curriculum, expressed complete satisfaction with this level of activity around teaching improvement. The annual budget to support faculty research is a substantially higher $80,000. Finally, a public urban comprehensive we visited had been awarded funding from the Fund for the Improvement of Post-Secondary Education (FIPSE) to assist faculty in improving a core course on world civilizations. There was absolutely no state funding for teaching improvement available.

At one of our community colleges, a well-funded one, each of the three campuses has only $10,000 per year for small grants of $1,000 to faculty to improve their courses. There is also a professional development program that includes occasional free seminars on teaching methods.

Interestingly, even at institutions that reward teaching, the evaluation process appears to leave much to be desired. The results of Carnegie's faculty survey indicate that observation of teaching by colleagues and/or administrators does not always occur. Only 56 percent of faculty at comprehensive universities said observation of teaching is important for granting tenure in their department; it rose to 67 percent at liberal arts colleges and to 75 percent at community colleges. A mere 32 percent at comprehensive universities said syllabi for courses taught are important for granting tenure. The percentages were 50 percent at liberal arts colleges and 44 percent at community colleges. Student evaluations of courses taught appear to be the most common form of evaluation: 77 percent of faculty at comprehensive universities said they are important for granting tenure; 87 percent at liberal arts colleges, and 64 percent at community colleges.[19] These data suggest, then, that students are playing a substantial role in faculty rewards for teaching, possibly a larger role than evaluation by colleagues and peers. If this is the case, faculty are abdicating an important responsibility.

In sum, few institutions are investing adequately in training their faculty to teach more effectively. Even the best efforts are relatively modest, given the magnitude of the task. Excellence in teaching requires the opportunity to review and revise courses, and to develop new courses. It requires knowing how people learn and mastering a wide range of methods and techniques to facilitate increasingly diverse learning styles. We believe that it requires, also, both a commitment to fostering intellectual community in the classroom and beyond, and the ability to connect with students and help them connect to others in the shared inquiry that constitutes the best in education. Ways must be found to enable and motivate faculty to learn how to teach better. The limits on students' learning and experience of intellectual community will not expand without major efforts in this direction.

Academic Advising

Institutions should place a high priority on assisting students in making sound and informed decisions. Such decision making is a prime opportunity for learning. It is also a means to affirm the existence and importance of academic community. Although faculty are the logical facilitators of academic planning, they rarely play a prominent role in the process. Only 25.4 percent of faculty responding to Carnegie's survey thought that academic advisement is important in the granting of tenure in their departments. The percentages ranged from 11.1 percent in research universities to 48.2 percent in liberal arts colleges.[20]

At the research institutions we visited, faculty almost never advise undergraduates until they are juniors, and, even then, a few "unlucky" faculty are usually given the task. At both our midwestern and mid-Atlantic flagships, only one "departmental undergraduate advisor" provides advising, often to hundreds of student majors. At a private research institution in the East, although faculty, in theory, provide mandatory advising to majors, in reality, the students often forge signatures or have a secretary sign their registration forms; most of the faculty have little contact with undergraduates. Although this institutional pattern seems to be typical of many research campuses nationally, we were surprised to learn that the faculty self-perception is quite different: 93.3 percent of faculty at these institutions thought that faculty had primary academic advising responsibility at research institutions, according to the Carnegie faculty survey.[21]

At the comprehensive institutions we visited, student advisement is still part of the defined role of faculty. For example, at our impecunious public comprehensive in the South, the university has made advising mandatory. Advising in the first two years is provided by a university college with staff advisors, but in the upper years, faculty advise. In the criminal justice department, one faculty member was advising over one hundred students.

At our teaching institutions, faculty also accept the role of advising students. At our well-to-do, private comprehensive in the South, and our liberal arts schools, faculty provide individual advice to students, both freshmen and upperclassmen, and everyone seems to be happy with the experience. At community colleges, many faculty are very active in advising and feel strongly that they should play a proactive, even "intrusive" role by monitoring students of all ages closely.

Faculty-Student (Dis)Connections

Overall, relations between faculty and undergraduate students in the 1980s were calm and devoid of conflict. There were neither strong points of connection nor of disconnection. On a given campus, at a given time, among given individuals, of course, dynamics are complex. The differences between students and faculty have always been great. On both sides, ever stronger forces pull students and faculty away from the teaching and learning experience that is the presumed center of the undergraduate enterprise and that has the potential to create a sense of common purpose. There are external factors: students' increasing need to work while attending college, which reduces time and energy available to engage academically; and economic demands on institutions, which keep class size large thus diminishing meaningful contact. There are also differences in socialization: faculty who, for the most part, pursue knowledge for its own sake; students whose goals are more instrumental. On many campuses, there is a sense that faculty and students are engaged in parallel play. Although both faculty and students express satisfaction with each other in national surveys, this perceived satisfaction masks a de facto agreement not to ask much of each other.

The student body, itself, has become larger and more fragmented. In addition to increased racial and ethnic diversity, there is greater age diversity. Students are increasingly divided between residents and commuters, part-timers and full-timers, day students and night students. Campus life is more tangential to more students than ever before.

Among themselves, faculty seem to have less and less in common. There is little interaction across disciplines or among schools, and too often, there is a division between those whose highest priority is research and those whose highest priority is teaching.

Disconnections

The great majority of faculty, even those who value teaching, view themselves as highly trained professionals and are happiest practicing their specialty. Nonmajors and, even more, poorly prepared students, are not partners in these professionally oriented pursuits. In the research culture, undergraduates are often an inconvenience to be tolerated.

More generally, faculty are professional intellectuals. The life of the mind is their career. The *practical* careerism of most students represents a difference in values that is substantial and creates some distance. We frequently heard faculty say, with varying degrees of discouragement, that students are not interested in things intellectual. There is no doubt that academic pursuits do not hold a place of choice in the priorities of most undergraduates. Studying is one activity among many and faculty often feel their courses are marginal to students. We often found either an irritating gap in expectations about the amount of work appropriate in a course or a resignation among faculty who have reduced the work load and no longer assign papers, for example, because students perform so poorly.

The increased diversity among students is another source of distance and occasional friction. Age has always been a great divide and remains so. Although there are more adults on campus, there are also more women and minorities. Since faculty have done little to understand their special needs and perspectives, cultural dissonance hovers just below the surface. But, because significant contact is rare and assimilation still the rule in the academic arena, conflict is uncommon.

Connections

A number of faculty and students *do* connect around academics. We saw various strong manifestations of this. For many faculty and students, the major department is a place of connecting, even partnering, through shared research, professional societies and clubs, and social events such as dinners, picnics, and softball games. Although much smaller in scale, honors programs bring students and faculty together in smaller classes and decrease the gap that lower intellectual ability and/or interest creates.

Judging from our sample, at liberal arts and community colleges the ubiquitous rhetoric of "the campus as community" still finds concrete expression. Here, we found frequent contact between faculty and students, thanks primarily to small classes, and some sense of common purpose. At community colleges, students experienced their faculty as allies in the struggle to "make it." Faculty saw themselves as enablers and counselors. The boundaries between the academic and the personal tended to blur. There were faculty who made dinner for their classes, took phone calls after midnight, and gave students bus money so they could get to class and to internships.

Charles Sykes, in his acerbic book *ProfScam,* proposes another form of faculty-student connection, a kind of conspiracy of silence to promote mediocrity in undergraduate teaching: "an unspoken bargain throughout nearly the entire curriculum: Don't ask too much of me, and I won't ask too much of you."[22] Mr. Sykes targets the universities, particularly the research ones, where the research culture is inimical to teaching. In that setting, his assertions come uncomfortably close to the mark. Large classes and low expectations are the norm, at least for the first two years.

Certainly, there is much data to indicate that most students are "satisfied" with their academic experience and most faculty are "satisfied" with their jobs. Thus there is little perceived need for change. In Carnegie's survey, a substantial number of faculty expressed interest in teaching undergraduates. But, experience shows that many fewer professors actually take advantage of teaching improvement opportunities, even when they are available on campus. Likewise, many faculty endorsed the idea of a core curriculum, yet the state of general education, especially, in our country is alarming and few institutions are doing anything about it. Just as raising academic standards will require that students spend more time studying, so raising teaching standards will require that teachers spend more time preparing and learning how to teach. Just as expanding learning beyond specialized majors will require that students take general education courses seriously, so offering rigorous general education courses will require that faculty do the work to revise courses or learn to teach new ones.

Conclusion

In the course of our visits, a number of students and faculty compared their institutions to a fast-food restaurant: "We're kind of like a McUniversity. Fast food." This is a disturbing leitmotif. There is much to be said for the cleanliness, efficiency, and profitability of fast food restaurants. But the fare they serve is mediocre. Continuing the analogy, we remember the popular ad, "Where's the beef?" and ask, Where's the substance, the academic quality of undergraduate education in America?

Ultimately, it is not useful to lay the blame at the feet of a single constituency as Mr. Sykes does. The "scam" is not one of professors over students but of society over its own long-term interests. By mandating access to all without offering adequate public monies to support them, by rewarding research handsomely through massive federal aid and private industry support while starving teaching initiatives, the American public is doing itself a great disservice. It will take courage, leadership, and money to change America's higher education diet.

Part 5

Community, Complexity, Diversity:
Making the Connections

Introduction

Those who work to strengthen community on American campuses walk hand in hand with paradox. In the face of increasing complexity and diversity, they seek ways to connect individuals to subcommunities and subcommunities to community of the whole. Those aspiring to community have always possessed the ability to see the promise of wholeness in the apparent contradiction of competing individual and small-group needs and rights. Today, the challenge is greater than it has ever been.

In chapter 12, we share our impressions, drawn from our campus visits, of students' experience of community—community of the parts and community of the whole. We found numerous opportunities for students to connect and belong in small-group settings, ranging from extracurricular clubs to honors programs. We found traditional-age students the most likely to choose these options. Opportunities for students to feel connected to their institution were much rarer. We sensed that most students experience a minimal "community of interest or convenience," based on the common goal of securing a degree.

Few students found academics a source of community. We found opportunities for intellectual community on campus relatively rare, especially at research and comprehensive universities. When they did exist, few students chose to paticipate in them.

In chapter 13, we propose a structured approach for examining and renewing community on campus: creating and implementing a Compact for a Pluralistic Community. This process will involve all members of the institution in examining and making explicit the ethical underpinnings of all campus policies and practices. The core ethical principles that we propose are: (1) Colleges and universities are, first and foremost, committed to learning; (2) Colleges and universities are committed to protecting freedom of thought and expression; (3) Colleges and universities are committed to justice; and (4) Colleges and universities are committed to respecting difference.

We close this book with a set of recommendations built around these four principles. Whenever possible, we have included illustrations of initiatives from colleges and universities across the country. In developing these recommendations, we focus most on the first principle, commitment to learning, because it expresses the essence of the mission of higher education. We also offer recommendations for implementing the principles of freedom of thought and expression, justice, and respect for difference. However, since, in our visits, we found so little connection between faculty and students and so little concern about the absence of intellectual common ground, we felt compelled to highlight the obvious: renewing academic community should be at the heart of community in action.

CHAPTER 1 2

When We Touch Common Ground

> We really are a family here at the University. As a university on a personal scale, [the university] will help you make friends, find your niche, and gain a sense of community on the University's River Campus.
>
> —*1988/89 Viewbook,* small private research university

As we remarked at the beginning of this book, all colleges and universities evoke the metaphor of community in talking about themselves; sometimes it is evoked in its most ancient form, the family. One need only scan promotional materials and presidential commencement addresses to confirm that Americans, on and off campus, resonate to the language of community. The cynic may point to astute but empty marketing and publicity, but we believe it is more than that.

Our travels took us from a campus of six hundred students where the language of family reflected a moving reality, where faculty gave students bus money and groceries, to a campus of fifty thousand students where faculty-student relations were antagonistic and a recent report on university relations that recommended "greater emphasis by all—students, faculty, and staff—on a commitment to increasing sense of community" was received with indifference. Between these two extremes, we found a broad and complex middle ground. In this chapter we will conclude our *tour d'horizon* of undergraduate students' experience of community on campus by focusing on their sense of connection with subgroups and, then, with the institution as a whole.

Community of the Parts

We found a plethora of subgroups on campus. Students, faculty, and administrators, with whom we spoke about students' experience of community on campus, repeatedly evoked these subgroups as the principal source of campus community. It is hard to know what percentage of students actually

147

experiences community in the strong sense of the term—common values, practices, and goals, a sense of belonging, mutual caring and responsibility—through these campus-based groups. The percentage actively participating in extracurricular organizations is relatively small.

Participation in the formal extracurriculum has waned on American campuses in recent years. Twenty-nine percent of the student affairs administrators surveyed by the American Council on Education and NAPSA in 1989 believed that fewer students had been participating in campus events in the last five years.[1] Seventy-six percent of the presidents who responded to the Carnegie/ACE survey ranked the item "few students participate in campus events" as a moderate or major problem on their campuses.[2] In *Coming of Age in New Jersey,* Michael Moffatt suggests that an important reason for this decline in interest is the fact that this area, once the domain of the students themselves, has been taken over by the administration and no longer represents a means to express an autonomous student culture. Another reason, cited by Moffatt and others, is the evolution of society toward more individualistic, less group-based pursuits, focused on the small circle of family and/or friends.

Whatever the reasons, various estimates contend that only about 10 percent of today's undergraduates participate actively in formal extracurriculum. By extracurriculum we mean all out-of-classroom, nonacademic organized activity. By actively, we mean attend a meeting, program, or other event once a week. On campus, we heard the same story from students with whom we spoke, themselves invariably the joiners and doers. There was a sense that most student organizations were peopled by leaders with very few followers.

This does not mean we found a dearth of energy and activity. On the contrary, on every campus we found many extracurricular organizations, both institution run and student run. The American campus offers a dizzying array. For example, at a large western flagship, there were about 350 students organizations; at a large mid-Atlantic flagship, there were about 450. Often the funding for these activities comes from student fees levied at a rate decided by the students themselves and allocated by them. On many campuses, student unions serve as the hub of this multifaceted world. At a small liberal arts college in the East, the student jazz fans had organized the Bessie Smith Jazz Club. Students on several campuses had formed BACCHUS affiliates to raise awareness about the risk of alcohol abuse. Students spoke with us about a range of public service activities. Also, on a number of our campuses, the Greek societies were growing in popularity and numbers. Professional clubs and honor societies were commonly mentioned and endorsed activities, providing a bridge between the extracurricular and curricular.

It was clear everywhere that student affairs administrators were greatly concerned to enhance the extracurriculum, to provide something of interest to everyone that would engage and educate beyond the classroom. On a number of campuses we visited, ranging from a small liberal arts college to the largest state universities, there had been an increase in funding for student activities. These are conscious and concerted efforts at community building. Everywhere we visited, we encountered the belief that a strong extracurriculum made up of many subcommunities is an important component of a healthy community of the whole. The president of one public comprehensive university described this point of view as the "Velcro theory of community": the hope that students, thrown into an environment boasting a myriad of small groups, will stick somewhere and stay at the institution. However, the experiences of an elite comprehensive university in the South and a liberal arts college in the East show the limits of institutional efforts to understand and shape student culture. In the first instance, the school was spending nearly $36,000 a year to provide entertainment in a nonalcoholic pub it opened in its student center on Friday and Saturday nights. Despite these efforts, after two years, only a handful of students were showing up. At the liberal arts college, the administration had created a late-night snack bar/cafe in the basement of a resident hall and equipped it with stereo, large-screen television and stage and track lighting. The students had not warmed up to it.

We found that traditional-age residential students participate more in the extracurriculum than do older commuter students or even traditional-age commuter students. For the most part, commuters simply do not come back to campus once they have left, and they leave to go to paying jobs. The mother of a five year old, who was editor of the student newspaper at a public comprehensive in the South, was the exception that proves the rule. This university had made a concerted effort to provide some programming at the lunch hour. Still, for commuters, especially, the extracurriculum is tangential at best.

Most campuses we visited, with the exception of the community colleges, still provide relatively little programming specifically for nontraditional students, especially adults, despite their increasing numbers. A large public research institution in the Southwest was running a mentor program for older adults to help them connect to the institution and to provide contact with faculty. A rural mid-Atlantic community college was running a program for displaced homemakers.

We did not find great dissatisfaction among commuters, part-timers, and adults. Many clearly do not wish to connect to the institution. They have other priorities. A "typical" part-timer at a comprehensive university in the East summarized well the prevailing attitude: "I'm not into school spirit. I'm thirty-four years old. I'm here for a degree, that's all. I'm not here for the social life." He had heard about the Adult Students Organization on campus but had no interest in it. In the face of such widespread lack of interest, administrators can readily become discouraged or choose to focus on the more visible residential students.

The role traditional institutions should play for their commuter, part-time, and adult students is a problematic issue. Part of that debate is the question, how much should institutions endeavor to intermix separate student cultures? At present, the gulf between residential students and all others is the widest. The president of a private urban doctoral university evoked the separation of student cultures with a humorous and nonjudgmental metaphor: layers of lasagna.

Sororities and fraternities, the women's center, the student union, the newspaper, sports teams, the radio club, and the jazz club are not the only small groups about which students spoke with enthusiasm and intensity. They also spoke of connecting through living-learning centers, and through their academic majors and clubs. At two of our research institutions, engineering students spoke of the *esprit de corps* in their program, where academics combined with picnics and softball games. In the business school of the midwestern flagship, all undergraduates encounter a common core of courses that begins in the junior year with an experience that both students and professors liken to boot camp. Students work in teams outside of class and emerge with a strong sense of camaraderie. Often the teams buy T-shirts proclaiming "I survived A-core." At a community college, the allied health professions students, especially the nurses, were described as "a family." Programs of smaller scope also provided community: the year-long interdisciplinary programs for freshmen and sophomores at a liberal arts college, for example, or the program for women at a southern comprehensive university that combines academic and social activities.

Occasionally, students spoke of the classroom as a place for community. In our visits, this occurred at liberal arts and community colleges. At a midwestern urban community college, a student commented: "We are a community in a class and try to help each other. It is not competitive the way it is at [the local university]." However, generally, students did not mention the classroom itself as generating an experience of community.

We encountered some concern, mainly from administrators, about the potential negative effects of subgroups and "little loyalties." The most frequent concern was expressed about Greek social organizations and groups of students from the same racial or ethnic background. Were they not choosing to separate themselves too much from other students, and shouldn't one worry about the dynamics of "like choosing like"?

We believe it is an important goal to create and maintain bridges among campus subgroups, but we also acknowledge that subgroup identity is absolutely inevitable and neither inherently good nor bad. Certainly, many students from minority backgrounds experience a kind of culture shock on a campus that is run and peopled by members of the majority. This psychic distress is mitigated by interacting with similar students. Without such support, these students might not be able to cope and achieve their potential.

Such subcommunities may well be the prerequisite for success. We are more concerned about the lack of connection between most students and faculty.

In sum, students everywhere do find opportunities for community on campus: in purely social settings, in educational settings, and in cocurricular settings. Numerous subgroups accommodate a wide range of individual interests and needs. Often people commented to us that it takes initiative by students to create connection, especially at large schools. But we found no lack of opportunity. Another common theme was the differing interest in and need for community on the part of students, depending on their age and circumstances. More than once we heard: "If you work and have a family, you may have all the community you need outside of school."

Community of the Whole

In our travels, we found many people who share our concern that healthy subcommunities are not enough, that in today's complex and diverse world, more than ever, students, and everyone else working on our campuses, must connect with the institution. As the vice-chancellor of a western research university put it:

> There is a great deal of "orbital energy" among the many subgroups, a magnetism that tugs at these groups, pulling them away from any common agenda. The challenge in the face of those centrifugal forces is to try to maintain some loyalty to the center, to a sense of common purpose. It is rather like a Venn diagram, with intersecting circles, each circle representing a different group with its own priorities and agenda. The idea, accordingly, is to try to expand the overlapping portion of the circles, while respecting the legitimacy and contribution of the separate circles.

Several people articulated the idea that healthy subcommunities are the prerequisite for a healthy community of the whole. As a political scientist at this same extremely heterogeneous western institution remarked: "Loyalty to the institution develops only after these little loyalties." A student at an eastern liberal arts college of 1800 students echoed this view: "You can't have a community of the whole without the smaller groups."

We cannot know what percentage of students at the colleges and universities we visited felt a strong sense of belonging to the institution. We spoke, for the most part, with students significantly involved in at least one campus-based activity; they often expressed institutional attachment. On the Carnegie Foundation's 1984 student survey, the item "I feel a sense of community at this institution" received an affirmative from 61 percent of the students polled at all institutions; 58 percent at public institutions; 74 percent at private ones.³ However, since the item was structured as a binary "yes/no," one cannot locate responses on a continuum from a minimal community of interest or convenience to the more developed community of conviction.

As a result of our travels, our best guess is that many students, perhaps most, experience a minimal and utilitarian community of interest, or of convenience. The common ground they share with others is the wish to get ahead, the goal of acquiring a degree. And for many, this is perceived as positive and adequate. As a sophomore at a huge flagship university in the Southwest said: "Yes, I think of [this school] as a community. People have common goals. Everyone's here to get a degree."

In some cases, common ground is actually more negative and reactive than positive. For example, a student government officer at a western university suggested that the sharing of war stories about skirmishes with the bureaucracy provided some bonding among students. Here, and at several other large institutions, students commented on a shared experience of coping with and surviving "the real world," by which they meant complex and unresponsive bureaucracy.

In other cases, common ground has virtually nothing to do with education per se. In our sample, sports played an important role in creating identification with the institution. Our southwestern flagship's football team provides a common focus of interest; the midwestern flagship convened much of the university around basketball. A large, private research university in the East, which lacks any major sports team, looked longingly toward a neighbor across town with a championship basketball team.

Returning again to the academic arena, many students expressed pride in their school's academic reputation. This was common from students at elite or flagship institutions. As a student at the southwestern flagship university put it: "Everything here is part of the university. There is a community feeling, a sense of pride." And another: "Our departments are ranked high. The faculty win so many awards. This is such an amazing place." However, students from our comprehensive southern university also were proud, and compared themselves favorably to the flagship university in another town, declaring themselves to be more serious students. And students at the southern community college, which is in the same town as the state flagship, took great pride in its own programs as well as its caring atmosphere.

Sometimes, students expressed a sense of community of the whole by evoking their positive experiences with faculty. This degree of connection, born of gratitude to faculty, was especially apparent at the community colleges. As a student said of her rural mid-Atlantic community college: "You will never find such a family environment as you will find here. The professors are terrific. They spend a lot of time with you." This college, its faculty and its administration, self-consciously created a caring community. This ambience of caring enabled community. One of the students observed: "Our college is like a big family and the dean of student affairs is the papa." Caring can be common ground.

It was rare that most students shared a common academic experience. There were three striking exceptions. One comprehensive university had recently instituted a core curriculum. At one small liberal arts college, for a number of years, the faculty had been teaching according to a block plan that scheduled students in three-week single-subject modules. Another liberal arts college had structured its curriculum into collaboratively taught interdisciplinary courses quite a few years ago. In choosing these institutions, students had the opportunity to share a distinctive academic common ground.

On a number of our campuses, there was a concern about the need to strengthen or create integrating traditions. At our southern private comprehensive, the sense of tradition in the women's college was envied by the men. The dean of men had recently provided money for an annual senior/alumni dinner and was encouraging the men students to create other traditions as well. The large flagship university in the Southwest had added a December commencement, so that there would be an occasion to convene those graduating in mid-year for an act of completion. At one community college, we found an aspiration for traditions and an effort to maintain the few they have: graduation, Winterfest, the annual luncheon of the club for students over twenty-five. People worried that these traditions will die away because they are being carried on by just a few people and because in the next fifteen years most of the faculty will retire. At one 200–year-old liberal arts college that became coeducational about twenty years ago, a new administration was anxious to create new traditions attuned to the changed campus culture. These traditions have included greater attention to the freshman experience, fall- and spring-term opening convocations, arts festivals, and a College Follies, the brainchild of a young administrator.

We encountered great concern about the obstacles to community of the whole on many of our campuses. On all of our larger campuses, there was consensus about the negative impact of large scale for community of the whole. We heard numerous anecdotes about the time when the institution was smaller and community more tangible. Several campuses had experienced dramatic transformations not only in size but in mission. The historical marker at one of our comprehensive campuses speaks eloquently to the reality of change:

Site of:

Evangelical College, 1835–1837
Hometown Collegiate Institute, 1841–1867
Hometown State Normal School, 1867–1942
Hometown State Teachers College, 1942–1964
State College at Hometown, State College System, 1964–

Perhaps the most ubiquitous obstacle, however—one that can exist even on relatively small campuses—is the complexity and diversity characterizing the modern academy and our larger society. There is ever increasing disciplinary specialization and the need to serve more external constituencies (government, business, industry); students are more diverse in age, in racial and ethnic identity, and in their patterns of use of the campus. These many "orbital energies" find expression in myriad activities and myriad courses.

This variety is the pride of American higher education. Healthy and vigorous subgroups that provide the opportunity to experience community are critical. We found ample evidence that students who choose it can find community on campus through such groups. It is less clear to us how widespread and how strong students' experience of community of the whole is. We did find it everywhere to some degree. And we found the aspiration to enhance it among some administrators and faculty on all the campuses we visited. We hope this aspiration is more than rhetoric.

In the United States of the 1990s, implementing the aspiration to balance community of the parts and community of the whole is one of the greatest challenges facing higher education. We believe it will require rethinking the principles that should guide the interaction between and among individuals, small groups, and the community of the whole, and renewing agreement about what is important and what is possible. It is to this compact for a pluralistic community that we now turn.

CHAPTER 13

Compact for a Pluralistic Community

A House Divided Against Itself Cannot Stand.

—Abraham Lincoln, Speech in Springfield, Illinois*

Increased concern about the health of community on American campuses prompted our study. In visiting eighteen institutions, we found among a number of administrators and faculty the feeling that community of the whole had eroded during the 1980s or that it had never been strong. However, we did not find the quality of community on campus for students in precipitous decline.

The diversity and complexity of today's campuses, which have made the experience of community increasingly problematic, are the result of decades of change. Greater diversity and complexity will likely be the norm through the 1990s, as well, and into the next century, although the pace and nature of change will vary from state to state and even institution to institution. If so, colleges and universities will face an ever greater challenge to their sense of identity and mission.

Institutions that wish to strengthen community, to cope most effectively with diversity and complexity, need a renewed framework for thinking about the legal and ethical bases of policies and practices on campus. They need a way to make that ethical underpinning real and apparent to all who live and work on campus. *In loco parentis* defined the legal and ethical relationship between student and university until the 1960s. That principle is now, as we have seen, both ethically and legally dead.

De jure the courts have become the arbiters of disputes and the authors of guiding principles. However, their judgments, too, are often based upon confusions over constitutional rights, contractual obligations, and standards of due care. Decisions based upon constitutional doctrine are generally in the

---

Mark 3:13 states, "If a kingdom is divided against itself, that kingdom cannot stand. And if a house is divided against itself, that house will not be able to stand." *Oxford Annotated Bible* (New York: Oxford University Press, 1962), p. 1217.

155

areas of free speech and privacy. Court decisions, based on an analysis of contractual obligations, have defined the relationship between students and their institutions in regards to claims in college bulletins and obligations set out in residence hall contracts. The courts have set standards of due care in tort cases that have arisen out of alcohol-related incidents and fraternity hazing actions.[1]

On campus, there are *de facto* agreements about rules and practices that may change in response to the latest crisis. In the larger society, law and ethics often run on parallel tracks, but do occasionally converge. Legislators and courts often draw on campus practices and justifications to inform their judgments. Although we cannot begin to clarify the law, we do wish to explore the ethical basis of policies for American campus life. We now turn to a vision based on a core agreement that should inform strategies and tactics for creating pluralistic communities.

We talked to hundreds of people about community on their campuses: students, faculty, administrators, and alumni. Everywhere we went, our conversation partners immediately responded with interest to queries about community. They instantly understood that we were concerned about whether they felt part of their campus and whether they had a share in decisions about its future and theirs. Although community is a complex concept, no one felt the need to spend long hours debating its meaning. Instead, the discussion was about how to improve community on campus and deal with the tension between communities of the parts and the community of the whole. We found a commitment to making campuses work by creating a self-conscious sense of community, with its opportunities and limitations.

To build on this interest in community we propose that campuses begin structured conversations about the issues we have been considering and the recommendations we make in chapter 14. We commend the drafting and endorsement of a campus-specific Compact for a Pluralistic Community. We believe this act of renewal must involve all stakeholders in the future of the campus, and that it needs to be informed by scholarly self-examination of the realities of the campus. Such a conversation can be a process of creative renewal and recommitment to a few core values by the whole institution and by all of its subcommunities.

The Concept of Compact

We use the language of compact to describe this vision, because the compact has a long and venerable history that is central to our American heritage of a constitutional democracy. The contract of Hobbes, Locke, and Rousseau became the metaphor for citizenship in a large and diverse land; it posited the central values of and the ground rules for community. In the process of debating and endorsing the Constitution, the founders of this country placed agreement about core values into the foundation of the legal system. The Constitution left great latitude to subcommunities and individuals to disagree according to ground rules of fairness. Although, by contemporary standards, the diversity of the colonial times was limited, even then the divisions among religious subcommunities and the claims of individual rights required explicit and fundamental agreement about a small number of core values, and agreement to disagree about a range of equally important values. Today, diversity is far greater. It is even more important to understand where we agree, appreciate where we disagree, and accept the right of disagreement by others, if we are to live together in a civil society.

In constructing our constitutional system, with its federal structure and Bill of Rights, Americans created a basic legal and ethical compact that acknowledged the needs of individuals and society and recognized the fact that groups—subcommunities—mediate between the individual and the larger society. The Constitution structures the relationship between and among subcommunities and the community of the whole, while acknowledging the special needs and rights of individuals.

The concern with subcommunities—their own health and their threat to the health of the whole—that informed the federal design is instructive for contemporary colleges and universities. Madison, in "Federalist 10," worried aloud for the founding fathers about the implications of certain subcommunities when he spoke of faction:

> By a faction, I understand a number of citizens, whether amounting to a majority or minority of the whole, who are united and actuated by some common impulse of passion, or of interest, adverse to the rights of other citizens, or to the permanent and aggregate interests of the community.[2]

A faction is a subcommunity pursuing its own ends without due regard to the public interest. All subcommunities, much of the time, are factions. So the community of the whole must devise ways to constrain the subcommunities, while, at the same time, giving them the space to serve their members as only smaller communities can. How modern the challenge sounds! The solution of Madison, Hamilton, and Jay was to convene the community of the whole, in its many parts, to agree on the ground rules and to endorse a few fundamental principles. This is the continuing task of compact in a pluralistic community.

Principles for Campus Community

We strongly endorse the following four principles as the necessary basis of compact on America's pluralistic campuses. We believe they constitute the common ground that all academic institutions share in a democratic society:

1. Colleges and universities are, first and foremost, committed to learning. Learning involves the interaction of individuals and groups: student with faculty, faculty with faculty, students with students, administrators with students, administrators with faculty, administrators with administrators. The nature of the pursuit of learning and the interaction of subcommunities around this pursuit will vary according to the campus mission. For example, a research university may rank learning through the advancement of knowledge above learning through the transmission of knowledge in the undergraduate classroom. A community college will focus on undergraduate learning. The rest of American higher education locates itself between these poles. Defining the academic mission as learning for students, faculty, and staff establishes a core value that is essential to any campus compact.

A pedagogy of active engagement undergirds this principle of commitment to learning, and unites all types of campuses, from the research university through the community college. The very concept of compact itself requires active and reflective consent, which demands real engagement between the compacting parties. Therefore, the pedagogy of the individuals who join through the compact must be participatory and collaborative. This pedagogy is especially important to communities with diverse participants, because active engagement will draw into the community those who are newly arrived. The norms of passive learning that characterize most of higher education today are inconsistent with the aspiration of the Compact for a Pluralistic Community.

Those subcommunities that enable learning, and serve the academic mission of the campus best, should be those that garner the greatest support. All campus subcommunities should regularly present evidence that they are serving the community of learners. This requires social clubs to be judged not by the quality of their parties, but by their contribution to an environment supporting learning for their members.

The *de facto* agreement about learning that Sykes portrays in *Profscam,* between professors who prefer not to put effort into teaching and students who prefer not to do hard academic work, must be made explicit, and then criticized by new standards articulated in the process of creating campus compacts.[3] When implicit agreements become explicit compacts, we have a powerful tool for changing current realities. The crafting of this language of standards for supporting learning is the most important contribution a campus compact can make to the quality of subcommunities on campus.

2. Colleges and universities are committed to protecting freedom of thought and expression.[4] The campus must be the place where even the most outrageous views are tolerated, as long as they are not expressed in a manner that deprives others of the right to express their views. Policies that restrict freedom of speech while protecting against racial and sexual harassment cannot be viewed as the means to control these reprehensible realities. The

philosophical underpinning of this principle is John Stuart Mill's understanding that freedom of expression does not necessarily guarantee the truth, but that it does guarantee an opportunity for all to learn from the clash between freely expressed views.

3. Colleges and universities are committed to justice. Throughout the twentieth century, meritocracy has been a form of justice that has assured equality of opportunity. In recent years, justice has also included a commitment to affirmative action. The campus compact needs to commit to both of these different conceptions of justice, giving up neither but recognizing the compromises demanded by each.

In 1972, John Rawls' book *A Theory of Justice* renewed the modern debate about justice. In his book, Professor Rawls articulated principles of justice based upon the agreement that would emerge between freely agreeing individuals *if they did not know what role they would play in society.*[5] This theory provides a helpful frame for just campus decision-making. When making ethical decisions affecting others, individuals and groups would put themselves in these others' position(s) in order to understand the full impact of their decisions on everyone. Take, for example, the task of revising the rules governing the grievance committee on sexual harassment. Students participating in this task would have to be willing to imagine themselves as faculty members against whom a grievance had been filed; faculty would have to be willing to imagine themselves as aggrieved students; women would have to imagine themselves as men and men as women.

4. Flowing from higher education's commitment to justice is the principle that colleges and universities are committed to respecting difference. The respect for difference is a modern statement of the Kantian principle that persons must be treated as ends not means; that is, people wishing to celebrate their difference deserve to be respected for that autonomous choice, not treated as instruments for the goals of others. Acknowledging the legitimacy of claims for resources by groups wishing to celebrate their difference is central to the practice of respect. The principle of justice as fairness requires that, in respecting difference, one acknowledge the special claims for resources of those who have been least served in the past. When the principle of justice is specified in the principle of respect for difference, civility in argument and social intercourse becomes the major ground rule. Although our campus compact cannot legislate civility, for it guarantees freedom of expression, it demands that expressions of bigotry be strongly condemned.

Another element of respect for difference is actually making pluralism operative. The Brown University 1986 report on racism on campus calls for reciprocity of understanding as the basis of a pluralistic community. It asks "that members of both majority and minority groups step beyond their respective cultural and intellectual boundaries."[6] We believe colleges and universities have the best opportunity to make pluralism operative if they: (1)

respect organized difference; (2) develop strategies to build meaningful bridges among the diverse subcommunities; (3) find ways to connect the subcommunities with the whole; and (4) celebrate community of the whole.

The campus compact must also guard against faction and its excesses. It can do so by establishing clear boundaries on: (1) the way in which subcommunities select members (Who gets into a fraternity and why? Who gets promoted to full professor of physics and why?); (2) the manner in which members are inducted (Is hazing educational?); (3) the way subcommunities interact with each other (Is debate about profound disagreements civil? Are the expectations for one group of students substantially different from those for others?); and (4) the means of distributing university resources among them (Does the student activities committee receive $100,000 for rock concerts while the history club receives $1,000 for the year?). The compact must establish clearly the priorities of the community of the whole so that the actions of subcommunities can be judged by them.

Campuses establish priorities and communicate them in a variety of ways. First and foremost, campus budgets are the evidence of campus values. We allocate scarce resources to reflect our operative values. Second, and equally important, we have a collection of *de facto* policies and practices that guide our community lives. We seldom review these policies and practices *en banc* and assess their consistency with our community values. Creating the Compact for a Pluralistic Community can become the occasion for evaluating our resource allocation, policies, and practices in the context of the principles we have suggested. This will require the explicit conversation about community that is the necessary though not sufficient condition of meeting the challenge of community.

Of course, in order to implement all of the preceding principles, the participants in the compact must approach it in the spirit of honesty and integrity. This commitment to honesty is owed to those who contract equally, because it is a further way to demonstrate respect for those who are different, and a firm demonstration that they are truly equal. The integrity of a Compact for a Pluralistic Community demands action as well as rhetoric; the nexus between them is honest implementation and indeed honesty throughout campus life.

Creating the Compact for a Pluralistic Community

Explicit agreement about the centrality of learning, freedom of expression, justice, and respect for diversity becomes the basis of ethical judgment about future policy and practice. The fact that all estates have agreed to a few central values means that the compact is the basis of approbation and condemnation: consent becomes the ethical basis of all actions. Such an explicit agreement, in itself, will not solve problems, but it will better guide concerted action. There will still be disagreement, even conflict, but the compact provides a structure to contain and manage these. The difficult issues that diversity, the regulation of behavior, and the disconnections between students and faculty raise on today's campuses can best be addressed if there is a core agreement, minimal common ground.

An explicit Compact for a Pluralistic Community also becomes the fundamental document confirming the ethical basis of the governance of the university. In the United States, the law clearly vests legal authority in the trustees, who often delegate it to the president and, on some occasions, to the faculty as well. But the ethical authority of governance on American campuses is usually *de facto,* not *de jure.* The creation of a compact that acknowledges the shared governance responsibilities of trustees, faculty, students, and indeed the larger society, can become the ethical basis of decision making that can then influence the legal distribution of authority. Without a form of governance that respects all of the stakeholders (although it need not vest veto power to any or equal voice to all), commands may be issued and followed but will not carry the ethical force that collegial decision making enjoys. The compact can be the beginning, but only responsive and responsible governance can actually implement the principles of community.

The details of the compact will vary depending upon the institution's size, the diversity of its members, and the complexity of its mission. Each institution will have to adapt the substance of the compact to its unique campus culture.

A large campus will need to address issues of scale through structure. Such a campus must affirm the centrality of its subcommunities, for it is through these that people are most likely to connect to the whole. In addition, a large campus could choose to create a variety of cross-cutting learning communities, no larger than five hundred members (students, faculty, staff), in order to reduce the scale of the institution. These intermediate networks could connect the smaller subcommunities to the campus as a whole.

A campus with substantial minority and working-class enrollments or a California campus with no majority but a confederation of minorities will approach the creation of community of the whole from a different perspective than a women's college, a religiously affiliated college, or an historically black college. At especially diverse institutions, every initiative in the compact must respond to the sensitivities of its many constituencies. In more homogeneous institutions, the campus can build upon the greater shared values and goals of its members.

The complexity of mission will also distinguish institutions. A flagship university landgrant institution that self-consciously embraces the missions of research, teaching, and service faces the difficult task of specifying the balance between and among the missions, and translating those choices into workable rules for decisions on resource allocation and promotion and tenure. Drafting a compact that does more than parrot rhetoric about all three poses a major political challenge and equally daunting requirements for follow-through. A predominantly teaching institution, either liberal arts college or community college, can define more easily its learning community as one in which small classes and collaborative learning are the highest priority. The tasks of creation and implementation will be quite institution specific.

The actual process of creating a Compact for a Pluralistic Community will vary according to the size, complexity, and nature of the campus as well. A commuter college will have to involve many people in small groups at different times. A small liberal arts college could convene the whole community from time to time to explore and ultimately ratify the compact. A huge research university will depend upon formal representative systems to create the compact, but still must invite the multitude of represented subcommunities to comment on and refine the compact. The work of creating the compact will be the work of learning together. The process of convocation— whether through representatives or of the whole—is the theater of compact and is necessary to its approval and celebration. This is the drama of a campus renewing itself. Specific guidelines for creating the Campus Compact for a Pluralistic Community follow.

Drafting the Compact

1. Undertake a careful assessment of the health of community on campus. Broad participation in this assessment is essential.
2. Convene a Campus Compact for a Pluralistic Community Task Force composed of students, faculty, administrators, alumni, and trustees to draft a campus compact.
3. Draft a Campus Compact for a Pluralistic Community that explicitly states the major values and goals of the campus and sets forth guidelines for the application of each principle that are consistent with the institutional mission. The Campus Compact for a Pluralistic Community should also spell out the structures for governance on the campus and the ground rules for subcommunities.
4. Circulate the draft Campus Compact for a Pluralistic Community to each of the major subcommunities for consultation and revision.
5. Reconvene the task force to revise the Campus Compact for a Pluralistic Community.

Endorsing the Compact

1. Convene a Campus Constitutional Convention to consider the new Campus Compact for a Pluralistic Community, as reported by the task force. This convention should be chaired jointly by the president and the chair of

the board of trustees and should include representatives of each of the campus estates elected by their peers. This ad hoc representative body should review, revise, and vote on the Campus Compact for a Pluralistic Community.

2. Submit the approved campus compact to the representative body of each estate (student government, faculty senate, administrative staff senate, alumni association, senior administration) for formal approval. After review by each estate, the Campus Compact for a Pluralistic Community should be adopted by the board of trustees as official policy of the campus.

Inviting Informed Consent

1. Disseminate the campus compact to all prospective members of the institution and adapt all publications to reflect the centrality of the compact.
2. Evaluate all prospective members in the community—either students or employees—by the standards of the compact.
3. Include an explicit reference to the Campus Compact for a Pluralistic Community in all faculty and administrative contracts, with a stipulation of willingness to abide by the compact's prescriptions.
4. During new student, faculty, and administrators' orientations provide mandatory workshops explaining the Campus Compact for a Pluralistic Community. Each entering student should be asked to sign a copy of the Campus Compact for a Pluralistic Community and state his/her willingness to abide by it. If there is a campus honor code, the compact should be viewed as part of the regulations that are enforced by the honor code judiciary.

Implementing the Compact for a Pluralistic Community

The process of implementing the compact must take into account a number of important goals: enabling healthy subcommunities while at the same time empowering community of the whole; recognizing the ubiquitous nature of disagreement, and even conflict, in healthy communities while encouraging harmonious community of the whole; controlling factions while protecting individual and group rights and opportunities. In sum, to implement the compact is to act in a principled fashion, while confronting the complexity created by diverse participants and varied goals.

All four principles—the centrality of learning, the priority of freedom of thought and expression, the priority of justice, and the importance of mutual respect—must become operative on campus, but they themselves will conflict from time to time in application. In these cases, the judgment calls will vary from campus to campus depending upon the priority given to each principle. The elevation of one above another requires special justification: e.g., our discussion of harassment rules established the priority of the principle of freedom of expression over the principle of respect for difference, and justified that priority by reference to the necessity of freedom of thought for meeting the educational goals of the campus community. Such conflicts can best be accommodated on campuses with strong and collegial systems of governance, campuses that have in place procedures for representatives of various constituencies to work out their differences through debate and compromise. Autocracy is inconsistent with the principles and inimical to the practice of community on campus. Campuses where community of the whole is already strong will best be able to resolve these conflicts between and among principles.

The campuses most able to implement the compact will be those where the principles are already embodied in day-to-day campus activities. For example, the principle of respect for difference will be the strongest on campuses that encourage regular interaction between and among their various members, both individuals and subcommunities, not those that merely legislate rules of tolerance. The very process of making the principles explicit will reinforce existing constructive campus cultures. It will be an impetus for change, for modifying those factors that are impediments to a principled community, only if there is enough shared commitment to change.

Our suggestions for implementing the principles of the campus compact assume a number of preconditions that, if not met, will make the compact and its principles little more than rhetorical wallpaper for a wall already covered with rhetorical graffiti. The preconditions for community include: adequate personal safety; adequate facilities, such as classrooms, library space, meeting spaces, and secure personal storage; access to required courses in popular areas of specialization; and adequate institutional services such as health care and access to public transportation. In addition, society as a whole must provide financial support for students and faculty at a level that allows them to invest time in the campus community and its central principles without putting at risk their economic security; this means adequate financial aid for students and middle-class wages for all faculty and staff.

We close this book on community on campus with a set of recommendations born of study, observation, and discussion with many committed individuals across the country.

CHAPTER 14

Recommendations for Community in Action

The following recommendations are those we believe most relevant to making the principles of the Compact for a Pluralistic Community operative. We have grouped them around the four principles: the centrality of learning, the priority of freedom of thought and expression, the priority of justice, and the importance of respecting difference. Of course, each recommendation has implications not only for the other recommendations grouped under the same principle, but also for all of the other principles and recommendations. Different institutions interested in enhancing community on campus will have somewhat different needs, goals, and constraints, and will adapt these recommendations accordingly. We offer them for discussion and action, and hope they contribute to strengthening community on American campuses.

A Learning Community: Colleges and universities are, first and foremost, committed to learning.

1. Strengthen the connections between students and faculty both in the classroom and out of the classroom.

The interaction of faculty members and students around academics is the heart of campus community. There is no substitute. We found these connections often sadly lacking, although few professors or students seemed concerned about their absence. There are many ways to better connect students with professors.

a. Minimize large classes.

Size has long been recognized as a critical factor in creating a sense of community. For many individuals, large groups diminish the possibility of feeling they belong and are committed to group goals. Those who seek to enhance students' higher-order learning and long-term retention know the value of smaller classes. These facilitate interactive teaching and learning.

Direct exchange with faculty members (as well as fellow students) can reinforce common interests and even create the human connection that will spark a new interest. We found that the majority of today's students, especially in their freshman and sophomore years, must take courses that are too large to connect them with faculty or peers. At liberal arts and community colleges, this was less likely to be the case. We propose, therefore, that colleges and universities seek ways to enable every student every semester to take at least one course of under thirty students taught by a regular faculty member. The potential for classroom community would thus be threaded throughout every student's career.

Institutions are most likely to recognize the need for smaller classes in particular circumstances: remedial classes, foreign language classes, labs, honors programs, and, increasingly, writing-intensive courses and freshman seminars. We invite colleges and universities to expand their commitment to smaller classes beyond such programs.

Smaller classes, by themselves, do not guarantee greater and more effective faculty-student interaction. As we saw from our examination of freshman seminars as a strategy for increasing faculty-student interaction, standard operating procedures—"Come see me at my office hour. The door is always open."—do not change longstanding habits or expectations. Small classes *and* greater faculty initiative in working with students individually and in small groups could have real impact.

b. Create learning environments where faculty and students interact more collaboratively.

Those interested in improving collegiate teaching have been advocating this for more than twenty years. Research has confirmed the effectiveness of such pedagogy. Moreover, a pluralistic academic community must endorse and promote active and interactive learning. Unfortunately, we found teacher-centered, lecture-based instruction still to be the norm everywhere. There are many resources colleges and universities can call on to make changes, ranging from teaching faculty to facilitate discussion-based and group problem-solving classes to establishing faculty-student research programs, curriculum revision projects, and/or teaching opportunities. The POD and CUE networks are two such resources. (See recommendation 4.)

At Brown, since 1982, the Odyssey Project has paired faculty and students to collaborate over the summer in the creation of new courses. Odyssey II, begun in 1986, has focused on including the experience or perspectives of racial and ethnic minorities. Students frequently act as teaching assistants in the courses they have helped revise or reconceive. Brown also makes extensive use of students as tutors in science and foreign language courses, as well as in facilitating writing across the curriculum (Karen Romer, Associate

Dean, 401–863–2538). SUNY Oswego has also developed collaborative faculty-student curriculum development projects.

In the Freshmen Explorations Program at Tufts, in existence for over fifteen years, pairs of upperclassmen teach for-credit courses of their own design to freshmen under the supervision of a faculty member and the staff of the Experimental College. Peer teachers receive semester-long training in teaching methodology. Every fall, about seventy students are selected to teach five hundred freshmen, close to half the entering class (Robyn Gittleman, Director, Experimental College, 617–381–3384). Involving students in research and/or teaching is a vital investment in the professoriate of tomorrow as well as the learning community of today.

The educational philosophy undergirding many "learning communities" (a cohort of students taking two or more courses together) tends to be collaborative. Faculty work together to create cohesive programs. And there is often a greater opening to active student participation in intellectual analysis than in traditionally conceived courses. The Washington Network is a learning community of learning communities. (See recommendation 4.)

c. Make academic advisement a more important faculty responsibility.

Institutions should place a high priority on assisting students in making sound and informed decisions. Such decision making is a prime opportunity for learning. It is also a means to affirm the existence and importance of academic community. Although faculty are the logical facilitators of academic planning, they rarely play a prominent role in the process. Students have long expressed dissatisfaction with academic advising. A recent poll, Alexander Astin's follow-up study *The American College Student, 1985,* reported that only 44 percent of seniors were satisfied or very satisfied with academic advising. We found faculty advising most common in liberal arts and community colleges. On the larger campuses we visited, more often than not, faculty do not advise freshmen or sophomores. Although we found some efforts to improve freshmen and sophomore advising, faculty did not figure prominently in the plans.

Faculty advising is not peripheral. It is a powerful symbol of the belief in shared academic values. We propose that all students have easy access to at least one faculty member with whom they can discuss their academic plans and aspirations throughout their college career. What is essential in the student-faculty connection, specifically, is not the details of graduation requirements, but the opportunity to affirm the importance of learning and to extend the partnership around it outside the classroom. There are a number of ways to implement this recommendation. The model of Columbia or the Claremont colleges, where each student has the same faculty advisor for four years, maximizes one-to-one connection. Combining professional advisors and trained faculty advisors in college-based advising centers is one of the models in use at Penn State, where there are extensive services provided to faculty to facilitate and improve their advising (James Kelly, Assistant Director, Division of Undergraduate Studies, 814–865–7576).

d. Allocate more resources to out-of-classroom academically oriented programs.

There is much evidence that substantial learning occurs outside the classroom. With the guidance of student affairs professionals, colleges and universities have put significant effort into enriching student life, especially for residential students. The standards of the extracurricular repertory—student government, newspaper, magazines, radio station, sports, clubs, and organizations—have been joined by leisure and wellness programs, self-defense classes, and race- and gender-awareness workshops. Some institutions have tried to increase faculty participation in such activities.

However, we found that students and faculty alike took greater interest in interacting around academic issues than around the extracurriculum. Such interaction is the logical extension and enrichment of the primary relationship between faculty and students. We believe that out-of-classroom academically oriented activities deserve more attention: disciplinary, multidisciplinary, and professional clubs and societies, and special projects such as a model United Nations or debating group, for example. Programs that integrate the academic with the residential life on campuses are underutilized opportunities. George Washington University, for example, in its Technology and Society Program, offers two sequential courses for residential students in a university town house, where a graduate assistant lives with the undergraduates and the students have in-house computers. The academic becomes central to the out-of-classroom experience for students.

The out-of-classroom can also be integrated into the classroom experience. The Leadership Program at Duke asks each student to undertake a volunteer project and then write about it in relation to issues raised in the academic course on leadership. An interested trustee initiated and funded this venture.

Institutions should promote the shared interest that majors or enthusiasts have with their faculty to strengthen academic subcommunity. One way would be to establish a grants competition for student-run organizations affiliated with programs or departments, where the best applicants would receive funds to implement special projects such as workshops, round tables, or simulations, or to carry out some research project. One criterion of success would be evidence of faculty involvement. All such academically oriented activities should have institutional support for necessary services (secretarial, photocopying, etc.) and materials (access to computers and to video facilities, for example).

2. *Raise the standards of academic achievement and establish expectations of greater commitment of student time and effort to academic work.*

The central mission of the undergraduate college or university has been and should continue to be the structured transmission of knowledge through an academic curriculum that serves both utilitarian and liberal education goals. The heart of community on campus is the interaction of students and faculty around intellectual growth. Like any relationship, this one requires the commitment of time and effort from both parties.

On the campuses we visited, we found pervasive academic disengagement among both students and faculty. On average, most students committed one hour a week to study for every hour in class. They had many other competing priorities, some imposed, some chosen: paid work, socializing, family responsibilities, and, for a small minority, participation in campus or community organizations. Many faculty, too, had priorities that competed with teaching, the most important one being research. Rewards for research far outweigh rewards for teaching almost everywhere. We found no explicit discussion of the issue of low academic expectations for and by students on our campuses.

We propose that institutions affirm the primacy of academic work, and that they take serious steps to reshape expectations about the time students and faculty will allocate to academic work and the standards of learning and teaching they must meet. To do so is to self-consciously counter many of both higher education's and society's existing norms. Large classes, machine-graded multiple-choice exams, textbooks rather than original sources, "gut" courses to maintain FTEs, parties that begin Thursday night and continue all weekend—these are part of the reality of many of our colleges and universities. All undermine the potential for a learning community.

At the University of Michigan, Ann Arbor, the discussion of the issue of low academic expectations has begun. The Curriculum Committee, under the leadership of Professor Henry Griffin of the Department of Chemistry, proposed to the Executive Committee of the School of Arts and Sciences a typology of courses that would guide the assignment of credit hours: (1) intellectually intensive seminars and lectures that would require two and one-half hours of weekly study per contact hour; (2) labs and studios where most of the work would be done in the course of a faculty-supervised educational experience; and (3) experiential learning where all of the learning would be part of an internship or other experience not structured by a faculty member. Courses in the first category would receive one credit hour for each weekly contact hour. Those in the second category would receive less than one credit hour per weekly contact hour. Those in the last category would require four or five hours of weekly experience for each credit hour. The Curriculum

Committee and the Executive Committee agreed that the expectation for each Michigan student should be an average of two and one-half hours of weekly out-of-classroom study for each credit hour. This average would require that most of a student's courses fall into the first category. Anecdotal evidence at Michigan suggested that the average student studies only thirty hours per week, including fifteen hours of in-class attendance (with engineers and natural scientists working much longer hours than humanities and social sciences students). We strongly recommend the Michigan Curriculum Committee's typology for assigning academic credit to courses and its expectation of an average of two and one-half hours of weekly study per credit hour.

Other institutions are taking some steps to raise the academic standards and improve the intellectual climate on their campuses. Berkeley, for example, raised the minimum grade for courses meeting distribution requirements from D- to C-. Depauw University has focused upon its freshman year and built-in common intellectual experiences, in part to create a counterweight to the Greek system, which claims 80 percent of the student body as members. First at freshman orientation, and then in the three-week winter term, freshmen engage in a thematic common intellectual experience. Throughout the year, the student affairs staff and faculty work together to provide educational programming in the freshmen residence halls (John White, Associate Dean of the University, Depauw University, 317–658–4025).

The work of the Holmes Group in schools of education is another manifestation of campuses focusing upon improving standards. The Holmes Group has recommended five years of preparation for students who wish to teach, so that the students can complete full preparation in general education and an academic major as well as master the essentials of pedagogy. In a number of large landgrant institutions, the work of Holmes Group members has upgraded faculty of education requirements and courses. Similarly, a number of liberal arts colleges have strengthened the integration of teacher training in their liberal arts curriculum in a manner that has made teacher preparation more rigorous. The arena of education is nationally unique in its discipline-based movement to improve standards. Of course, this movement originated in public dissatisfaction with the quality of teaching in schools.

This public concern has also generated attention in the past few years to outcome assessment and accountability. A number of states have imposed exams at the end of the sophomore year that test a set of basic skills. Certainly this concern about standards is justified by the reality we have reported. However, the assessment movement, with its emphasis on multiple-choice test instruments, does not encourage higher-level learning skills such as analysis and synthesis, or address the critical problem of self-expression. As always, teaching to tests is only a partial answer.

3. Create a significant academic experience shared by all students and faculty.

One of the most powerful ways to enhance the experience of intellectual community on campus is to create shared learning experiences for all students. Few institutions have taken the route of creating academic common ground for students and faculty. The most frequent model of general education, for example, has been the reinstitution of some form of Chinese menu, guaranteeing a sampling of disciplines, but no widely shared experience. Distinctive structures or pedagogies that affect the entire campus are likewise rare, representing as they do, a high level of risk taking. A number of institutions have experimented with subgroups such as schools or programs. The Western College of the University of Miami in Ohio is one example.

We believe campuses that wish to make a serious commitment to community of the whole must create some form of academic common ground. Engaging a campus in decisions about this common ground means reaching compromises that transcend the inevitable disagreements.

a. Construct a "minimalist" core set of courses that all students take and that all faculty teach from time to time.

The most venerable and extensive shared academic experience is the core curriculum. With its roots in the trivium and quadrivium, the modern history of the core curriculum owes much to the creation of courses at Columbia during and after the First World War to help new students, particularly immigrant Jews, better understand what caused the war. To this day, Columbia continues to teach Contemporary Civilization and Humanities. Robert Hutchins' Chicago also continues its modified core curriculum, created to overcome the fragmentation of the disciplines. Of course, St. John's College of Annapolis and Santa Fe has the most imperial core, where all of the students spend their four undergraduate years reading the great books. Today, according to a recent National Endowment for the Humanities report, only 2 percent of colleges and universities have any core curriculum.

In spite of the fact that core curricula are rare, there is evidence that even large and complex institutions can create cores that reflect contemporary realities. City College of the City University of New York installed a substantial core curriculum with the initiative of its president, Bernard Harleston, and with the agreement of its faculty. City College has built its core around two major courses, World Humanities and World Civilizations. More than seventy-five faculty teach classes with no more than thirty-five students in them, where each student writes a number of essays totaling at least 2500 words during the term.

We strongly recommend that all campuses, regardless of size or complexity, look to the institutions that have, for many decades, maintained strong academic cores, and create a small number of required courses that all students must take. Such a minimalist core is the embodiment of shared values and its exact content may vary substantially from campus to campus. It can be built on a modest multidisciplinary base in the humanities, social sciences, or sciences. It could be historical or it could be topical. We believe it should be substantial and rigorous. The most successful cores—those at Columbia, Chicago, and St. John's—are remembered by succeeding generations of students as among the most demanding academic experiences of their undergraduate years.

b. Create a required academic course that focuses student attention on the nature of community and connects an understanding of the history and philosophical analysis of community with the realities of the campus and society.

Making a study of community the centerpiece of the minimalist core could construct academic community around the reflective understanding of the concept itself. The "CC" course at Columbia has been a partial model of such an enterprise, since the historical evolution of the concept of community has been an integral part of its design over the decades. A course that makes the understanding of community its goal could connect a rich history with the very nature of the particular campus community.

Such a course could be either an initiating experience for freshmen, or an opportunity for sophomores to connect their previous year's campus experience to a larger reality. In order for the course to be an experience of community, as well as a reflection on community, it should be taught in small seminar settings and students should participate very actively.

c. Establish distinctive structures and/or pedagogies.

A campus-wide commitment to an approach to teaching and learning, whether structural or pedagogical, can become the source of community of the whole.

For example, Cornell College in Iowa and Colorado College in the Rockies both use a distinctive course sequencing arrangement to create intense academic experiences. At both institutions, students generally take one course at a time for about three weeks and spend four to six hours a day with the same professor and fellow students. Both students and faculty on these campuses testify to the effectiveness of this approach and to the fact that this structure of time creates very intense communities among students in the classes and between students and faculty in each time period.

The Evergreen State College in Washington State has combined structure and pedagogy to create interdisciplinary team-taught learning communities. The curriculum is not based in departments but in year-long CORE programs for freshmen and sophomores and Specialty Areas for upperclassmen. Students receive written evaluations, not grades.

Alverno College in Milwaukee has created a community around a distinctive pedagogy. Alverno has installed a competency-based curriculum where both faculty and students participate in an enterprise that is nationally unique and significant. Alverno is one of the few campuses in the United States where a pedagogy has structured the curriculum and been the center of gravity of the community.

d. Create campus-wide programming around a common theme each quarter, semester, or year.

Another form of shared academic experience that is both curricular and cocurricular is one that explores a common theme for a substantial period of time. Departments, programs, particular courses, student organizations, in short, all the campus subgroups focus on this cross-cutting topic in one way or another and provide some programming open to the entire campus. This builds a web of opportunities for different individuals and groups to interact and learn.

A common theme can also be a way of integrating the whole year for a class of students. Using themes to tie the experiences of freshmen, sophomores, juniors, and seniors together could be a powerful means of creating community. As one moved through one's four years, there would be intellectual common ground with both one's own cohort and with the three other classes in different stages of the same sequence.

We did not find examples of quite these levels of campus-wide coordination. However, each year Ohio Wesleyan picks a topic that is then examined and discussed in a variety of ways: in a year-long master seminar, in a speaker series, in corollary courses, and in student projects, which are presented in the spring to all of the students and faculty. In recent years, Ohio Wesleyan has explored topics such as "Sport, Culture, and Public Values," "The Pursuit of Happiness: Personal Choice and Public Interest," and "The Impact of Technology on Culture." The College of Wooster in Ohio in its leadership program has taken a similar approach.

4. Provide opportunities for all faculty and graduate teaching assistants to improve their teaching.

As we have said before, the interaction of faculty and students around learning is the heart of campus community. Creating intellectual connection takes hard work and requires a special commitment to (re)designing both course content and classroom climate. When the curriculum and the process of learning are adequately student-centered, students will know they are responsible and valued partners in learning. Only then will the classroom be a community. This means challenging the long-standing norm of both students and faculty that students should be the passive recipients of pre-existing knowledge. It means acknowledging that the professoriate has had little opportunity to seriously learn how to teach and that the growing diversity of the student body increases the complexity of an already complex art.

On the campuses we visited we found a range of levels of commitment to improving faculty teaching. Virtually everywhere, however, there was greater support for faculty research than for teaching, even at liberal arts colleges.

The American Association of Higher Education's Collaboration in Undergraduate Education (CUE) network, and the Professional and Organizational Development Network in Higher Education (POD) are both committed to improving faculty teaching and provide expertise and collegiality. CUE's focus has been on collaborative pedagogy and learning communities (Karen Romer, Associate Dean, Brown University, 401–863–2538). POD brings together individuals interested in instructional development and faculty development efforts (Delivee Wright, University of Nebraska, Lincoln, 402–472–3079).

The Washington Center, a consortium of thirty-nine institutions (twenty-four community colleges; fifteen four-year institutions) in Washington State, constitutes an interinstitutional learning community for faculty. Located at the Evergreen State College and grounded in the Evergreen curricular approach of multidisciplinary team-taught learning communities, the center supports curricular reform and faculty development statewide. The primary approach is faculty exchange and the pairing of novices with colleagues experienced in team teaching (Barbara Leigh Smith, Director, 206–866–6000, ext. #6606).

Individual institutions making an above-average commitment to instructional and faculty development include Berkeley, Ohio State, the University of Washington Seattle, Syracuse, and Texas A&M.

5. Reward faculty for their contributions to the learning community.

a. Make good teaching, good academic advising, and participation in other activities that enhance student learning part of the review process for promotion and tenure.

A leitmotif throughout this book has been the importance of rewarding participation in the learning community; another leitmotif has been the absence or token nature of this reward. The reality at both the research and comprehensive universities we visited was summed up in this statement from a curriculum reform report at a flagship institution:

Administrators regularly profess that teaching, along with research and service, are the triad of faculty activities which are evaluated to determine tenure, promotion, and annual salary raises. This is current campus policy. By word and deed, however, most campus administrators at all levels, with the complicity of most faculty, reinforce the commonly held perception that research and scholarly productivity are by far the dominant factors in these decisions.

The report went on to quote from an accrediting self-study:

A majority of professorial faculty (69 percent) believes that teaching does not now have substantial importance in the distribution of rewards on campus (e.g. tenure, promotion, and salary increases), but 85 percent believe that it should. Ten percent or less of the faculty respondents regard teaching evaluations as very important in contract renewal, promotion, tenure, and salary decisions and teaching assignments; yet, over 90 percent of the faculty respondents believe evaluations should be important or very important in these decisions.

Still, there are occasional campuses where teaching is rewarded. For example, Fort Hays State University in Kansas changed the formula for promotion and tenure: teaching, research, and service had received equal consideration; now the formula is 60 percent teaching, 20 percent, research, and 20 percent service. Also, the faculty increased their workload from three courses per semester to four, in order to reduce class size and increase faculty-student contact.

Of course, rewarding teaching is only one part of rewarding faculty contribution to academic community. Franklin and Marshall, a small liberal arts college, has an explicit commitment to consider participation in activities such as campus governance and regular out-of-classroom contact with students; these account for up to 25 percent of the standard for promotion and tenure.

Rewarding teaching and other contributions to the learning community requires evaluating the quality of both. In regard to teaching, there is currently heavy reliance on student opinion gathered through multiple-choice instruments. Berkeley is one institution that has developed a thoughtful "Sourcebook for Evaluating Teaching" that provides a structured set of options for evaluating teaching quality.

Substantially increasing the reward given for teaching and service to the learning community provides the best single strategy for improving faculty participation in both these activities. Occasional teaching awards or plaques for service at retirement offer little incentive to affect faculty culture, where research is the most important activity. Only when the institution changes the reward structure will the faculty culture itself evolve into one that is more responsive to the learning community.

b. Establish endowed chairs for service to the learning community.

Revising promotion and tenure criteria and enlarging teaching award programs both can contribute substantially to rewarding contributions to the learning community. Another rare but useful way to reward those who contribute most to the learning community and also to celebrate these contributions is to establish endowed chairs explicitly for quality teaching and service to the learning community. Only one of the campuses we visited had such chairs.

The State University of New York system has, for more than two decades, offered Distinguished Teaching Professorships and Distinguished Service Professorships to outstanding faculty who have made their contributions through either teaching or service. These chairs pay more than other senior faculty positions; moreover, the lines are added to the complement of departmental resources, not taken from existing departmental budgets.

We recommend that institutions enrich 10 percent of senior faculty lines and designate them as chairs for teaching and service excellence. Significant rewards will help reshape faculty culture.

6. Reward staff who contribute to community, with special attention to improving the status and compensation of student affairs administrators.

Faculty are the key facilitators of the learning community. But the overall experience of campus community is affected by all members of the administrative and support staff. On a number of the campuses we visited, we found new sensitivity to the importance of all employees in creating a welcoming and caring environment. Two campuses had undertaken campuswide campaigns to develop a friendlier administrative climate for students.

Various campuses across the United States have implemented programs to reward friendliness by all staff, from the president to the janitors. The University of Tennessee at Knoxville, for example, has created a "Courtesy Benefits Everyone" program that is led by the Personnel Training and Development department. Staff who are nominated by students and colleagues receive rewards ranging from money to an especially convenient parking place.

Perhaps the most committed community builders on campus are the student affairs personnel. On the campuses we visited, we found the student affairs staff to be thoughtful, creative, and generally overworked and underappreciated.

We were unable to collect hard data on the salaries and benefits of student affairs personnel on our campuses, and the national student affairs organizations do not have systematic data about numbers of student affairs people and their salaries and benefits. However, we have reason to believe that student affairs administrators are less well compensated and certainly given less in other resources than regular faculty.

We believe that campuses for whom community is truly important will offer student affairs administrators salaries and benefits comparable to those of regular faculty, including opportunities for sabbatical leaves. They will also provide them with the other resources they need to do their work well. These professionals build and maintain student community. At present, they are virtually alone on campus in this endeavor. And many of the programs they create in student unions, residence halls, and advising and counseling centers serve a campus public broader than students.

7. *Offer programs that educate new students about participating responsibly in the learning community.*

The greater diversity of today's students has increased the need for acculturation into the learning community, from offering basic skills instruction and setting clear standards as to what constitutes university-level work, to providing opportunities to experience the excitement of intellectual inquiry early on.

Integrated and systematic freshman orientation programs now exist in some form on virtually every campus we visited. One of the largest and oldest programs in the country is the freshman year experience at the University of South Carolina. In addition to a substantial summer orientation program, University 101, a year-long course, enables students to come to understand the campus and think reflectively about the experience of being a college student. Topics include library skills, academic survival skills, information on learning, and tips on better interaction with faculty. About one-third of the instructors are regular faculty. One indicator of the success of University 101 is the fact that the attrition rate of participants is 7 percent lower than that of the freshman class as a whole. The higher retention is noteworthy because participants' aptitude scores are lower than the average. All "at risk" students must take the course. Information about the national movement to enrich the freshman year is now disseminated through the National Center for the Study of the Freshman Year Experience at the University of South Carolina (John Gardner, 1–800–522–3932).

A Free Community: Colleges and universities are committed to protecting freedom of thought and expression.

8. *Protect freedom of speech, publication, and association.*

Freedom of speech, publication, and association are all principles encapsulated in the First Amendment to the U.S. Constitution that have special moral force in the university. We cannot advance and share knowledge unless these freedoms and their corollary, academic freedom, are alive and well on campus. The only limitations on students, faculty, and invited speakers should be those associated with time, place, and manner, never substance.

In the course of preparing this book, we found that on a number of campuses we visited and on campuses identified in the press, the right of speech had been the subject of controversy. One egregious example of the limitation of speech was the withdrawal of an invitation to an African-American performer in a one-woman show called *N*gg*r Cafe* in response to the demands of African-American faculty and students to stop the show because it was insulting. This limitation of speech cuts to the heart of freedom on campus and does not advance the values of equality and civility.

It is imperative that all campus leaders stand up for the right of free speech, even in the face of objections based on lack of civility and bigotry. President Kirwin, at the University of Maryland, for example, allowed Louis Farrakhan to speak despite objections from Jewish students. The president stated his objections to some of Farrakhan's views, but defended his right to speak and the university's obligation to provide sufficient security to allow him to give his talk, in spite of the probability of large crowds of picketing students. President Bok at Harvard also took a stand for free expression by not censoring a blatantly sexist letter written by a student club. He vigorously condemned it publicly, thus reasserting the expectations for civility at Harvard.

9. Make sure that harassment policies do not restrict free expression.

Free expression is the sine qua non of the academy. However, those who benefit from it may inflict great pain upon others who experience themselves as the targets of prejudice. We understand their claims for respect and a civil environment. We believe that universities and colleges must rely more on persuasion by example and ongoing education than on regulation to create tolerance of and respect for difference.

Drafting harassment policies requires balancing different and conflicting principles. These regulations must protect persons from harassment yet not unduly limit speech and chill legitimate expression of opinion. The policy should only proscribe speech that leads directly to discriminatory conduct, such as changing grades, threatening to dismiss, offering money for sex, or a pattern of saying objectionable epithets to the same person. It should require that a particular person, particular persons, or an identifiable campus organization be the target of the harassment (e.g., the Black or Jewish student union, an individual in a class, roommates). Moreover, the policy or code should have different criteria for the public plaza, the classroom, and the dorm room. For example, one must allow a racist speech in the major student and faculty plaza; one will allow an off-color joke by a faculty member when it is part of a classroom presentation, but not when it is extraneous to the subject matter. One will protect also against someone coming repeatedly to a woman's dorm room and making sexist jokes if that woman is always offended and tells the person making the jokes to leave.

We found few institutional harassment policy statements or sets of regulations that we believe adequately protect free speech and balance other interests. The Federal District Court in Michigan struck down one of the better codes we reviewed, that of the University of Michigan, because it was too broad. The Stanford University Interpretation of the Fundamental Standard in relation to free expression and discriminatory harassment provides the best policy we saw. The interpretation, outlined in chapter 7, requires that the offender intend to insult or stigmatize, directly address an identifiable individual or small group of individuals, and use insulting or "fighting words" or nonverbal symbols commonly understood to convey direct and visceral hatred or contempt (Sally Cole, Judicial Affairs Officer, 415–723–9610).

Perhaps the most eloquent policy statement concerning the issue of freedom of expression in relation to offensive language was the 1975 Report of the Committee on Freedom of Expression at Yale, chaired by Professor C. Vann Woodward, and incorporated into the Yale Undergraduate Regulations. The committee wrote:

> No member of the community with a decent respect for others should use, or encourage others to use, slurs and epithets intended to discredit another's race, ethnic group, religion, or sex. It may sometimes be necessary in a university for civility and mutual respect to be superseded by the need to guarantee free expression. The values superseded are nevertheless important and every member of the university community should consider them in exercising the fundamental right to free expression.... The conclusions we draw, then, are these: even when some members of the university community fail to meet their social and ethical responsibilities, the paramount obligation of the university is to protect their right to free expression.... If the university's overriding commitment to free expression is to be sustained, secondary social and ethical responsibilities must be left to the informal processes of suasion, example, and argument.[1]

Our recommendation requires campus leaders at all levels to take stands that are unpopular: guaranteeing free expression to those who are uncivil and sometimes bigoted. But, at the same time, these leaders must urge civility by the force of their own example and educate their various constituents to respect difference.

A Just Community: Colleges and universities are committed to justice.

10. Recruit and retain more students and faculty of color.

One of the most important contributions universities and colleges can make to justice in American society is to offer higher education to the full diversity of our population. During the last twenty years, the student population has grown more diverse, but some groups are still underrepresented—particularly African-American males.

Institutions should strive for campus populations that mirror their larger communities: regional campuses should set themselves goals that approximate the demography of the region, elite national campuses should set goals that correspond to national populations.

Professor Richard Richardson and his colleagues, in their national study of African-American student retention, have shown the importance of calibrating recruitment of minority students to the norms of the larger campus. They have also found that it is important there be a large enough number of minority students to guarantee "comfortability" for them and some sense of subcommunity.

The Developmental Studies Program at Memphis State University, which is part of a state-mandated basic skills program, has contributed to a particularly high retention rate for minority students. It offers a broad range of coordinated support and advising services to minority students.

Ohio State has put in place a Teaching for Black Student Retention program through its Center for Teaching Excellence. This program, with a direct allocation of $50,000, will help faculty and teaching assistants better understand the needs and experiences of African-American students in the educational environment and develop teaching strategies that will enhance the academic success of these students.

At San Antonio Community College, the Women's Center focuses on reentry women, most of whom come from minority groups. The center provides academic and financial aid counseling, personal counseling, and a single parents and homemakers program. It maintains a textbook lending library for women who cannot afford to buy books. Such centers provide critical support for a growing campus population.

If many campuses have made measured progress in relation to the recruitment of minority students, the record in regard to recruitment of minority faculty is much less positive. The fact is that the pool of potential minority faculty is small. An extreme case is mathematics, where, in 1989, there were four Ph.D.s awarded to African-Americans. Two of them were in mathematics education, which would not qualify the recipients for a tenure-track appointment in a mathematics department. Most campuses, all of which have faculty affirmative action programs, are competing among themselves for the same few faculty.

A few campuses have especially strong records in recruiting minority faculty. Ohio University in Athens, for example, has been effective in recruiting more minority faculty than similar institutions. National observers suggest that the commitment of the president there has been the most important ingredient in its success.

Only by increasing the professional pool can American higher education create faculty diversity to serve student diversity. Mentoring of minority faculty, as eloquently advocated by Professor James Blackwell of the University of Massachusetts in *Academe* (September/October, 1989: 8–14) is essential for retaining and enhancing the skills of minority faculty on campus.

It is clear that the long-term solution to the problem of minority faculty recruitment will be student recruitment and retention, with special attention to academically talented students. Faculty mentoring of promising minority students may provide the best strategy for attracting more minorities into the professoriate. The United Black Scholars program at Memphis State is a good example of mentoring outstanding students. The university invites fifty students to be part of this elite group and each student is assigned a faculty or administrative mentor.

11. Invest in honors programs for especially talented students.

Just as it is essential to assist those who do not come fully prepared to participate equally in the campus community, it is also important to challenge and support those with special intellectual abilities. Honors programs can be important subcommunities for especially talented students in open admissions, comprehensive, and large, diverse research institutions. These programs attract students who wish to devote greater energy to learning and faculty who enjoy teaching.

We found honors programs on a number of the campuses we visited. Some were based in departments, others were campus-wide programs with separate identities. Both approaches seemed to work, although on some campuses, programs were having difficulty recruiting students, in part because of the lack of interest of many students in academic achievement. The programs with substantial independent resources and identifiable physical spaces had developed as strong subcommunities that in turn contributed to the community of the whole by raising the academic tone of the campus.

A vigorous campus-wide program exists at the University of Arkansas at Little Rock (UALR). The Scholars Program recruits traditional-age and adult students. They receive scholarship aid from a private foundation—more scholarship money than any other students on campus, except for the basketball players. The students take year-long team-taught core courses together. The faculty get double released time to teach in the program. A unique aspect of the UALR honors program is that each student must develop some competency in a foreign language and receives scholarship support to spend a few weeks in the country of his or her choice. This international dimension helps define the academic community of the scholars program.

The Lee Honors College at Western Michigan University is a free-standing honors college and uses a cluster course approach for its students. It draws its faculty from the larger university but develops its own curriculum as well as using department-based courses. In their senior year, honors students complete a thesis project in their major area and then have to defend the thesis orally. A section of a dormitory has been designated for students in the Lee Honors College, so those that choose to can live in the same space.

Community colleges also have honors programs. Frederick Community College in Maryland initiated an honors program seven years ago. Each year 100 students, out of 3500, participate in the program. The students range in age from fifteen to fifty-four. They take a combination of department-based and general education honors courses. An Honors Student Association, using student fees, sends students to national conferences and subsidizes tickets to concerts and the theater. Eighty to ninety percent of the honors students go on to four year colleges, while only 33 percent of the regular Frederick students go on.

The national organization of honors programs, the National Collegiate Honors Council, offers a national network for honors programs and provides useful guidance to those wishing to create or strengthen their campus' approach to serving the outstanding students. "Beginning in Honors: A Handbook," by Dr. Samuel Schuman, is a helpful guide to the practice of honors programs.

12. Make all institutional services available early in the morning and in the evenings to accommodate the scheduling needs of all students.

Class schedules have expanded to accommodate the increasing number of students who are unable to attend during traditional hours and whose time on campus is severely limited. There are classes early in the morning, in the evening, and on weekends at many institutions across the country. However, necessary support services, the prerequisite to any experience of campus community, are not as readily available. This means an important and growing number of students are second-class citizens. The needs of these students are an important priority.

On the campuses we visited, everyone acknowledged the needs of these nontraditional students but few actually met them. Even an urban comprehensive university that is completely commuter provided few services after 5:00 P.M. despite the fact that some students felt the need to spend the night in labs rather than risk venturing home alone late. At a rural community college, the counseling center was open at night, but the cafeteria, the bookstore, and the business office were not.

At Piedmont Virginia Community College, service offices remain open until 7:00 P.M., when the evening block of classes begin. Administrators also serve on evening rotations so that one is available until 9:00 P.M. each evening during the week.

The University of Louisville's ACCESS program (Adult Commuter Center; Evening Student Services) offers quite a comprehensive approach to the delivery of services to nontraditional students. On most week nights, all major campus services—admissions, registration, financial aid, career planning and placement—are provided through the ACCESS office until 8:00 P.M., when the evening classes begin. The services are also available on Saturday morning. ACCESS has a lounge and study area where there are always staff and other support services available, including forms for every university function. There are one full staff person, one secretary, and a graduate assistant to run ACCESS.

13. Provide affordable child care to the members of the campus community who most need it.

Students who are over twenty-five years old are now a majority. This has made the provision of child care a significant issue on many campuses. A caring community considers its members within the parameters of their family responsibilities. Therefore, colleges and universities have the responsibility to help their most needy students provide for their children's care while they are in class, lab, or the library. As the demographics change, the need for elder care will be added to the need for child care. Most of the campuses we visited had some child care, although not always for students. Nowhere was there sufficient child care to meet the demand.

The scale of child care varies substantially from campus to campus. American University, for example, with a student body of about 8,500, runs a child-care center for thirty children (one place per 283 students). Ohio State has the largest center in the country with three hundred children on a campus with 52,000 students (one place per 173 students). Many of the campuses operate on a user fee basis, with most of the costs met by the parents of the children but with the campus often providing rent-free space.

Cuyahoga Community College in Cleveland offers child care to students on its campuses through its Early Childhood Education Program. Its Early Learning Centers are supported by federal grants and user fees. They combine child care with learning opportunities for students who wish to pursue careers in early childhood education. This is a typical model on many campuses around the country.

Nationally, the University of California system has been a leader in providing child care for students. Most of the California campuses have quite large child-care centers, funded in part directly by the state, in part by the campuses, and substantially from user fees. In May 1989, Berkeley published a major study of child-care services that recommended a significant expansion of services to provide faculty and staff child-care services as well. This report included an exhaustive needs analysis and specified the importance (and expense) of providing subsidized child care, since few students, faculty, or staff could afford the real cost of developmental child care. It also documented some often overlooked needs such as temporary sick-child-care facilities and family health assistance leave.

At Montgomery Community College in Pennsylvania, students took the lead in expanding child-care facilities to include a cooperatively run program for toddlers. Student initiative has also made a difference at the University of Austin. There, the Student Child Care Association, a cooperative of more than two hundred families, has run for several years a facility for student parents who need child care from 3:00 P.M. to 10:00 P.M. week days and on weekend evenings. The operating budget is about $58,000, out of which the university provides more than half.

The national association addressing the provision of child care is the National Coalition for Campus Child Care, PO Box 258, Cascade, WI 53011.

14. Promote voluntary service by all members of the campus community.

The Campus Compact and the Campus Outreach Opportunity League (COOL) have given national impetus in the last several years to an important expression of community caring—organized voluntary service. By serving—on the campus itself, in adjoining neighborhoods, and even far away—individuals connect to other individuals and through them to the experience of interdependence and compassion without which there can be no community. Alverno College, Berea College, and Mt. St. Mary's (Los Angeles) require public service for graduation.

On Compact campuses, a 1986 survey of students showed 10 percent to 20 percent taking part in volunteer activities. There is anecdotal evidence that participation rates are now much higher. For example, 2200 out of 5100 Yale undergraduates do some sort of community service work. More than 60 percent of Harvard's students are said to be involved, up from 33 percent in 1983. The Compact, based at Brown, has about 140 institutional members. COOL, based at the University of Minnesota, offers community service advice to students and staff on more than 450 campuses (James Kielsmeier, National Youth Leadership Council, 612–624–3700).

When Guilford College in Greensboro, N.C., had to move all of its books from an old library to a new one, more than eight hundred volunteer students, faculty, and alumni together moved 250,000 books from one building to the other. "The book move is a bit of community magic based on the spirit of Guilford College," the president observed. Even modest voluntary service often leads to "community magic."

We strongly endorse the further growth of community voluntary action programs where students, faculty, and staff can work together. Connecting academic work with voluntary service is a high priority and to date has not received adequate attention and support.

A Community That Respects Diversity: Colleges and universities are committed to respecting difference.

15. Establish and enforce clear standards of civil and tolerant behavior for all students, faculty, and staff.

A pluralistic campus community will respect and safeguard the individual and group differences that are its building blocks. Setting expectations about behavior is fundamental. Establishing harassment codes is one way to put the members of the institution on notice. However, we believe these codes should not infringe upon freedom of expression (see recommendations 8 and 9). Thus, their enforcement will have limited application, for example, sanctions on those who engage in patterns of harassment of identifiable individuals. Regulation, then, is not enough. Institutions must also find every occasion to provide affirmative and concrete models of civility and tolerance as well as timely condemnation of acts of bigotry. In this way, institutions set standards as much, if not more, by sustaining a clear campus ethos as by regulation. We invite campus leaders at all levels to take thoughtful and visible stands on the ethical imperative of respect for diversity.

16. Provide ongoing noncredit programming to help all individuals and groups on campus understand and respect diversity.

Pluralism is more of an ideal than a reality on the nation's campuses. Therefore, institutions committed to creating a community that understands and respects diversity must take every opportunity to provide ongoing education about and reinforcement of these values. This requires comprehensive initiatives.

The most problematic differences on campus are race, ethnicity, and gender. On the campuses we visited, for the most part, programming in these areas had only recently begun. Nowhere did we find substantial programming more than a year or two old.

Nationally, some good work has started. For example, Indiana University at Bloomington has created a Unity and Diversity Week. Latinos Unidos, the Black Student Union, the Asian-American Student Association, and the Commission on Racial Understanding present a series of activities such as Gay, Lesbian, and Bisexual Day, a day focusing on the Holocaust, poetry reading for Asian-American Day, an international festival of music, dance and food, Latino Day with special music, and a dance celebrating African-American Day.

The University of Massachusetts, Amherst, in the wake of the racially motivated riot in 1986, created Civility Week. Events have ranged from a discussion of racial and ethnic celebrations to classes and lectures on sexism and sexual orientation. The highlight of the week has been a human "Hands Around UMass," where up to three thousand students have joined hands and encircled a lake on campus.

At the University of California at Santa Barbara, an Educational Program to Increase Racial Awareness (EPIRA) has created two video tapes as the focus of several hundred workshops during the past three years. The video tapes use students to talk about the experience of being African-American or Latino on campus. EPIRA was preparing a similar video on the Asian-American experience on campus.

The University of Rochester has a Human Relations Advocates program, where students are trained to offer small workshops and become facilitators of student discussions of racial and gender issues. The students are trained to lead these groups through both noncredit and credit-bearing classes.

The University of New Hampshire has put substantial energy into educating students about gender civility. Its Sexual Harassment and Rape Prevention Program (SHARP) includes a range of programs offered in residence halls and classes. Fraternity and sorority pledges must attend sessions. A mock sexual assault trial drew eight hundred students last year.

At Franklin and Marshall, a new college physician developed an ongoing seminar on sexuality as an extension of freshman orientation. A range of students attend these seminars throughout part of the fall semester. The seminar deals with date rape and sexual harassment but moves beyond these problems to an exploration of the complexities of individual relationships.

Creative programming to improve racial, ethnic, and gender understanding on campus is clearly a new campus priority. Since most of these initiatives are in their infancy, there is much room for further expansion and improvement in this critical area of campus life.

17. Create responsive support systems for individuals who have experienced the effects of bigotry.

A caring campus community will have in place the means of alleviating the distress of individuals. Although many campuses are creating new regulations to discourage and punish bigotry, we found that few as yet have strong and prompt support for those who have experienced racial harassment. A number of campuses have created support systems for victims of sexual harassment and/or assault. The University of New Hampshire, for example, has trained a group of forty student, staff, and faculty advocates who are on call on a rotation system.

At Indiana University in Bloomington, the dean of students office has created a racial incidents response team of administrators and faculty to respond promptly to student needs. The dean's office has published a brochure, "IU Against Racism," that gives students guidelines on how to recognize racism and information on how to contact the response team.

18. Make a major commitment to educating students about cultures different from their own and about the United States as a multicultural society.

Since most American undergraduates have grown up in a segregated and insular society, average students know little about Americans from racial and ethnic groups or from social classes different from their own, much less about foreign cultures. Students must study cultural difference to be responsible citizens of the campus and the larger society. Such study is integral to an understanding of community. We found few of our campuses giving a high priority to teaching about a multicultural society in an interdependent world.

On some campuses in the United States, there are exciting initiatives underway. For example, City College of the City University of New York's core curriculum includes the history and literatures of many of the cultures from which its students come.

A small number of other institutions across the country already require a course or courses in multiculturalism for graduation. For many years, the University of Minnesota has had a pluralism requirement. Students take at least two courses where the primary focus is on any of four American cultures. Courses focus on significant factors in those cultures such as class, gender, age, and sexuality, and on the concepts of race, ethnicity, sexism, and racism. Tufts University, UC Santa Cruz, and Washington State University also have some form of ethnic or non-Western studies requirement. Dennison requires either an ethnic studies or women's studies course.

Berkeley's faculty senate passed a Proposal for an American Cultures Breadth Requirement that requires every undergraduate to choose one course for graduation from a number of courses that substantially consider at least three of the five main racial/cultural groups in American society: African-American, native American, Asian-American, Hispanic, and European-American.

SUNY/Brockport, in the past few years, has begun an initiative to integrate global and multicultural studies across the curriculum. With the leadership of the president and provost, each school and program of the university has prepared a plan to include the study and appreciation of global interdependence and cultural diversity into its academic programs. The university has provided a modest grant program (growing to about $50,000 in three years) to fund initiatives to integrate these concerns into the curriculum.

A number of campuses are responding to the challenge of educating for diversity by creating new courses that draw on a number of disciplines and scholars from diverse backgrounds. What is often a political challenge on campus becomes the occasion for real educational creativity.

19. Integrate women into the curriculum.

Women have long been a significant portion of the undergraduate student body. In 1929–30, women already constituted 44 percent of enrollments. Yet, it is only in the last decade that there have been serious efforts to integrate the experience, perspectives, and scholarship of women into the college and university curricula. Even today, when they represent the absolute majority, at most institutions women students are not equal members in the learning community. The prism of sex still shapes curricular reality; faculty, both men and women, still transmit knowledge from the traditional perspective of white men, a perspective that marginalizes women.

College and universities will not become pluralistic learning communities until they teach a pluralistic curriculum. A pluralistic curriculum will weave cultural and gender differences throughout its fabric, exposing all students to many strands of reality, many prisms. The inclusion of the new scholarship on women is one must.

Most of the campuses we visited had made little progress toward integrating women into their curricula. This is particularly unfortunate since there are now abundant resources, materials, and models.

The work has begun on more than one hundred campuses. The University of Arizona, the University of Delaware, Hunter, the University of Maine, Orono, Montana State University, Rutgers, Smith, Spelman, Towson State, Wellesley, Wheaton, and Yale, for example, have instituted instructional development projects. The National Endowment for the Humanities and the Fund for the Improvement of Post-Secondary Education, as well as the Ford, Lilly, Mellon, and Rockefeller foundations, have supported curriculum revision. The Wellesley College Center for Research on Women, one of the oldest of these centers nationally, has special expertise in curriculum integration (Peggy MacIntosh, 617–431–1453). The Women's Center at Memphis State has a strong program in women of color (Lynn Cannon, Director, Center for Research on Women, 901–678–2770).

20. Provide opportunities to collaborate on and participate in campus-wide programming.

On the campuses we visited, students had ample opportunity to experience a sense of community through participation in a large variety of small groups. There were fewer opportunities to participate in all-campus events that affirm and celebrate community of the whole, especially academic community. Yet the orbital energy of subgroups, the energy that can pull them away from a common agenda, has intensified in the last twenty years, at the same time that most institutions have substantially increased in size. We believe it is imperative that colleges and universities find ways to involve the entire campus regularly in common events that are meaningful and that provide the concrete experience of collaboration toward some worthwhile end. We are particularly concerned that the various subgroups on campus have the opportunity to work together toward common ends. Campus-wide intellectual and civic interaction should be embedded in the culture.

Part of the challenge of creating opportunities to experience community of the whole is setting aside time. For many years, Philander Smith College in Little Rock, Arkansas, has set aside Thursday mid-day for an all-college assembly. Weber State in Utah also sets aside one afternoon a week to allow for a campus-wide convocation. A few years ago, the University of Rochester reviewed the health of campus community and as a result instituted a similar University Day. It also began the Rochester Conference, an annual affair for gown and town that focuses on a large issue such as power, creation, and time.

Traditions such as matriculation and commencement can be collaboratively planned. So can programs to educate about cultural diversity, to do public service work, to promote wellness, to clean up the environment. Important issues will inevitably address both the entire campus as community and the relation of the campus to the larger world. For example, students from state-supported institutions in Kentucky organized a rally for higher education at the state capitol. Faculty, staff and administrators joined students and school mascots. Lobbying on behalf of the campus became a collaborative activity.

With careful planning, events can serve both to educate and to entertain. Opportunities for campus-wide celebration are important ways to create and renew bonds that are sorely needed on our campuses.

Conclusion

"A house divided against itself cannot stand." At a time of constitutional crisis, Abraham Lincoln, quoting the Bible, drew on ancient wisdom that has informed political and religious traditions for centuries. The founders of this country were no less aware of the wisdom embodied in this saying, and crafted the Constitution as a response to the challenge of creating unity in diversity. Since its inception, the United States has based its national identity on the promise inherent in this paradox.

Over the decades, higher education has played a dual role in the construction of America: providing citizens a common core of skills, knowledge, and principles, while at the same time meeting the needs of ever more diverse constituents. In the last twenty years, the reality of a common curriculum and the ideology of assimilation that sustained it have almost disappeared. The 1980s especially were a decade of rethinking pluralism.

In her 1987 book *Democratic Education,* Princeton political philosopher Amy Gutmann includes a chapter on the purposes of higher education in which she reviews a number of twentieth-century formulations of the ideal university community and proposes her own ideas. "Universities are more likely to serve society well not by adopting the quantified values of the market but by preserving a realm where the nonquantifiable values of intellectual excellence and integrity, and the supporting moral principles of nonrepression and nondiscrimination flourish," says she.[2] Gutmann rejects any single institutional model as an appropriate democratic ideal, be it ivory tower or multiversity:

> Because no single kind of university community can offer everything that is democratically valuable in higher education to everyone, the democratic ideal of a university community is best conceived as a "principled pluralism" of universities, each of which is dedicated to nonrepression and nondiscrimination, and all of which together foster freedom of academic association.[3]

Many institutions, many houses; yet they share a common ground of commitment to intellectual excellence and integrity, freedom of thought and expression, and respect for difference. The four principles we have proposed are similar: the centrality of learning, the protection of freedom of thought and expression, the commitment to justice, and the respect for difference. "A house divided against itself cannot stand"; but our pluralistic houses must contain rooms of their own for the many subcommunities that wish to express their difference.

The creation and implementation of a Compact for a Pluralistic Community is a response to the paradox and promise of community on today's campuses. Making explicit the ethical principles that structure the relationship between and among individuals, small groups, and the institution as a whole, and then embodying them in carefully crafted policies and programs, is to affirm the possibility of encompassing apparent contradictions in a larger context, balancing centripetal and centrifugal forces through "principled pluralism."

Renewing academic community should be at the heart of community in action. The promise of academic community, of teachers and learners connected by the commitment to intellectual and civic growth, is a promise American higher education must keep.

Notes

Chapter 1

1. Unpublished data on students' allocation of time collected by the Higher Education Research Institute's follow-up surveys in 1985 to 1988 corroborate this impression.

Chapter 2

1. Oscar and Mary Handlin, *The American College and American Culture* (New York: McGraw-Hill, 1970), p. 5.

2. 2: U.S. Department of Education, Table 116: "Historical summary of faculty, students, degrees, and finances in institutions of higher education: 1869–70 to 1985–86," *Digest of Educational Statistics: 1988* (Washington, D.C.: Government Printing Office, 1988), 141.

3. Ibid., Table 116: "Postsecondary Education: College Enrollment," p. 141.

4. "The Specialized College Faculty," *The Nation,* 26 March, 1908; 278.

5. Helen Lefkowitz Horowitz, *Campus Life* (New York: Alfred A. Knopf, 1987), p. 76.

6. *Digest of Educational Statistics,* Table 116, p. 141.

7. Barbara Miller Solomon, *In the Company of Educated Women* (New Haven: Yale University Press, 1985), p. 189.

8. Ibid., p. 194.

9. *Digest of Educational Statistics,* Table 151, p. 175.

10. Ibid., Table 146, "Total enrollment in institutions of higher education, by type of institution and race/ethnicity of student: Fall 1976 to Fall 1986," p. 170.

11. Ibid.

12. *Educational Record, Fall 1987–Winter 1988* (Washington, D.C.: American Council on Education, 1988), p. 80.

13. *Digest of Educational Statistics,* Table 146, p. 170.

14. Ibid.

15. Israel Zangwill, *The Melting Pot* (1908).

16. Christopher Jencks and David Riesman, *The Academic Revolution* (Garden City, New York: Anchor Books, 1969), pp. 51–60.

17. Frederick Rudolph, *The American College and University: A History* (New York: Random House, 1962), p. 103.

18. Jencks and Riesman, p. 36.

19. Horowitz, p. 24.

20. Calvin B. T. Lee, *The Campus Scene: 1900–1970* (New York: McKay, 1970), p. 98.

21. Rudolph, p. 33.

22. Seymour Martin Lipset and Philip G. Altbach, eds., *Students in Revolt* (Boston: Houghton Mifflin, 1969) and John Searle, *The Campus War* (Middlesex, England: Penguin Books, 1972).

23. Horowitz, p. 29.

24. Jencks and Riesman, p. 30.

25. American Association of University Professors, *Policy Documents and Reports,* 1984 Edition (Washington, D.C.: American Association of University Professors, 1984).

Chapter 3

1. Gerald David Jaynes and Robin M. Williams, Jr., eds., *A Common Destiny: Blacks and American Society* (Washington, D.C.: National Academy Press, 1989), p. 4.

2. *"Newsweek* on Campus Poll: Racial Issues," reprinted with permission in the *Educational Record,* Fall 1987–Winter 1988 (Washington, D.C.: American Council on Education, 1988), p. 76.

3. The Carnegie Foundation for the Advancement of Teaching and the American Council on Education, *National Survey of College and University Presidents,* 1989.

4. Jaynes and Williams, pp. 113–160.

5. Ibid., pp. 122–23.

6. Ibid., p. 117.

7. Stanford University Committee on Minority Issues, *Building a Multiracial, Multicultural University Community,* (Stanford: Stanford University Press, 1989), p. 158.

8. Ibid., p. 181.

9. Edward B. Fiske, "The Undergraduate Hispanic Experience: A Case of Juggling Two Cultures," *Change* (May/June, 1988): p. 31.

10. Ibid.

11. *The Racial Climate on the MIT Campus,* A report of the Minority Student Issues Group (Cambridge: Massachusetts Institute of Technology, September, 1986), p. 10.

12. Ibid., p. 9.

13. "Final Report on Recent Incidents at Ujamaa House." *Stanford Daily,* 18 January, 1989: 7.

14. Michael Moffatt, *Coming of Age in New Jersey* (New Brunswick, N.J.: Rutgers University Press, 1989), p. 146.

15. Sharon Gwyn, "Muzzle the Stanford Bigots." *New York Times,* 12 May, 1989.

16. James C. McKinley, Jr., "Thousands from CUNY Hold Tuition Protest at Federal Hall," *New York Times,* 3 May, 1989, section B.

17. Bob H. Suzuki, "Asian Americans in Higher Education: Impact on Changing Demographics and Other Social Forces." Paper prepared for a National Symposium on the Changing Demographics of Higher Education, The Ford Foundation, New York, April 8, 1988, p. 41.

18. "Proposal for an American Cultures Breadth Requirement," Report by the Special Committee on Education and Ethnicity, Berkeley Division, Academic Senate, University of California, March 29, 1989, p. 4.

19. Ibid., p. 18.

20. Mary Jo Frank, "Racism Course Proposal Stalls; Faculty Ask for Alternatives," *The University Record* (Ann Arbor: University of Michigan, April 10, 1989, p. 1.

21. Laura B. Randolph, "Black Students Battle Racism on College Campuses." *Ebony* (December, 1988): 126, 128–130; Bob Secter, "A New Bigotry Ripples Across U.S. Campuses." *Los Angeles Times,* 8 May, 1988; Philip G. Altbach, "Racial Problems on Campus Reflect Political Trends." *Buffalo News,* 15 January, 1989; Denise K. Magner, "Blacks and Whites on the Campuses: Behind Ugly Racist Incidents, Student Isolation and Insensitivity." *The Chronicle of Higher Education,* 26 April, 1989: A1, A28–31; "Race, Racism, and American Education: Perspective of

Asian Americans, Blacks, Latinos, and Native Americans." *Harvard Educational Review* 58, no. 3 (1988).

22. Stanford University Committee on Minority Issues. *Building a Multiracial, Multicultural University Community*. Stanford: Stanford University, 1989; and Brown University Visiting Committee on Minority Life and Education. *The American University and the Pluralist Ideal*. Providence, Rhode Island: Brown University, May 9, 1986.

23. University of Michigan. *The Michigan Mandate: A Strategic Linking of Academic Excellence and Social Diversity*. (Ann Arbor: University of Michigan, April 1989), p. 10.

24. *The American University and the Pluralist Ideal*, p. 5.

Chapter 4

1. Alexander W. Astin, *The American College Student, 1985: National Norms for 1981 and 1983 College Freshmen* (Los Angeles: Higher Education Research Institute, University of California, 1988).

2. Carol S. Pearson, Donna L. Shavlik, and Judith G. Touchton, eds. *Educating the Majority: Women Challenge Tradition in Higher Education* (New York: American Council on Education/MacMillan, 1989), pp. 32–45.

3. Peter S. Prichard, ed., "Crime on Campus: Schools Fail Safety Test." *USA Today*, October 4–7, 1988: 6.

4. Ailenn Adams and Gail Abarbanel, *Sexual Assault on Campus: What Colleges Can Do*. (Santa Monica: Rape Treatment Center, Santa Monica Hospital Medical Center, 1988), p. v.

5. *1988 National Campus Violence Survey*, A complete report from the Center for the Study and Prevention of Campus Violence (Towson, Maryland: Towson State University, December, 1988).

6. Daniel Goleman, "When the Rapist is not a Stranger: Studies Seek New Understanding," *New York Times*, 29 August, 1989: section C.

7. Michael Freitag, "Rape Crisis Alters Life at Syracuse," *New York Times*, 20 November, 1989, section B.

8. Carnegie Foundation and the American Council on Education.

9. The American Council on Education (ACE) and the National Association of Student Personnel Administrators (NASPA). *National Survey of Chief Student Affairs Officers*, 1989.

10. Carnegie Foundation and the American Council on Education.

11. ACE and NASPA.

12. Mary M. Leonard and Brenda Alpert Sigall, "Empowering Women Student Leaders: A Leadership Development Model," in Carol S. Pearson, Donna L. Shavlik, and Judith G. Touchton, eds. *Educating the Majority: Women Challenge Tradition in Higher Education* (New York: American Council on Education/MacMillan, 1989), p. 231.

13. Association of American Colleges. *On Campus with Women* (Washington, D.C.: Association of American Colleges, Project on the Status of Women, Spring 1984), Vol. 13, no. 4.

14. *Sexual Harassment on Campus: A Legal Compendium* (Washington, D.C.: National Association of College and University Attorneys, 1988), p. 35.

15. Ibid., p. 36.

16. Ibid., p. viii.

17. *John Doe v. University of Michigan,* No. 89–71683, U.S. District Court, Eastern District of Michigan, Southern Division, 1989.

18. "Students Protest Policy to Limit Speech Practices." *New York Times,* 17 September, 1989, Campus Life section.

19. E. T. Hall, *The Silent Language* (Garden City, N.Y.: Doubleday, 1959) and *The Hidden Dimension* (Garden City, N.Y.: Doubleday, 1966).

20. Ray Birdwhistell, *Kinesics and Context* (Philadelphia: University of Pennsylvania Press, 1970).

21. Robin Lakoff, *Language and Woman's Place* (New York: Harper and Row, 1975).

22. *Body Politics: Power, Sex and Nonverbal Communication* (New York: Prentice Hall, 1977).

23. Roberta M. Hall and Bernice R. Sandler, *Out of the Classroom: A Chilly Campus Climate for Women?* A publication of the Project on the Status and Education of Women (Washington, D.C.: Association of American Colleges, October, 1982); Hall and Sandler, *The Classroom Climate: A Chilly One for Women?* A publication of the Project on the Status and Education of Women (Washington, D.C.: Association of American Colleges, February, 1984); and Sandler and Hall, *The Campus Climate Revisited: Chilly for Women Faculty, Administrators, and Graduate Students.* A publication of the Project on the Status and Education of Women (Washington, D.C.: Association of American Colleges, October, 1986).

24. Claudia Wallis, "Onward, Women!" *Time,* 4 December, 1989: 82.

25. Lisa Belkin, "Bars to Equality of Sexes Seen as Eroding, Slowly," *New York Times,* 20 August, 1989, section A.

Introduction to Part Three

1. William A. Kaplin, *The Law of Higher Education*, second edition (San Francisco: Jossey-Bass, 1985), p. 224).

2. Virginia Davis Nordin, "The Contract to Educate: Toward a More Workable Theory of the Student-University Relationship." *The Journal of College and University Law* 8, no. 2: 141–181.

Chapter 5

1. "Students Still Drink, Fewer Drive Drunk." *Notes,* newsletter of the Association of Governing Boards of Universities and Colleges (Washington, D.C.: Association of Governing Boards of Universities and Colleges, February/March, 1989): 1.

2. Carnegie Foundation and the American Council on Education.

3. The Carnegie Foundation for the Advancement of Teaching, *The Condition of the Professoriate: Attitudes and Trends, 1989* (Princeton, N.J.: Carnegie Foundation for the Advancement of Teaching, 1989).

4. ACE and NASPA.

5. "Students Still Drink, Fewer Drive Drunk," p. 1.

6. *Alcohol and Other Substance Abuse: Resources for Institutional Action,* Self-Regulation Initiatives: Resource Documents for Colleges and Universities, No. 5 (Washington, D.C.: American Council on Education, August, 1988), p. 9.

7. *Bradshaw v. Rawlings,* 612 F.2d 137 (3rd Cir. 1979).

8. *Alcohol and Other Substance Abuse,* p. 10.

9. *Beach v. University of Utah,* 726 P.2d 413 (1986).

10. *Alcohol and Other Substance Abuse,* p. 10.

11. Ibid., p. 10.

12. "Students Still Drink, Fewer Drive Drunk," p. 1.

13. *Alcohol and Other Substance Abuse,* p. 1.

Chapter 6

1. Horowitz, p. 245.

2. Susan J. Curry, "Hazing and the 'Rush' Toward Reform: Responses from Universities, Fraternities, State Legislatures and the Courts." *Journal of College and University Law* 16, no. 1: 94.

3. Moffatt, pp. 64–65.

4. Chuck V. Loring, "A Time for Action—A Message from the President." *National Interfraternity Conference Annual Report, 1988* (Indianapolis, Indiana: National Interfraternity Conference, 1988).

Chapter 7

1. *John Doe v. University of Michigan.*

2. *John Doe v. University of Michigan.*

3. Stanford University, *Stanford University Student Conduct Policies* (Palo Alto: Office of the President, Stanford University, 1990), p. 4.

4. Stanford University Student Conduct Policies, pp. 5–6.

5. Ibid., p. 6.

6. Howard J. Ehrlich and Cornel Morton, *Ethnoviolence on Campus: The UMBC Study,* Institute Report No. 2 (Baltimore: National Institute Against Prejudice and Violence, 1987).

7. Ibid., p. 4.

8. Derek C. Bok, "Reflections on Free Speech: An Open Letter to the Harvard Community." *Educational Record* (Washington, D.C.: American Council on Education, 1985), p. 6.

9. *Meritor Savings Bank, FSB v. Vinson,* 106 S. Ct. 2399 (1986).

10. *Cooper v. Aaron,* 358 U.S. 1(1958).

11. Bok, "Reflections on Free Speech," p. 6.

Chapter 8

1. Prichard, pp. 1–2.

2. Federal Bureau of Investigation, *Uniform Crime Reports of the United States,* 1972 and 1988 editions (Washington, D.C.: Federal Bureau of Investigation, 1972 and 1988).

3. *National Campus Violence Survey, General Report,* 1985, 1986, 1987, 1988 editions (Towson, Maryland: Center for the Study and Prevention of Campus Violence, Towson State University, 1985, 1986, 1987, 1988).

4. Prichard, pp. 1–2.

5. Federal Bureau of Investigation, "Table 1—Index of Crime, United States, 1977–1986," *Uniform Crime Reports of the United States* p. 41.

6. Michael Clay Smith, *Coping With Crime on Campus* (New York: Macmillan, 1988), p. 20.

7. Kelly W. Bhirdo, "The Liability and Responsibility of Institutions of Higher Education for the On-Campus Victimization of Students," *Journal of College and University Law* 16, no. 1: 120–121.

8. Federal Bureau of Investigation, "Table 7—Number of Offenses Known to Police, Universities and Colleges, 1988." *Uniform Crime Reports of the United States,* p. 123.

9. Federal Bureau of Investigation, "Table 1—Index of Crime, United States, 1977–1986," *Uniform Crime Reports of the United States,* p. 41.

10. *National Campus Violence Survey.*

11. Smith, p. 94.

Chapter 9

1. ACE and NASPA.

Part IV Introduction

1. Carnegie Foundation for the Advancement of Teaching, *The Condition of the Professoriate.*

2. Ibid.

Chapter 10

1. Table 174, "Bachelor's degrees conferred by institutions of higher education, by discipline division: 1970–71 to 1985–86," *Digest of Education Statistics 1988,* CS 88–600 (Washington, D.C.: U.S. Department of Education, Office of Educational Research and Improvement, September, 1988), p. 210.

2. Horowitz, pp. 272, 292.

3. Project on Redefining the Meaning and Purpose of Baccalaureate Degrees. *Integrity in the College Curriculum: A Report to the Academic Community.* (Washington, D.C.: Association of American Colleges, 1985) and Robert Zemsky, *Structure and Coherence: Measuring the Undergraduate Curriculum* (Washington, D.C.: Association of American Colleges, 1989).

4. Carnegie Foundation for the Advancement of Teaching, "Academe and the Boom in Business Studies," *Change* (September/October 1987): 37–42.

5. "Table 174," *Digest of Educational Statistics.*

6. Robert E. Beck, *Career Patterns: The Liberal Arts Major in Bell System Management* (Washington, D.C.: Association of American Colleges, 1981), p. 13.

7. Clifford Adelman, "On the Paper Trail of the Class of '72," *New York Times,* 22 July, 1989: 25.

8. Zemsky.

9. Horowitz.

10. Moffatt, p. 6.

11. Alexander W. Astin, "Follow-up Trends for 1985-1988, Four Years After Entry," unpublished information provided to the authors.

12. Robert C. Pace, *Measuring the Quality of College Student Experiences* (Los Angeles: University of California, Higher Education Research Institute, Center for the Study of Evaluation, 1988), p. 58, table 7.

13. "More College Students Combine Work and Study." *ACE News Release,* 4 September, 1989 (Washington, D.C.: American Council on Education).

14. Ibid.

15. Anne-Marie McCartan, "Students Who Work." *Change* (September/October, 1988): 13.

16. *The American College Student, 1985: National Norms for 1981 and 1983 College Freshmen* (Los Angeles: Higher Education Research Institute, University of California, 1988), p. 3.

17. Carnegie Foundation for the Advancement of Teaching, "Trendlines—College and Changing Values: Two Year and Four Year Institutions." *Change* (September/October 1988): 21–26.

18. Richard C. Richardson, Jr., and Elizabeth Fisk Skinner, *Achieving Quality and Diversity: Universities in a Multicultural Society* (New York: American Council on Education/MacMillan, 1991).

19. Wilber J. McKeachie, *Teaching Tips: A Guidebook for the Beginning College Teacher.* 8th ed. (Lexington, Mass.: D.C. Heath, 1986), p. 182.

20. Donald H. Wulff, Jody D. Nyquist, and Robert D. Abbott, "Students' Perceptions of Large Classes." *New Directions for Teaching and Learning* (Winter 1987): 28–29.

21. Michele N-K Collison, "Student Group Seeks a Sharper Focus on Undergraduate Teaching." *The Chronicle of Higher Education* (November 1, 1989): A37.

22. William G. Perry, Jr., *Forms of Intellectual and Ethical Development in the College Years* (New York: Holt, Rinehart and Winston, 1970).

23. Derek Bok, "Toward Education of Quality." *Harvard Magazine* (May/June 1986): 54.

Chapter 11

1. Carnegie Foundation for the Advancement of Teaching, *The Condition of the Professoriate.*

2. Ibid.

3. Ibid.

4. Ibid.

5. Carnegie Foundation for the Advancement of Teaching, *The Classification of Institutions of Higher Education* (Princeton: Carnegie Foundation for the Advancement of Teaching, 1987).

6. Carnegie Foundation for the Advancement of Teaching, *The Condition of the Professoriate.*

7. Charles Sykes, *ProfScam* (Washington, D.C.: Regnery Gateway, 1988).

8. Carnegie Foundation for the Advancement of Teaching, *The Condition of the Professoriate.*

9. Ibid.

10. Gerald Grant and David Riesman, *The Perpetual Dream* (Chicago: University of Chicago Press, 1978), p. 371.

11. Carnegie Foundation for the Advancement of Teaching, *The Classification of Institutions.*

12. Carnegie Foundation for the Advancement of Teaching, *The Condition of the Professoriate.*

13. Burton R. Clark, *The Academic Life: Small Worlds, Different Worlds* (Princeton: Carnegie Foundation for the Advancement of Teaching, 1987), pp. 114–115.

14. Carnegie Foundation for the Advancement of Teaching, *The Classification of Institutions.*

15. Carnegie Foundation for the Advancement of Teaching, *The Condition of the Professoriate.*

16. Ibid.

17. Ibid.

18. Anne Paolucci, ed., *The Doctor of Arts Degree: Re-Assessing Teaching and Research Priorities* (Whitestone, N.Y.: Council on National Literatures, 1989).

19. Carnegie Foundation for the Advancement of Teaching, *The Condition of the Professoriate.*

20. Ibid.

21. Ibid.

22. Sykes, p. 86.

Chapter 12

1. ACE and NASPA.

2. Carnegie Foundation and the American Council on Education. This was the largest degree of agreement found in a list of twenty-nine potential problems. Alcohol abuse, at 67 percent, was the second most common concern.

3. Ernest L. Boyer, *College: The Undergraduate Experience in America* (New York: Harper and Row, 1987), p. 192.

Chapter 13

1. Nordin.

2. Alexander Hamilton, John Jay, and James Madison, *The Federalist* (New York: Random House, 1787), p. 54.

3. Sykes.

4. The centrality of learning requires great freedom for faculty and students. In nineteenth-century Germany, Wilhelm von Humboldt articulated the Prussian guarantee of freedom for both: *lehrfreiheit,* faculty freedom to teach and do research; and *lernfreiheit,* student freedom to learn.

5. John Rawls, *A Theory of Justice* (Oxford: Clarendon Press, 1972).

6. *The American University and the Pluralist Ideal.*

Chapter 14

1. Yale Undergraduate Regulations, 1990–91 edition, pp. 10–12.

2. Amy Gutmann, *Democratic Education* (Princeton: Princeton University Press, 1987), p. 183

3. Ibid., p. 193.

Bibliography
List of Works Cited and Consulted

Abrahamson, Judith Pounds. *The Influences of Student Involvement by Sorority Membership*. Bloomington, Indiana: Center for the Study of the College Fraternity, Indiana University, 1987.

American Association of University Professors. *Policy Documents and Reports,* 1984 edition. Washington, D.C.: American Association of University Professors, 1984.

Adams, Ailenn, and Gail Abarbanel. *Sexual Assault on Campus: What Colleges Can Do*. Santa Monica, California: Rape Treatment Center, Santa Monica Hospital Medical Center, 1988.

Adelman, Clifford. "On the Paper Trail of the Class of '72." *New York Times.* 22 July, 1989.

Alcohol and Other Substance Abuse: Resources for Institutional Action, Self-Regulation Initiatives: Resource Documents for Colleges and Universities, No. 5. Washington, D.C.: American Council on Education, 1988.

Alinsky, Saul D. *Rules for Radicals*. New York: Random House, 1971.

Allen, Walter R. "Black Students in U.S. Higher Education: Toward Improved Access, Adjustment, and Achievement." *Urban Review* 20, no. 3: 165–188.

Allmendinger, David F., Jr. *Paupers and Scholars: The Transformation of Student Life in Nineteenth-Century New England*. New York: St. Martin's Press, 1975.

Altbach, Philip G. "American Student Activism: The Post-Sixties Transformation." In *Student Political Activism,* ed. Philip G. Altbach. Westport, Connecticut: Greenwood Press, 1989.

———. "Perspectives on Student Political Activism." *Comparative Education* 25, no. 1: 97–110 June, 1981.

———. "Racial Problems on Campus Reflect Political Trends." *Buffalo News,* 15 January, 1989.

American Council on Education and the National Association of Student Personnel Administrators. *National Survey of Chief Student Affairs Officers.* Washington, D.C.: American Council on Education and the National Association of Student Personnel Administrators, 1989.

American Council on Education. "Sexual Harassment on Campus: Suggestions for Reviewing Campus Policy and Educational Programs." Washington, D.C.: American Council on Education, December, 1986.

———. *The New Agenda of Women for Higher Education.* Washington, D.C.: American Council on Education, Commission on Women in Higher Education, 1987.

———. *One-Third of a Nation.* Washington, D.C.: Education Commission of the States, 1988.

———. *Survey on the Quality of Campus Life,* Survey of college and university presidents. American Council on Education for *The Campus as Community* Special Report. Washington, D.C.: American Council on Education, Spring, 1989.

Annotated Bibliography: Research Studies and Articles, 1980–1985. Bloomington, Indiana: Center for the Study of the College Fraternity, Indiana University, 1985.

Annotated Bibliography: Research Studies and Articles, 1950–1970. Bloomington, Indiana: Center for the Study of the College Fraternity, Indiana University. (Originally published by the Commission on Fraternity Research, 1970.)

Appleton, James R., Channing M. Briggs, and James J. Rhatigan. *Pieces of Eight.* Portland, Oregon: National Association of Student Personnel Advisors' Institute of Research and Development, 1978.

Apps, Jerold W. *Higher Education in a Learning Society: Meeting New Demands for Education and Training.* San Francisco: Jossey-Bass, 1988.

———. *The Adult Learner on Campus: A Guide for Instructors and Administrators.* Chicago: Follett, 1981.

Association of American Colleges. *A New Vitality in General Education: Planning, Teaching, and Supporting Effective Liberal Learning.* Washington, D..C.: Association of American Colleges, 1988.

Association of American Colleges. *The Problem of Rape on Campus,* Washington, D.C.: Association of American Colleges, Project on the Status and Education of Women, undated.

Association of American Colleges. *On Campus with Women* 13, no. 4. Washington, D.C.: Association of American Colleges, Project on the Status of Women. Spring 1984.

Association of American Colleges Project on the Status and Education of Women. *Selected Activities Using "The Classroom Climate: A Chilly One for Women?"* Washington, D.C.: Association of American Colleges, Project on the Status and Education of Women, 1984.

Astin, Alexander W. "Follow–up Trends for 1985–1988, Four Years After Entry," unpublished information provided to the authors.

———. *The American College Student, 1985: National Norms for 1981 and 1983 College Freshmen.* Los Angeles: Higher Education Research Institute, University of California, 1988.

———. *Achieving Educational Excellence.* San Francisco: Jossey-Bass, 1985.

Astin, Helen S., and Werner Z. Hirsch. *The Higher Education of Women.* New York: Praeger Publishers, 1978.

Baltzwell, E. Digby. *The Search for Community in Modern America.* New York: Harper and Row, 1968.

Barringer, Felicity. "Drives by Campuses to Curb Race Slurs Pose a Speech Issue." *New York Times,* 25 April, 1989: A1, A20.

Batson, Steve W. "Minimizing Liability for the College Administrator: Female Student Protection." *School Law Update,* 1986: 120–128.

Bauer, Brian. "Police Tighten Yale Security." *Yale News,* 2 November, 1988: 1, 5.

Beach v. University of Utah, 726 P.2d 413 (1986).

Beck, Robert E. *Career Patterns: The Liberal Arts Major in Bell System Management.* Washington, D.C.: Association of American Colleges, 1981.

Behrens, Anna Jo. *Higher Education with Fewer Teachers: Some Examples of Current Practice.* Washington, D.C.: Management Division, Academy for Educational Development, 1972.

Belenky, Mary Field, et al. *Women's Ways of Knowing.* New York: Basic Books, 1986.

Belkin, Lisa. "Bars to Equality of Sexes Seen as Eroding, Slowly." *New York Times,* 20 August, 1989: A1, A26.

Bellah, Robert N., et al. *Habits of the Heart: Individualism and Commitment in American Life.* Berkeley: University of California Press, 1985.

Bender, Thomas. *Community and Social Change in America.* Baltimore: Johns Hopkins University Press, 1978.

Berger, Joseph. "Campus Racial Strains Show Two Perspectives on Inequality." *New York Times,* 22 May, 1989: A1, A15.

———. "Slowing Pace to Doctorates Spurs Worry on Filling Jobs." *New York Times,* 3 May, 1989: A1, B7.

Berke, Richard L. "Census Predicts Population Drop in Next Century." *New York Times,* February 1, 1989: A1, A18.

Bernstein, Richard J. *Beyond Objectivism and Relativism Science.* Philadelphia: University of Pennsylvania Press, 1985.

Bhirdo, Kelly W. "The Liability and Responsibility of Institutions of Higher Education for the On-Campus Victimization of Students." *Journal of College and University Law* 16, no. 1: 119–135.

Bickel, Alexander M. *The Morality of Consent.* New Haven: Yale University Press, 1975.

Biddle, William W. and Loureide J. Biddle. *The Community Development Process: The Rediscovery of Local Initiative.* New York: Holt, 1965.

Birdwhistell, Ray. *Kinesics and Context.* Philadelphia: University of Pennsylvania Press, 1970.

"Blacks in Higher Education: The Climb Toward Equality," *Change,* special issue (May/June 1987).

Blake, Elizabeth S. "Classroom and Context: An Educational Dialectic." *Academe* (September, 1979): 280–292.

Bloom, Allan. *Closing of the American Mind.* New York: Simon and Schuster, 1987.

Bok, Derek C. "Toward Education of Quality." *Harvard Magazine* (May/June 1986): 49–64.

————. "Reflections on Free Speech: An Open Letter to the Harvard Community." *Educational Record* (Winter 1985): 4–8.

Bowen, Howard R., and Jack H. Shuster. *American Professors: A National Resource Imperiled.* New York: Oxford University Press, 1986.

Boyer, Ernest L. *College: The Undergraduate Experience in America.* New York: Harper and Row, 1987.

Boyte, Harry C. *Community is Possible.* New York: Harper and Row, 1984.

Brademas, John. *Washington, D.C. to Washington Square.* New York: Weidenfeld and Nicolson, 1986.

Bradshaw v. Rawlings, 612 F.2d 137 (3rd Cir. 1979)

Brokfield, Stephen D. *Understanding and Facilitating Adult Learning.* San Francisco: Jossey-Bass, 1986.

Brown University Visiting Committee on Minority Life and Education. *The American University and the Pluralist Ideal.* Providence, Rhode Island: Brown University, May 9, 1986.

Brownell, Baker. *The College and the Community.* New York: Harper and Brothers, 1952.

Bureau of the Census, U.S. Department of Commerce. *Statistical Abstract of the United States 1989.* 109th ed. Washington, D.C.: Government Printing Office, 1989.

Cahn, Steven M. *The Philosophical Foundation of Education.* New York: Harper and Row, 1970.

Carmody, Deirdre. "Increasing Rapes on Campus Spur College to Fight Back." *New York Times,* 1 January, 1989.

The Carnegie Council on Policy Studies in Higher Education. *Three Thousand Futures: The Next Twenty Years for Higher Education.* San Francisco: Jossey-Bass, 1980.

The Carnegie Foundation for the Advancement of Teaching. *The Condition of the Professoriate: Attitudes and Trends, 1989.* Princeton: Carnegie Foundation for the Advancement of Teaching, 1989.

————. "Trendlines—College and Changing Values: Two Year and Four Year Institutions." *Change* (September/October 1988): 21–26.

————. *The Classification of Institutions of Higher Education.* Princeton: Carnegie Foundation for the Advancement of Teaching, 1987.

————. "Academe and the Boom in Business Studies," *Change* (September/October 1987): 37–42.

————. *The Control of the Campus: A Report on the Governance of Higher Education.* Washington, D.C.: Carnegie Foundation for the Advancement of Teaching, 1982.

The Carnegie Foundation for the Advancement of Teaching and the American Council on Education. *National Survey of College and University Presidents, 1989.*

Carter, Deborah, Carol Pearson, and Donna Shavlik. "Double Jeopardy: Women of Color in Higher Education." *Educational Record* (Fall 1987–Winter 1988): 98–103.

Casey, John. "At Dartmouth: The Class of '89." *New York Times Magazine* (26 February, 1989): 28–30, 66–.

Cheit, Earl F. *The Useful Arts and the Liberal Tradition.* New York: McGraw Hill, 1975.

Churgin, Jonah R. *The New Woman and the Old Academe: Sexism and Higher Education.* New York: Libra, 1978.

Clark, Burton R. *The Academic Life: Small Worlds, Different Worlds.* Princeton: The Carnegie Foundation for the Advancement of Teaching, 1987.

————. *The Distinctive College: Antioch, Reed and Swarthmore.* Chicago: Aldine, 1970.

————. *The Open Door College: A Case Study.* New York: McGraw-Hill, 1960.

Clowes, Darrel A., Dennis E. Hinkle, and John C. Smart. "Enrollment Patterns in Postsecondary Education, 1961–1982." *Journal of Higher Education* (March/April 1986): 121–133.

Cohen, Arthur M., and Florence B. Brawer. *The American Community College.* San Francisco: Jossey-Bass, 1982.

Cole, Sally. "Beyond Recruitment and Retention: The Stanford Experience." In *The Racial Crisis in Higher Education*, eds. Philip Altbach and Kofi Lomotey. Buffalo: SUNY Press, 1990.

"Colleges Take Two Basic Approaches in Adopting Anti-Harassment Plans." *The Chronicle of Higher Education*, 4 October, 1989: A38.

Collison, Michele N-K. "Student Group Seeks a Sharper Focus on Undergraduate Teaching." *The Chronicle of Higher Education*, 1 November, 1989: A37.

———. "At Greensboro: Blacks Chafe at Stereotyping, White Students Assail Emphasis on Race." *The Chronicle of Higher Education*, 26 April, 1989: A28, A33.

———. "For Some Students, Spring Break Offers Chance to Aid the Needy." *The Chronicle of Higher Education*, 22 March, 1989: A33–34.

Commission on the Future of Community Colleges. *Building Communities*. Washington: American Association of Community and Junior Colleges, 1988.

Conlin, Joseph R. *The Morrow Book of Quotations in American History*. New York: William Morrow, 1984.

Connell, Christopher. "Drinking on Campus, The Twenty-One Year-Old Drinking Age: Education or Enforcement?" *Change* (January/February 1985): 44–51.

Cooper v. Aaron, 358 U.S. 1 (1958).

Cowan, Alison Leigh. "Women's Gains on the Job: Not Without a Heavy Toll." *New York Times*, 21 August, 1989: A1, A14.

Crocker, Lester G. *Rousseau's Social Contract: An Interpretive Essay*. Cleveland: Case Western Reserve University Press, 1968.

Curry, Susan J. "Hazing and the 'Rush' Toward Reform: Responses from Universities, Fraternities, State Legislatures, and the Courts." *Journal of College and University Law* 16, no. 1: 93–117.

Dalton, Jon C. *Promoting Values Development in College Students*. Vol. 4. Washington, D.C.: National Association of Student Personnel Administrators, 1985.

"Danger on Campus." *Los Angeles Times* editorial, 23 September, 1988.

Daniels, Lee A. "Some Top Universities in Squeeze Between Research and Academics." *New York Times*, 16 May, 1989: B1, B8.

DeLoughry, Thomas J. "At Penn State: Polarization of the Campus Persists Amid Struggles to Ease Tensions." *The Chronicle of Higher Education*, 26 April, 1989: A30, A33.

Delworth, Ursula, et al. *Student Services: A Handbook for the Profession*. 2nd ed. San Francisco: Jossey-Bass, 1989.

Department of Education and Science. *Aspects of Higher Education in the United States of America*. London: Her Majesty's Stationery Office, 1989.

Dewey, John. *Democracy and Education*. New York: Macmillan, 1963.

Diner, Steven J. *A City and Its Universities: Public Policy in Chicago, 1882–1919*. Chapel Hill, North Carolina: University of North Carolina Press, 1980.

John Doe v. University of Michigan. No. 89–71683, U.S. District Court, Eastern District of Michigan, Southern Division, 1989.

Drukman, Mason. *Community and Purpose in America: An Analysis of American Political Theory*. New York: McGraw-Hill, 1971.

Eggins, Heather, ed. *Restructuring Higher Education*. Milton Keynes, England: The Society for Research into Higher Education and Open University Press, 1987.

Ehrhart, Julie K., and Bernice R. Sandler. *Campus Gang Rape: Party Games?* A publication of the Project on the Status and Education of Women. Washington, D.C.: Association of American Colleges, November, 1985.

Ehrlich, Howard J., and Cornel Morton. *Ethnoviolence on Campus: The UMBC Study*, Institute Report No. 2. Baltimore: National Institute Against Prejudice and Violence, 1987.

El-Khawas, Elaine. *Campus Trends, 1989*. Higher Education Panel Report Number 78. Washington, D.C.: American Council on Education, 1989.

———. *Campus Trends, 1988*. Higher Education Panel Report Number 77. Washington, D.C.: American Council on Education, 1988.

Epstein, Richard A. *Takings: Private Property and the Power of Eminent Domain*. Cambridge: Harvard University Press, 1985.

Etzioni, Amitai. *The Moral Dimension*. New York: The Free Press, 1988.

Faragher, John Mark, and Florence Howe. *Women and Higher Education in American History*. New York: W. W. Norton, 1988.

Farrell, Charles S. "Black Students Seen Facing 'New Racism' on Many Campuses: Environment at 'White' Colleges Viewed as Hostile to Minorities." *The Chronicle of Higher Education*, 27 January, 1988: A1, A36.

———. "Stung by Racial Incidents and Charges of Indifference, Berkeley Trying to Become Model Integrated University." *The Chronicle of Higher Education*, 27 January, 1988: A36–37.

Federal Bureau of Investigation. "Table 7—Number of Offenses Known to the Police, Universities and Colleges, 1988." *Uniform Crime Reports of the United States*. Washington, D.C.: Government Printing Office, 1989, pp. 116–123.

———. "Table 7—Number of Offenses Known to the Police, Universities and Colleges, 1987." *Uniform Crime Reports of the United States*. Washington, D.C.: Government Printing Office, 1987, pp. 110–117.

———. "Table 1—Index of Crime, United States, 1977–1986." *Uniform Crime*

Reports of the United States. Washington, D.C.: Government Printing Office, 1987, p. 41.

————. "Table 7—Number of Offenses Known to Police, Universities and Colleges, 1985." *Uniform Crime Reports of the United States.* Washington, D.C.: Government Printing Office, 1986, pp. 111–118.

————. "Table 68—Number of Offenses Known to Police, 1971, Universities." *Uniform Crime Reports of the United States.* Washington, D.C.: Government Printing Office, 1972, p. 219.

————. Uniform Crime Reports of the United States. Washington, D.C.: Government Printing Office, 1988.

Feldman, Kenneth A., and Theodore M. Newcomb. *The Impact of College on Students.* San Francisco: Jossey-Bass, 1970.

Fields, Cheryl M. "College Advised to Develop Strong Procedures to Deal with Incidents of Racial Harassment." *The Chronicle of Higher Education,* 20 July, 1988: A11–12.

"Final Report on Recent Incidents at Ujamaa House." *Stanford Daily,* 18 January, 1989, 7–10.

Fiske, Edward B. "The Undergraduate Hispanic Experience: A Case of Juggling Two Cultures." *Change* (May/June 1988): 28–31.

Francis, Roy G. *Crumbling Walls.* Cambridge, Massachusetts: Schenkman, 1970.

Frank, Mary Jo. "Racism Course Proposal Stalls; Faculty Ask for Alternatives." *The University Record.* Ann Arbor: University of Michigan, 10 April, 1989: 1.

Freitag, Michael. "Rape Crisis Alters Life at Syracuse." *New York Times,* 20 November, 1989: B1, B2.

Fromm, Erich. *The Anatomy of Human Destructiveness.* New York: Fawcett Crest, 1973.

Gardner, Howard. *Frames of Mind.* New York: Basic Books, 1985.

Gardner, John N., and A. Jerome Jewler. *College is Only the Beginning: A Student Guide to Higher Education.* 2nd ed. Belmont, California: Wadsworth, 1989.

Garforth, F. W. *Educative Democracy: John Stuart Mill on Education in Society.* New York: Oxford University Press for the University of Hull, 1980.

Goleman, Daniel. "When the Rapist is not a Stranger: Studies Seek New Understanding." *The New York Times,* 29 August, 1989: C1, C6.

Goodman, Paul. *The Community of Scholars.* New York: Random House, 1962.

Gottfredson, Michael, and Travis Hirschi. "Criminal Behavior: Why We're Losing the War on Crime." *New York Times,* 10 September, 1989: C3.

Grant, Gerald, and David Riesman. *The Perpetual Dream.* Chicago: University of Chicago Press, 1978.

Grant, W. Vance, and Leo J. Eiden. *Digest of Education Statistics 1982.* Washington, D.C.: U.S. Department of Education, National Center for Education Statistics, 1982.

Green, Elizabeth. "At Oberlin: Liberal Traditions, Intentions Are No Guarantee of Racial Harmony." *The Chronicle of Higher Education,* 26 April, 1989: A31–32.

————. "Minority-Affairs Officials, Picked to Help Campuses Improve Racial Climate, Report Some Progress." *The Chronicle of Higher Education,* 22 March, 1989: A32–34.

Green, Madeleine F. *Minorities On Campus: A Handbook for Enhancing Diversity.* Washington, D.C.: American Council on Education, 1989.

Griffith, Marlene, and Ann Connor. "To Extend Opportunities to All, Colleges Need to Redefine Remedial Education." *The Chronicle of Higher Education,* 27 September, 1989: B2.

Gutmann, Amy. *Democratic Education.* Princeton: Princeton University Press, 1987.

Gwyn, Sharon. "Muzzle the Stanford Bigots." *New York Times,* 12 May, 1989.

Hacker, Andrew. "Affirmative Action: The New Look." *New York Review,* 12 October, 1989: 63–64.

Hall, E. T. *The Hidden Dimension.* Garden City, New York: Doubleday, 1966.

————. *The Silent Language.* Garden City, New York: Doubleday, 1959.

Hall, Roberta M., and Bernice R. Sandler. *The Campus Climate Revisited: Chilly for Women Faculty, Administrators, and Graduate Students.* Washington, D.C.: Association of American Colleges Project on the Status and Education of Women, October, 1986.

————. *The Classroom Climate: A Chilly One for Women?* Washington, D.C.: Association of American Colleges Project on the Status and Education of Women, 1984.

————. *Out of the Classroom: A Chilly Campus Climate for Women?* Washington, D.C.: Association of American Colleges Project on the Status and Education of Women, October, 1982.

Hamilton, Alexander, John Jay, and James Madison. *The Federalist.* New York: Random House, 1787.

Handlin, Oscar, and Mary F. Handlin. *The American College and American Culture.* New York: McGraw-Hill, 1970.

Harris, Seymour E. *A Statistical Portrait of Higher Education.* New York: McGraw-Hill, 1972.

Hayden, Dolores. *Redesigning the American Dream*. New York: W. W. Norton, 1984.

Heller, Jack F., C. Richard Puff, and Carol J. Mills. "Assessment of the Chilly College Climate for Women." *Journal of Higher Education*. (July/August 1985): 446–461.

Hendrix, Kathleen. "Rape on Campus: It's on Rise Across U.S., Report Experts Who Say That Schools Don't Know How to React." *Los Angeles Times*, 23 August, 1988.

Henley, Nancy. *Body Politics: Power, Sex and Nonverbal Communication*. New York: Prentice Hall, 1977.

Hevesi, Dennis. "Students at Ten CUNY Campuses Vote to End Their Tuition Protests." *New York Times*, 5 May, 1989: B3.

Hodgkinson, Harold L., and L. Richard Meeth. *Power and Authority*. San Francisco: Jossey-Bass, 1971.

Horowitz, Helen Lefkowitz. *Campus Life*. New York: Alfred A. Knopf, 1987.

————. *Alma Mater*. New York: Alfred A. Knopf, 1984.

Howe, Florence, ed. *Women and the Power to Change*. New York: McGraw-Hill, 1975.

Hsia, Jayjia. *Asian Americans in Higher Education and at Work*. Hillsdale, New Jersey: Lawrence Earlbaum Associates, 1988.

The Hudson Institute. *Workforce 2000: Work and Workers for the Twenty-first Century*. Indianapolis: The Hudson Institute, 1987.

Hughes, Jean O'Gorman, and Bernice R. Sandler. *Peer Harassment: Hassles for Women on Campus*. Washington, D.C.: Association of American Colleges Project on the Status and Education of Women, September, 1988.

————. *"Friends" Raping Friends: Could it Happen to You?* A publication of the Project on the Status and Education of Women. Washington, D.C.: Association of American Colleges, April, 1987.

————. *In Case of Sexual Harassment: A Guide for Women Students, We Hope It Doesn't Happen to You, But If It Does...* A publication of the Project on the Status and Education of Women. Washington, D.C.: Association of American Colleges, April, 1986.

Jaynes, Gerald David, and Robin M. Williams, Jr., eds. *A Common Destiny: Blacks and American Society*. Washington, D.C.: National Academy Press, 1989.

Jencks, Christopher, and David Riesman. *The Academic Revolution*. Garden City, New York: Anchor Books, 1969.

Kaplin, William A. *The Law of Higher Education*. San Francisco: Jossey-Bass, 1985.

Katchadourian, Herant A., and John Boli. *Careerism and Intellectualism Among College Students*. San Francisco: Jossey-Bass, 1985.

Katz, Montana, and Veronica Vieland. *Get Smart: A Woman's Guide to Equality on Campus*. New York: The Feminist Press at The City University of New York, 1988.

Kerr, Clark. *The Uses of the University*. Cambridge, Massachusetts: Harvard University Press, 1963.

Knapper, Christopher. "Large Classes and Learning." *New Directions for Teaching and Learning* (Winter 1987): 5–15.

Knox, Alan B. *Helping Adults Learn*. San Francisco: Jossey-Bass, 1986.

Kolbert, Elizabeth. "Cuomo's Veto of Tuition Rise Draws Attack: Lawmakers Say 'Hole' in Budget Must Be Filled." *New York Times,* 4 May, 1989: B1, B10.

Kuh, George D. *Enhancing the Quality of Greek Life*. Bloomington, Indiana: Indiana University Center for the Study of the College Fraternity, February, 1982.

Lakoff, George, and Mark Johnson. *Metaphors We Live By*. Chicago: University of Chicago Press, 1980.

Lakoff, Robin. *Language and Woman's Place*. New York: Harper and Row, 1975.

Lamont, Lansing. *Campus Shock*. New York: E. P. Dutton, 1979.

Lasser, Carol, ed. *Educating Men and Women Together: Coeducation in a Changing World*. Urbana: University of Illinois Press in conjunction with Oberlin College, 1987.

Leatherman, Courtney. "Louis Farrakhan's Controversial Campus Visits: Inspirational for Blacks, Abhorrent to Jews, a Headache for College Officials." *The Chronicle of Higher Education,* 17 May, 1989: A35–37.

Lee, Calvin B. T. *The Campus Scene: 1900–1970*. New York: David McKay, 1970.

Leonard, Mary M., and Brenda Alpert Sigall. "Empowering Women Student Leaders: A Leadership Development Model." In *Educating the Majority: Women Challenge Tradition in Higher Education,* eds. Carol S. Pearson, Donna L. Shavlik, and Judith G. Touchton. New York: American Council on Education/MacMillan, 1989.

Levine, Arthur, ed. "Special Report: Hispanics and the Academy." *Change*. (May/June 1988).

Levine, Arthur. *When Dreams and Heroes Died*. San Francisco: Jossey-Bass, 1980.

Lipset, Seymour Martin, and Philip G. Altbach, eds. *Students in Revolt*. Boston: Houghton Mifflin, 1969.

Lipson, Leslie. *The Democratic Civilization*. New York: Oxford University Press, 1969.

Little, Frank Graham. *Faces on the Campus: A Psycho-Social Study*. Carlton, Victoria: Melbourne University Press, 1975.

Loring, Chuck V. "A Time for Action—A Message from the President." *National Interfraternity Conference Annual Report 1988.* Indianapolis, Indiana: National Interfraternity Conference, 1988.

Lovett, Clara M. Review of "Educating Men and Women Together: Coeducation in a Changing World," ed. Carol Lasser. *Journal of Higher Education* (January/February, 1989): 118–121.

Lubove, Roy. *The Urban Community Housing and Planning in the Progressive Era.* Englewood Cliffs, New Jersey: Prentice-Hall, 1967.

Lyall, Sarah, "Rape Charge Splits Stony Brook Campus." *New York Times,* 7 April, 1989: B1, B3.

McCartan, Anne-Marie. "Students Who Work." *Change* (September/October, 1988): 11–20.

McGrath, Earl J. *Should Students Share the Power?* Philadelphia: Temple University Press, 1970.

McKeachie, Wilber J. *Teaching Tips: A Guidebook for the Beginning College Teacher.* 8th ed. Lexington, Massachusetts: D. C. Heath, 1986.

McKenna, Teresa, and Flora Ida Ortiz, eds. *The Broken Web: The Educational Experience of Hispanic American Women.* Berkeley: The Tomas Rivera Center and Floricanto Press, 1988.

McKinley, James C., Jr. "Thousands from CUNY Hold Tuition Protest at Federal Hall." *New York Times,* 3 May, 1989: B1, B6.

———. "CUNY Protests Spread to More Schools" *New York Times,* 28 April, 1989: B3.

McMillen, Liz. "Ford Fund Programs Look at Campus Race Relations and Minority Schoolteachers; The Mellon Fund Evolves." *The Chronicle of Higher Education,* 17 May, 1989: A33–34.

Magner, Denise K. "Blacks and Whites on the Campuses: Behind Ugly Racist Indicents, Student Isolation and Insensitivity." *The Chronicle of Higher Education,* 26 April, 1989: A1, A28–31.

———. "'Life Gets Better' Program; 'Multicultural Awareness' at Temple U.; More." *The Chronicle of Higher Education,* 12 April, 1989: A32.

Maihoff, Nancy, and Linda Forrest. "Sexual Harassment in Higher Education: An Assessment Study." *Journal of NAWDAC* (Winter 1983): 3–8, reprinted with permission in *Sexual Harassment on Campus: A Legal Compendium.* Washington, D.C.: National Association of College and University Attorneys, 1988.

Mangan, Katherine S. "At Texas: An Undercurrent of Hostility Amid Efforts to Promote Multiculturalism." *The Chronicle of Higher Education,* 26 April, 1989: A28, A32.

Martin, Warren B., Harold L. Hodgkinson, and Patricia K. Cross. *Education Task Force Papers.* Vol. 2 of *Occasional Papers.* Berkeley: Center for Research and Development in Higher Education, University of California, 1971.

Massachusetts Institute of Technology Minority Student Issues Group. *The Racial Climate on the MIT Campus.* Cambridge, Massachusetts: Massachusetts Institute of Technology, September, 1986.

Meritor Savings Bank FSB v. Vinson, 106 S. Ct. 2399 (1986).

Miller, Jean Baker. *Toward a New Psychology of Women.* Boston: Beacon Press, 1976.

Minnich, Elizabeth, Jean O'Barr, and Rachel Rosenfeld, eds. *Reconstructing the Academy Women's Education and Women's Studies.* Chicago: University of Chicago Press, 1988.

Moffatt, Michael. *Coming of Age in New Jersey.* New Brunswick, New Jersey: Rutgers University Press, 1989.

Mooney, Carolyn J. "Only Four Black Americans Said to Have Earned Math Ph.D's in 1987–88." *The Chronicle of Higher Education,* 2 August, 1989: A11–12.

Moore, Molly. "West Point Graduates Defend Honor Code: Commission Studies Possible Revisions." *Washington Post,* 25 January, 1989: A8.

"More College Students Combine Work and Study." *ACE News Release,* 4 September, 1989. Washington, D.C.: American Council on Education.

Morrill, Richard L. *Teaching Values in College.* San Francisco: Jossey-Bass, 1980.

Myrdal, Gunnar. *An American Dilemma,* 2 volumes. New York: Harper Torchbooks, 1944–1962.

National Association of College and University Attorneys. "Sexual Harassment on Campus: A Legal Compendium." Washington, D.C.: National Association of College and University Attorneys, 1988.

National Association of Student Personnel Administrators. *Points of View: A Perspective on Student Affairs.* Washington, D.C.: National Association of Student Personnel Administrators, 1989.

1988 National Campus Violence Survey, A complete report from the Center for the Study and Prevention of Campus Violence. Towson, Maryland: Towson State University, 1988.

National Campus Violence Survey, General Report 1988, A report of the Center for the Study and Prevention of Campus Violence. Towson, Maryland: Towson State University, 1988.

National Campus Violence Survey, General Reports 1985, 1986, 1987, A report of the Center for the Study and Prevention of Campus Violence. Towson, Maryland: Towson State University, 1987.

Nelson, Robert C. "Changing Public Values: An Interview with Daniel Yankelovich." *The Kettering Review* (Fall 1988): 40–48.

Nettles, Michael T., ed. *Toward Black Undergraduate Student Equality in American Higher Education*. New York: Greenwood Press, 1988.

Newman, Frank. *Higher Education and the American Resurgence*. Princeton: The Carnegie Foundation for the Advancement of Teaching, 1985.

Newman, Oscar. *Community of Interest*. Garden City, New York: Anchor Press/Doubleday, 1980.

Newsweek "On Campus Poll: Racial Issues," reprinted with permission in *Educational Record* (Fall 1987–Winter 1988): 76.

Nordin, Virginia Davis. "The Contract to Educate: Toward a More Workable Theory of the Student-University Relationship." *The Journal of College and University Law* 8, no. 2: 141–181.

Office of Educational Research and Improvement, U.S. Department of Education. *The Condition of Education: Postsecondary Education 1988*. Vol. 2. Washington, D.C.: U.S. Department of Education, 1988.

Olivas, Michael A., ed. *Latino College Students*. New York: Teachers College Press, 1986.

"On Changing Academic Culture From the Inside: An Interview with Donna Shalala." *Change* (January/February 1989): 20–29.

Orfield, Gary. "Opportunities for Minorities: New Focus of Concern for Higher Education." *Change* (May/June 1989): 50–53.

Pace, C. Robert. *Measuring the Quality of College Student Experiences*. Los Angeles: University of California, Higher Education Research Institute, Center for the Study of Evaluation, 1988.

———. *Measuring Outcomes of College*. San Francisco: Jossey-Bass, 1979.

Palmer, Parker. *To Know as We are Known*. New York: Harper and Row, 1983.

Paolucci, Anne, ed. *The Doctor of Arts Degree: Re-Assessing Teaching and Research Priorities*. Whitestone, New York: Council on National Literatures, 1989.

Pateman, Carole. *Participation and Democratic Theory*. Cambridge, England: Cambridge University Press, 1970.

Pearson, Carol S., Donna L. Shavlik, and Judith G. Touchton, eds. *Educating the Majority: Women Challenge Tradition in Higher Education*. New York: American Council on Education/MacMillan, 1989.

Pelikan, Jaroslav. *Scholarship and Its Survival: Questions on the Idea of Graduate Education*. Princeton: The Carnegie Foundation for the Advancement of Teaching, 1983.

Perry, William G., Jr. *Forms of Intellectual and Ethical Development in the College Years: A Scheme.* New York: Holt, Rinehart and Winston, 1970.

Peterson, Marvin W., et al. *Black Students on White Campuses.* Ann Arbor: The University of Michigan Press, 1978.

Plisko, Valeno White, ed. *The Condition of Education 1983.* Washington, D.C.: U.S. Department of Education, National Center for Education Statistics, 1983.

Prichard, Peter S., ed. "Crime on Campus: Schools Fail Safety Test," special report. *USA Today,* 4–7 October, 1988.

Project on Redefining the Meaning and Purpose of Baccalaureate Degrees. *Integrity in the College Curriculum: A Report to the Academic Community.* Findings and Recommendations. Washington, D.C.: Association of American Colleges, 1985.

Project on the Status and Education of Women and the Women's Studies Program at Duke University. *Evaluating Courses for Inclusion of New Scholarship on Women.* Washington, D.C.: Association of American Colleges, 1988.

Quandt, Jean B. *From the Small Town to the Great Community: The Social Thought of Progressive Intellectuals.* New Brunswick, New Jersey: Rutgers University Press, 1970.

"Race, Racism, and American Education: Perspective of Asian Americans, Blacks, Latinos, and Native Americans." *Harvard Educational Review* 58, no. 3 (1988).

Randolph, Laura B. "Black Students Battle Racism on College Campuses." *Ebony* (December, 1988): 126, 128–130.

Rawls, John. *A Theory of Justice.* Oxford, England: Clarendon Press, 1972.

The Recruitment and Retention of Minority Students at MIT, A report of the Minority Student Issues Group. Cambridge, Massachusetts: Massachusetts Institute of Technology, March 1989.

Report of the Task Force on Child Care Services. Berkeley: University of California, May, 1989.

Reynolds, Charles H., and Ralph Y. Norman, eds. *Community in America: The Challenge of Habits of the Heart.* Berkeley: University of California Press, 1988.

Richardson, Richard C., Jr., and Louis W. Bender. *Fostering Minority Access and Achievement in Higher Education.* San Francisco: Jossey-Bass, 1987.

Richardson, Richard C., Jr., and Elizabeth Fisk Skinner. *Achieving Quality and Diversity: Universities in a Multicultural Society.* New York: American Council on Education/MacMillan, 1991.

Rivers, Caryl, Rosalind Barnett, and Grace Baruch. *Beyond Sugar and Spice: How Women Grow, Learn and Thrive.* New York: Ballantine Books, 1979.

Rousseau, Jean Jacques. *The Social Contract and Discourses.* New York: E. P. Dutton and Company, 1950.

Rudolph, Frederick. *The American College and University: A History*. New York: Random House, 1962.

Sandler, Bernice R., and Roberta M. Hall. *The Campus Climate Revisited: Chilly for Women Faculty, Administrators, and Graduate Students*. Washington, D.C.: Association of American Colleges Project on the Status and Education of Women, October, 1986.

Schlossberg, Nancy K. *Improving Higher Education Environments for Adults*. San Francisco: Jossey-Bass, 1989.

Schrecker, Ellen W. *No Ivory Tower: McCarthyism and the Universities*. New York: Oxford University Press, 1986.

Schuman, Samuel, "Beginning in Honors: A Handbook." Greensboro, North Carolina: National Collegiate Honors Council, 1989.

Scranton, William W. *President's Commission on Campus Unrest, 537*. Washington, D.C.: U.S. Government Printing Office, 1970.

Searle, John. *The Campus War*. Middlesex, England: Penguin Books, 1972.

Secter, Bob. "A New Bigotry Ripples Across U.S. Campuses." *Los Angeles Times*, 8 May, 1988.

Sharpe, William, and Leonard Walleck, eds. *Visions of the Modern City*. New York: Columbia University Press, 1983.

Smith, Daryl G. *The Challenge of Diversity: Involvement or Alienation in the Academy?* ASHE-ERIC Higher Education Report No. 5. Washington, D.C.: ASHE-ERIC, 1989.

Smith, Michael Clay. *Coping with Crime on Campus*. New York: Macmillan, 1988.

Snyder, Thomas D., Project Director. *Digest of Education Statistics 1988*. Washington, D.C.: U.S. Department of Education, National Center for Education Statistics, 1988.

Snyder, Benson R. *The Hidden Curriculum*. New York: Alfred A. Knopf, 1971.

Solomon, Barbara Miller. *In the Company of Educated Women*. New Haven: Yale University Press, 1985.

"The Specialized College Faculty." *The Nation* (26 March, 1908): 277–278.

Stanford University Committee on Minority Issues. *Building a Multiracial, Multicultural University Community*. Stanford: Stanford University, 1989.

Stanford University. *Stanford University Student Conduct Policies*. Palo Alto: Office of the President, Stanford University, 1990.

State University of New York Standing Committee on Women's Issues. *Taking Women Students Seriously: A Study of the College Experience of Women*. Brockport: State University of New York, Spring, 1989.

Statistical Abstract of the United States 1989, 109th ed. Washington, D.C.: U.S. Department of Commerce, Bureau of the Census, 1989.

Steele, Charles Thomas, Jr. "Mandatory Student Fees at Public Universities: Bringing the First Amendment Within the Campus Gate." *Journal of College and University Law* 13, no. 4 (1987): 353–374.

Steele, Shelby. "The Recoloring of Campus Life: Student Racism, Academic Pluralism, and the End of a Dream." *Harpers* 278, no. 1665: 47–57.

Stein, Maurice R. *The Eclipse of Community.* Princeton: Princeton University Press, 1960.

"Students Protest Policy to Limit Speech Practices," Campus Life—Tufts. *New York Times,* 17 September, 1989: 61–62.

"Students Still Drink, Fewer Drive Drunk." *Notes.* Washington, D.C.: Association of Governing Boards of Universities and Colleges, February/March 1989.

Suzuki, Bob H. "Asian Americans in Higher Education: Impact on Changing Demographics and Other Social Forces." Paper prepared for National Symposium on the Changing Demographics of Higher Education, for The Ford Foundation, New York, April 8, 1988.

Sykes, Charles J. *ProfScam.* Washington, D.C.: Regnery Gateway, 1988.

Thelin, John R. "Campus Life: Undergraduate Cultures from the End of the Eighteenth Century to the Present"—a book review. *The Journal of Higher Education* (March/April, 1989): 232–234.

Theus, Kathryn T. "Campus-Based Community Service: New Populism or 'Smoke and Mirrors?'" *Change* (September/October, 1988): 27–38.

Tobias, Marilyn. *Old Dartmouth On Trial: The Transformation of the Academic Community in Nineteenth-Century America.* New York: New York University Press, 1982.

Tocqueville, Alexis de. *Democracy in America.* New York: Vintage Books, 1945.

Trow, Martin, ed. *Teachers and Students: Aspects of American Higher Education.* New York: McGraw-Hill, 1975.

True, James A. "Campus Violence Crime Reports Security Standards." Presentation to the Third National Conference on Campus Violence, The Center for the Study and Prevention of Campus Violence, Towson State University, Towson, Maryland, January 10–12, 1989.

Truman, David B. *The Governmental Process.* New York: Alfred A. Knopf, 1960.

United States Department of Justice Statistics. *The Crime of Rape.* Washington, D.C.: Government Printing Office, 1985.

University of California. *Report of the Coordinating Committee on the Status of Women*. Berkeley: University of California, March, 1989.

University of California Committee on Admissions and Enrollment. *Freshman Admissions at Berkeley: A Policy for the 1990s and Beyond*. Berkeley: Academic Senate, University of California, 19 May, 1989.

University of California Special Committee on Education and Ethnicity, Academic Senate. *Proposal for an American Cultures Breadth Requirement*. Berkeley: University of California, 29 March, 1989.

University of Maryland. *Maryland Longitudinal Study*. Research Highlights, Research Reports 1–12. College Park, Maryland: University of Maryland, 1986–1989.

University of Maryland College Park Campus Senate Ad Hoc Committee on Undergraduate Education. *Promises to Keep: The College Park Plan for Undergraduate Education*, College Park, Maryland: University of Maryland, 14 September, 1987.

University of Michigan. *The Michigan Mandate: A Strategic Linking of Academic Excellence and Social Diversity*. Ann Arbor: University of Michigan, 1989.

University of Wisconsin-Madison. *The Madison Plan*. Madison: University of Wisconsin, February, 1988.

———. *The Madison Plan: One Year Later*. Madison: University of Wisconsin, February, 1989.

University of Wisconsin-Madison Steering Committee on Minority Affairs. *Final Report*. Madison: University of Wisconsin-Madison, November, 1987.

Upcraft, M. Lee, et al. *The Freshman Year Experience: Helping Students Survive and Succeed in College*. San Francisco: Jossey-Bass, 1989.

Veblen, Thorstein. *The Higher Learning in America*. New York: Hill and Wang, 1918.

Vera, Ronald T. "Texas Responds to the Office of Civil Rights: Progress Made Under the Texas Equal Educational Opportunity Plan for Higher Education." A Tomas Rivera Center Working Paper, Claremont, California, 1989.

Verhovek, Sam Howe. "Behind Tuition Fight: A Struggle to Gain Prestige." *New York Times,* 5 May, 1989: B3.

Veysey, Laurence R. *The Emergence of the American University*. Chicago: University of Chicago Press, 1965.

Vobejda, Barbara. "Two-Year Colleges: Mixed Success as Vehicle of Upward Mobility." *Washington Post,* 5 May, 1989: A1, A16.

———. "Competition for College Feeds Elitism: Well-Off Applicants Flood Prestigious Schools as Tuitions Rise." *Washington Post,.* 4 May, 1989: A1, A14.

———. "A Hierarchy of Institutions Reinforces Class Divisions: 'Level Playing Field' Never Achieved." *Washington Post,* 3 May, 1989: A1, A12.

Wallis, Claudia. "Onward, Women!" *Time* (4 December, 1989): 80–89.

Warren, Roland L. *Studying Your Community.* New York: Free Press, 1965.

Warshaw, Robin. *I Never Called it Rape.* New York: Harper and Row, 1988.

Watkins, Beverly T. "For Many Teachers, Classroom Lecture is Giving Way to Projects That Students Tackle in Small Groups." *The Chronicle of Higher Education,* 2 August, 1989: A9, A12.

What Can Be Done to Deal With Sexual Harassment, An institutional mode for addressing the problem of sexual harassment. University of New Hampshire, 1989.

Whyte, William H. *Organization Man.* New York: Simon and Schuster, 1956.

Williams, David D., et al. "University Class Size: Is Smaller Better?" *Research in Higher Education* 23, no. 3: 307–318.

Willie, Charles Vert. *The Ivory and Ebony Towers.* Lexington, Massachusetts: Lexington Books, 1981.

Wilson, Logan, ed. *Emerging Patterns in American Higher Education.* Washington, D.C.: American Council on Education, 1965.

Wilson, R. Jackson. *In Quest of Community: Social Philosophy in the United States.* New York: John Wiley and Sons, 1968.

Wilson, Reginald, and Deborah J. Carter. *Seventh Annual Status Report on Minorities in Higher Education.* Washington, D.C.: American Council on Education, Office of Minority Concerns, 17 October, 1988.

Wilson, Robert C., et al. *College Professors and Their Impact on Students.* New York: John Wiley and Sons, 1975.

Wilson, Robin. "Colleges' Anti-Harassment Policies Bring Controversy Over Free-Speech Issues." *The Chronicle of Higher Education,* 4 October, 1989: A1, A38–39.

Woolf, Virginia. *A Room of One's Own.* New York: Harvest/Harcourt Brace Jovanovich, 1929.

Wren, Scott C. *The College Student and Higher Education Policy: What Stake and What Purpose?* Washington, D.C.: The Carnegie Foundation for the Advancement of Teaching, 1974.

Wulff, Donald H., Jody D. Nyquist, and Robert D. Abbott. "Students' Perceptions of Large Classes." *New Directions for Teaching and Learning* (Winter 1987): 17–30.

Wyman, Roger E., et al. *Humanities Ph.D.'s and Nonacademic Careers: A Guide for Faculty Advisers.* Evanston, Illinois: The Committee on Institutional Cooperation, 1983.

Yen, Marianne. "Student Protests Crush Tuition Hike in New York." *Washington Post,* 4 May, 1989: A19.

Zangwill, Israel. *The Melting Pot.* 1908.

Zemsky, Robert. *Structure and Coherence: Measuring the Undergraduate Curriculum.* Washington, D.C.: Association of American Colleges, 1989.

Zwerling, L. Steven. "The Miami-Dade Story: Is it Really Number One?" *Change* (January/February 1988): 10–23.

Index